Learning Pentaho CTools

Acquire finesse with CTools features and build rich and custom analytics solutions using Pentaho

Miguel Gaspar

BIRMINGHAM - MUMBAI

Learning Pentaho CTools

First published: May 2016

Production reference: 1250516

Published by Packt Publishing Ltd.
Livery Place
35 Livery Street
Birmingham B3 2PB, UK.

ISBN 978-1-78528-342-0

www.packtpub.com

Credits

Author
Miguel Gaspar

Reviewers
Dan Keeley
Sadakar Pochampalli
Umang Shah

Commissioning Editor
Dipika Gaonkar

Acquisition Editor
Sonali Vernekar

Content Development Editor
Kirti Patil

Technical Editor
Jayesh Sonawane

Copy Editor
Ameesha Smith-Green

Project Coordinator
Sanchita Mandal

Proofreader
Safis Editing

Indexer
Monica Ajmera Mehta

Graphics
Disha Haria

Production Coordinator
Arvindkumar Gupta

Cover Work
Arvindkumar Gupta

About the Author

Miguel Gaspar started working at Webdetails about 3 years ago, some time before the acquisition of Webdetails by Pentaho. He was a consultant in the Implementation team and his work involved developing dashboard solutions as part of services. He is now acting as the technical owner of some of the Implementations projects as part of the Webdetails team in Pentaho. He likes to be as professional as possible, but in an informal way. One of his favorite hobbies is learning and his particular areas of interest are: business analytics, predictive analysis and big data, augmented reality, and cloud computing. He likes to play and is a huge martial arts fan and also one of the worst soccer players ever. He is married and a parent of two young and lovely daughters, who would like to spend more time playing like crazies with him. He also likes to spend time with friends or just having a drink and a good talk with someone else, if possible with his family at his side. He really hates liars.

I am really grateful to my wife for all the support and also to my daughters for letting me compensate them for the time I spent writing the book while I should be spending the time with them, playing and laughing. I also want to thank all the reviewers and the team that worked on the book to make it better.

About the Reviewers

Dan Keeley is an open source analytics advocate who has been working with Pentaho for nearly 10 years. He is now running his own company, building a team specializing in fast turnaround analytics. He has reviewed books on Pentaho Reporting and Pentaho Data Integration.

Sadakar Pochampalli has been working as a BI consultant, and has around 4 years of experience with the Pentaho BI suite (all the modules) and the Japsersoft BI suite (all the modules). He is a postgraduate with a masters in computer applications from Bankatlal Badruka College for IT, Hyderabad, Telangana. He was awarded by Badruka (BBCIT) college with E.Balagurusamy gold medal for his outstanding performance during his postgraduation. He has been involved in end-to-end BI solutions using the Pentaho BI suite to meet the customers' expectations. He is passionate about learning open source and enterprise BI technologies as well an enthusiast of working on big data technologies. He often says to his friends, colleagues, and family that *learning things never exhausts the mind*. He has successfully delivered around 20 end-to-end BI projects using Pentaho and Jaspersoft. He has also trained more than 200 folks, from freshers to the CEOs of companies.

This is the first book he has reviewed. He is the author of two active blogs: `http://pentaho-bi-suite.blogspot.in/` (Pentaho BI Suite) and `http://jasper-bi-suite.blogspot.in/` (Jaspersoft BI Suite).

> I would like to express my special thanks to the author of this book Miguel Gaspar and Packt Publishing for giving me this wonderful opportunity to review the content of book to make me part of this project. I enjoyed doing it as I have been working on the same technology for the past few years. Hope you find this book very useful and you will also enjoy learning CTools.

Umang Shah did his MSc (IT) at the Dhirubhai Ambani Institute of Information and Communication Technology (DA-IICT), which is among India's top tier institutes. After completing his masters of science, he worked in a startup firm, Cogbooks, as a BI-ETL developer and has working here for the last 3 years. As a startup culture, he worked on multiple roles and with multiple technologies. Pentaho, Amazon-EC2, and Cassandra are major parts of them. He writes a blog for helping Pentaho community: `https://shahumang.wordpress.com`.

This is the very first book I am reviewing, so I want to thank Packt Publishing for giving me this opportunity.

www.PacktPub.com

eBooks, discount offers, and more

Did you know that Packt offers eBook versions of every book published, with PDF and ePub files available? You can upgrade to the eBook version at `www.PacktPub.com` and as a print book customer, you are entitled to a discount on the eBook copy. Get in touch with us at `customercare@packtpub.com` for more details.

At `www.PacktPub.com`, you can also read a collection of free technical articles, sign up for a range of free newsletters and receive exclusive discounts and offers on Packt books and eBooks.

`https://www2.packtpub.com/books/subscription/packtlib`

Do you need instant solutions to your IT questions? PacktLib is Packt's online digital book library. Here, you can search, access, and read Packt's entire library of books.

Why subscribe?

- Fully searchable across every book published by Packt
- Copy and paste, print, and bookmark content
- On demand and accessible via a web browser

This book is dedicated to all the Pentaho Community contributors, and to the excellent Webdetails team for the excellent work they do. I hope all of you can keep the contributions coming and hope that the book can bring new ones.

Table of Contents

Preface

Using Pentaho allows you to build a complete analytics solution, and CTools brings an advanced flexibility to creating custom reports and making the most out of Pentaho. You can build your analytics dashboards/reports in an advanced and remarkable way. I can not avoid saying that Pentaho and CTools are two of the fastest and most amazing tools for building a complete solution that really takes your business to another level, and you probably would not be able to do with any other tool on the market.

CTools provides a way to use web technologies to deliver astounding data visualizations that are proven to create a huge visual impact, but the the learning curve can be quite slow; the documentation can be dispersed and sometimes not easy to obtain. So, this book will help overcome the problem, getting you up to speed and giving you basic and advanced concepts so that you can acquire all the knowledge you need.

By reading the book, you can learn not only how to understand how CTools work, but also the best way to make use of them. You will learn how to create custom dashboards to build incomparable analytics solutions. Throughout the book, your knowledge will increase, and at the end, you will be capable of creating your own custom and advanced analysis.

What this book covers

Chapter 1, Getting Started with CTools, gives a brief introduction to the history of CTools. It will also introduce the reader to the purpose of the tool and teaches the user what methods are needed to install Community Tools. It is important to take some time getting an introduction to some concepts before you start building dashboards with Community Tools, so this chapter is not optional. When developing a dashboard, the first step is to interact with the client and get the requirements. There is a need to understand what is the best way to display data on the dashboard, and of course, there are some techniques that can be used to have a clean and simple dashboard that is, at the same time, very informative and intuitive. Navigation inside the dashboard should respect the requirements, but should be easy to understand. There is also a need to use standard components with a custom style so that it can be a unique dashboard while being quick to develop. Understanding this and other concepts will make the difference when developing the dashboard, so this chapter exposes some considerations that should be taken into account while creating dashboards.

Chapter 2, Acquiring Data with CDA, is focused on the use of Community Data Access (CDA). Readers will find what kinds of Pentaho data sources we can use to acquire data using CDA, and also how to do it. How we can use parameters and all the other properties to get the desired results and how to manipulate the output that will be exposed to the dashboards or to the exports will also be covered.

Chapter 3, Building the Dashboard Using CDF, will cover the two ways to build Community Dashboards. To build a dashboard, readers can avoid the use of CDF, but to achieve better results and build incredible dashboards, users should know how it works. One of the most important parts when building a CTools dashboard is the life cycle, so readers will have the chance to know how the life cycle of the dashboards and the components works. Pentaho uses the CDF framework inside the platform, so some concepts will become clear to you. Readers will also be challenged to create their first dashboard using CDF to better understand the concepts of Community Dashboards Editor.

Chapter 4, *Leverage the Process with CDE,* will be focused on the advantages and disadvantages of using Community Dashboards Editor (CDE) and why to use CDE to build a dashboard. Here, we will learn how to create dashboards without writing code or leveraging the work without the need to write code. The reader will also learn how to build a responsive and interactive dashboard, starting with the main concepts, and how to use the available graphical interface. Among the other concepts, you will learn how to create a layout, use components, and set some queries to be used inside the components. The chapter will also teach what needs to be changed to quickly build dashboards when using CDE. An important part is how to add more resources to the dashboard, and include them in the execution of the dashboard.

Chapter 5, *Applying Filters to the Dashboard* , will show how to work with the most important and commonly used components. This chapter will cover filters and selectors that can be applied to the dashboard as one way to create interaction by filtering data for the full dashboard, or just some sections of it. A dashboard is meant to be easy to use and give good insights to get results at the first look. We can filter the information being displayed. This chapter covers the components we can use so that the user can have access to all the information, keeping it simple to understand and only providing information for the selected context.

Chapter 6, *Tables, Templates, Exports, and Text Components,* covers add-ins for both table and template components. An important part of building a dashboard is to find the best way to represent data on the dashboard. We should not focus on only showing a table, a chart, or any other component, but how to represent the data using that same component. So, this chapter covers the most commonly used components. There is also another component such as the exports and the text component. There are some tips on how to avoid performance issues in the dashboards.

Chapter 7, *Advanced Concepts Using CDF and CDE,* covers the advanced concepts when building dashboards with both CDF and CDE dashboards. CDF and CDE provide some really cool components that have more flexibility and allow you to build your own visualizations. So, we will also need to cover these components. You will face some requests to internationalize/localize dashboards, so we will also be covering it. There are some tips and advanced concepts that new CTools developers may not find easy to understand at first glance, but that more advanced users will find useful. The chapter also reinforces the concepts of references to components, parameters, and layout elements.

Chapter 8, *Visualizations Using CCC*, may be one of the most expected chapters. A dashboard is really useful and desirable when a user looks at it and can understand what is going on with the business without the need of having to look for quite a large amount of information. This is where visualizations become very useful. This chapter will teach the reader how to make customizations on the available charts produced by the Community Charts Components (CCC). This book will show how to apply properties that can be shared between multiple charts. Readers will get a better knowledge of how to customize charts, where to look for information, and see some more advanced features useful inside dashboards. I would like to cover all the aspects, concepts, and properties, but that's almost impossible. CCC is a huge tool with infinite customizations that can be applied, so we would need to focus on giving you what you really need to keep learning about CCC by yourself.

Chapter 9, *Pentaho App Builder*, talks about the one new feature created for Pentaho — the ability to create plugins without the need to create Java code. I would say this is one of the most interesting plugins created for Pentaho. By this time, readers already know how to create a dashboard. So, if you already know how to create jobs and transformations using Pentaho Data Integration, you should also be able to create plugins. We will need to understand the Community Plugin Kick-starter (CPK) and its relation with the Pentaho App Builder, and this chapter will explain it.

Chapter 10, *Embed, Deploy, and Debug*, will explain how to embed both CDF and CDE dashboards into third-party applications. Usually, one request from customers is how to embed a dashboard into one application. Using RequireJS, this is simple and very flexible. You can build mini dashboards that you easily embed into your application without interfering with its default behavior. This chapter will provide information on how you can do debugging on the dashboard using the developer's tools of your browser.

What you need for this book

The only requirements are to have a Pentaho 5.X installed, but it's recommended to install 6.X.

When installing Pentaho, there is the option to include some sample data, so please do it. Most of the samples make use of it, so to properly make use of samples, you will need to include them. It is known as the Steelwheels sample data. This includes a database of Metadata and Mondrian schemas.

To make proper use of Pentaho Builder Application Server, you will need a browser. Even if Pentaho, in some of its versions, supports Internet Explorer 8, we just can't use this version when building responsive dashboards or making use of CSS3. You will need to have a higher version, such as Internet Explorer 9 or even better, make use of Chrome, Firefox, or Safari.

The reader should have knowledge of JavaScript, JQuery, and Cascading Style Sheets (CSS). Not that it's mandatory to know the technologies, but it's the way the user will take the most out of some CTools.

Who this book is for

If you are a CTools developer and would like to expand your knowledge and create attractive dashboards and frameworks, this book is the go-to-guide for you. A basic knowledge of JavaScript and Cascading Style Sheets (CSS) is highly recommended.

Conventions

In this book, you will find a number of text styles that distinguish between different kinds of information. Here are some examples of these styles and an explanation of their meaning.

Code words in text, database table names, folder names, filenames, file extensions, pathnames, dummy URLs, user input, and Twitter handles are shown as follows: "We can include other contexts through the use of the include directive."

A block of code is set as follows:

```xml
<?xml version="1.0" encoding="UTF-8"?>
<CDADescriptor>
   <DataSources>
      <!-- HERE LIVES EACH ONE OF <Connection>-->
   </DataSources>
   <!-- HERE LIVES EACH ONE OF <DataAccess> -->
</CDADescriptor>
```

When we wish to draw your attention to a particular part of a code block, the relevant lines or items are set in bold:

```
[default]
exten => s,1,Dial(Zap/1|30)
exten => s,2,Voicemail(u100)
exten => s,102,Voicemail(b100)
exten => i,1,Voicemail(s0)
```

Any command-line input or output is written as follows:

```
# cp /usr/src/asterisk-addons/configs/cdr_mysql.conf.sample
    /etc/asterisk/cdr_mysql.conf
```

New terms and **important words** are shown in bold. Words that you see on the screen, for example, in menus or dialog boxes, appear in the text like this: "Clicking the **Next** button moves you to the next screen."

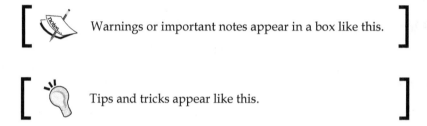

Warnings or important notes appear in a box like this.

Tips and tricks appear like this.

Reader feedback

Feedback from our readers is always welcome. Let us know what you think about this book—what you liked or disliked. Reader feedback is important for us as it helps us develop titles that you will really get the most out of.

To send us general feedback, simply e-mail feedback@packtpub.com, and mention the book's title in the subject of your message.

If there is a topic that you have expertise in and you are interested in either writing or contributing to a book, see our author guide at www.packtpub.com/authors.

Customer support

Now that you are the proud owner of a Packt book, we have a number of things to help you to get the most from your purchase.

Downloading the example code

You can download the example code files for this book from your account at
`http://www.packtpub.com`. If you purchased this book elsewhere, you can visit
`http://www.packtpub.com/support` and register to have the files e-mailed directly
to you.

You can download the code files by following these steps:

1. Log in or register to our website using your e-mail address and password.
2. Hover the mouse pointer on the **SUPPORT** tab at the top.
3. Click on **Code Downloads & Errata**.
4. Enter the name of the book in the **Search** box.
5. Select the book for which you're looking to download the code files.
6. Choose from the drop-down menu where you purchased this book from.
7. Click on **Code Download**.

You can also download the code files by clicking on the **Code Files** button on the
book's webpage at the Packt Publishing website. This page can be accessed by
entering the book's name in the **Search** box. Please note that you need to be logged in
to your Packt account.

Once the file is downloaded, please make sure that you unzip or extract the folder
using the latest version of:

- WinRAR / 7-Zip for Windows
- Zipeg / iZip / UnRarX for Mac
- 7-Zip / PeaZip for Linux

The code bundle for the book is also hosted on GitHub at `https://github.com/`
`PacktPublishing/Learning-Pentaho-CTools` . We also have other code bundles
from our rich catalog of books and videos available at `https://github.com/`
`PacktPublishing/`. Check them out!

Downloading the color images of this book

We also provide you with a PDF file that has color images of the screenshots/
diagrams used in this book. The color images will help you better understand the
changes in the output. You can download this file from `http://www.packtpub.com/`
`sites/default/files/downloads/LearningPentahoCTools_ColorImages.pdf`.

Errata

Although we have taken every care to ensure the accuracy of our content, mistakes do happen. If you find a mistake in one of our books—maybe a mistake in the text or the code—we would be grateful if you could report this to us. By doing so, you can save other readers from frustration and help us improve subsequent versions of this book. If you find any errata, please report them by visiting `http://www.packtpub.com/submit-errata`, selecting your book, clicking on the **Errata Submission Form** link, and entering the details of your errata. Once your errata are verified, your submission will be accepted and the errata will be uploaded to our website or added to any list of existing errata under the Errata section of that title.

To view the previously submitted errata, go to `https://www.packtpub.com/books/content/support` and enter the name of the book in the search field. The required information will appear under the **Errata** section.

Piracy

Piracy of copyrighted material on the Internet is an ongoing problem across all media. At Packt, we take the protection of our copyright and licenses very seriously. If you come across any illegal copies of our works in any form on the Internet, please provide us with the location address or website name immediately so that we can pursue a remedy.

Please contact us at `copyright@packtpub.com` with a link to the suspected pirated material.

We appreciate your help in protecting our authors and our ability to bring you valuable content.

Questions

If you have a problem with any aspect of this book, you can contact us at `questions@packtpub.com`, and we will do our best to address the problem.

Getting Started with CTools

We will start this chapter with a brief overview of the history of the CTools, and from there we will jump into the general concepts involved when building a dashboard. When building a dashboard, it's not enough to just start developing the dashboard — there is a process to follow and some tasks that you should know about in order to produce better work.

First, you will need to have a good understanding of the requirements, such as who is going to use the dashboard, what is the purpose, what it will be used for, and so on. The next step will be preparing a mock-up or design of the dashboard. It is essential that you understand the best way to display data on the dashboard, and of course there are some techniques that provide a clean and simple dashboard that is very informative and intuitive at the same time. Doing a functional breakdown of the entire dashboard will make a big difference when developing both the back end and front end of the dashboard.

When working in a team, you always need to know the responsibilities of each element of the project. This chapter will touch a little on each of these points. You can see this chapter as a way to demystify what you probably need to know and do before starting the development of the dashboard.

To be able to use the CTools, you need to install them, or if you already have the CTools, you need to learn how to update them, and how to check what version you have. To be able to follow the remaining chapters, we will also provide a brief introduction to the most important technologies and frameworks that the CTools use. This is really important, because for you to become an expert at developing dashboards using the CTools, you will need to know these technologies and frameworks, and have an idea what they are used for. You don't need to know the details about how they work just yet, so this chapter will not give you in-depth knowledge on each one of them.

Understanding these concepts and applying them will make all the difference while developing dashboards, so you should not consider this chapter as optional.

We will cover the following topics:

- A brief introduction to the CTools
- Considerations when creating the design of a dashboard
- The difference between dashboard design and mock-up
- Frameworks and libraries used when developing dashboards
- External tools to use while developing dashboards
- The processes available to install the CTools, and how to install them
- The process of developing a dashboard from beginning to end
- Interacting with clients and getting their requirements

Introducing the CTools

If you take a look at http://www.webdetails.pt/info/storywithtruth.html, you will find a great infographic with a timeline of the CTools.

Let's briefly talk about the CTools. The development of CTools started in the summer of 2008, just because the opinion of a client was, "That's great, but it's just too ugly." So, then there was a lot of work done on the development of the **Community Dashboard Framework (CDF)**, and in April 2009, the first CTool was adopted by Pentaho and integrated in version 3. But at that time, we needed to build a dashboard by writing all of the code, so in the second half of the same year, the first version of the **Community Dashboard Editor (CDE)** was released.

As the number of projects started to increase, it would have taken a huge amount of time to prepare a system for these projects. To tackle this issue, the **Community Build Framework (CBF)** was built. Then came the data layer abstraction, which was also adopted by Pentaho. This leveraged data access and at the same time, allowed to increase the number of accessible data systems.

The CTools became very popular, and the needs and interests of clients to have the best visualizations they could have increased, so a year after the first CTool, CDE started to include its own chart library, **Community Charts Components (CCC)**, which would later also be used in the visualizations produced by Pentaho Analyzer. Just four months after this, a series of CTools training sessions started. In the meantime, due to the needs of many clients, the possibility to export a chart as an image became reality with the **Community Graph Generator (CGG)**.

To increase the speed with which data is delivered to the user, and to improve the user experience when using the dashboards, the **Community Distributed Cache (CDC)** was released in January 2012. CDC, I believe, has some advantages compared to the two options that are currently provided and supported by Pentaho, particularly when it comes to cache management.

Pedro Alves, during one of his trips for the CTools training sessions, started a new plugin, the **Community Data Generator (CDG)**, which provided the functionality to set some options that made it possible to create dummy data to be used in the dashboards.

Another tool arrived in the summer of 2012, **Community Data Validation (CDV)**, which could be used to validate data and make sure it sends notifications to the right people. However, we are not going to cover this tool, because I believe we can achieve the same results using **Pentaho Data Integration (PDI)**.

I started to work at Webdetails in September 2012, and since then I have seen some other CTools, such as the **Community File Repository (CFR)**, which enables us to make use of files outside the solution repository.

Sometime later, **Sparkl**, nowadays known as Pentaho App Builder, was presented, which is built on top of the **Community Plugin Kickstart (CPK)**. Pentaho App Builder is a Pentaho plugin used to create Pentaho plugins without the need to know Java code. This made it possible for people who already knew how to use data integration and CDE to build a plugin. Now, there are a lot of plugins available on Pentaho Marketplace that were developed using this great tool.

In the meanwhile, **Pentaho Repository Synchronizer (PRS)** also arrived, and was created on top of Sparkl. It came out to be used with version 5 of Pentaho so users could avoid the inconvenience of having all their files and folders inside a database and not in the file system, as was the case in the previous versions.

 All the CTools have been built as open source projects and are available under Mozilla Public License, Version 2.0, licenses (`http://mozilla.org/MPL/2.0/`). All the projects are available under the public Git repository through `http:/www.github.com/webdetails`. Don't be shy to contribute.

Considerations before creating a dashboard

Nowadays, most business analytics tools have a way to create dashboards easily, but to this day, I have not encountered another that is capable of having the level of customizations that we can achieve with Pentaho and the CTools. Most business analytics solutions, like Pentaho, provide self-service business intelligence capabilities, but they don't provide capabilities for developers to build really customized dashboards.

I am sure that self-service capabilities are very important nowadays, when users can create their own dashboards/reports easily, but often we want to get some results that we are just not able to get using the self-service capability tools.

Pentaho provides the best of both worlds, the capability to create self-service reports/dashboards, but also to make use of the CTools to build high-customized visualizations and dashboards/reports. However, we should not think of custom and self-service reports as independent from each other, as they can live together and accomplish better results. A great example of this is the **Stream Line Data Refinery (SDR)** that Pentaho has implemented and made available to their clients. It uses a combination of a custom dashboard and Analyzer, where users are able to request and refine data to a small dataset that is modeled and published as a new data source, usable in the Analyzer to create self-service reports.

This solution solves a challenge in the area of Big Data. Data will be delivered to the end user through the Analyzer, but the request and control of the refinery process is done through a custom page, which is built like a dashboard using the CTools. We should see this custom dashboard as a web page that will make calls to ensure that it is getting a smaller dataset and will publish it. It's possible not only to make the selection, but also to fire some actions and control the status. At the end, it's possible to invoke an Analyzer report that can make use of the published data source. To get more details on this solution and how it works, you can take a look at `http://www.pentaho.com/Streamlined-Data-Refinery`.

Another example is CTools, used to embed the Analyzer by making use of its API. Highly customizable and embedded interfaces are just another example of where you can use the CTools, but this one is to the detriment of using self-service capabilities. As in the preceding SDR example, I really agree that self-service capabilities are very useful, but not always sufficient.

Dashboard Designer, like the Analyzer and Interactive Reports, is only available in the **Enterprise Edition** (EE). Dashboard Designer is a tool where, just by dragging-and-dropping, you are able to build a dashboard, create new content for the dashboard, or reuse some of the reports that you have already created. You can start building reports with the Analyzer, Interactive Reports, and Report Designer (after publishing them), and drag them onto a dashboard. This kind of dashboards is not very customizable, so you might need to use a custom dashboard that can be build with some of the CTools.

When using CTools you also have the ability to add filters to the dashboard and specify which elements will react to changes. Sometimes you just need to go further and create really custom reports that Analyzer and other business intelligence platforms are not capable of producing, and that is when most part of the CTools comes in. The CTools provide a way to create custom dashboards by offering very customizable data sources, components, and visualizations. This can lead to astounding dashboards. With them, you are able to create pixel perfect visualizations, without limits. I like to think that the only limit is our imagination.

So, one of the advantages of using the CTools is really to deliver custom dashboards with the visualizations that you need using the standard functionality, or by extending it. CTools dashboards are web pages built with **Hypertext Markup Language (HTML)**, **JavaScript**, and **Cascade Style Sheets (CSS)**. Like Dashboard Designer (the standard tool from Pentaho for building dashboards), Analyzer, and Interactive Reports, CTools dashboards are web-based and can be rendered in your browser, so there is no need to install a client application. The big difference between Analyzer, Interactive Reports, Dashboard Designer, and CTools dashboards is that the first three are self-service tools that allow you to build reports just by dragging-and-dropping, but you can face some limitations with them. You will not find these limitations when creating dashboards, reports, or web pages with the CTools.

Of course, you may face some difficulties when building some really custom visualizations, but even if you have some difficulties, you will be able to get them done, and that's where this book comes in—helping you to achieve great results. We are all conscious of the fact that it's very important for companies to have platforms that provide tools capable of creating insights and trends in an easy, but also flexible, way.

Let's suppose you want to create a dashboard as a landing page to launch other reports, but also provide **Key Performance Indicators (KPIs)** that can vary from user to user. You will not be able to do this with self-service tools, but you are able to achieve these goals using the CTools dashboards.

A very common request from final users is to have some kind of visualization that's not available out of the box, and using CTools, we are able to extend the tools to deliver the visualizations that users need and expect, such as a new selector, a map, or even a floor plan if needed.

Multi-tenancy, that is, the ability to serve multiple tenants on a unique server, is becoming very common in analytics, and when using CTools, you have a way to provide a custom interface (images, colors, fonts, and more) or whatever you need to the end user, just by knowing which user is logged in or which group the user belongs to. So based on a custom *property* that we can customize inside Pentaho, you are able to create the visualizations, dashboards, and reports that you have always dreamed of.

Top business analytics tools need to be able to provide machine learning/data mining/predictive capabilities. Not all are capable of this, but Pentaho is one of the tools that provides these capabilities. Think of the potential when using predictive analytics and custom visualizations to display the results. If we join the capability to mine data with the ability to provide user integrations and produce high custom visualizations, Pentaho and CTools are definitely the right choice. Let's suppose you want to create some simulations based on risk—for this you may provide the user with some interaction, process the risk analysis, and later provide a custom way to give the user the right information in a clearer way. Or, you may want to create a recommendation system that is able to provide this information to your end users with incredible visualizations.

When we look at some of the most successful business/companies over the last few years, such as Google, Facebook, LinkedIn, and Amazon, among others, we can see that they provide custom insights and trends to their clients, customers, and users. These insights are unique and focused on the business, and are getting better and better results every single day. Pentaho and CTools are the tools that allows us to get business further ahead just by using the combination of tools, plugins and capabilities.

For the first time it might not seem so easy to build a custom dashboard, but, if we put some effort in, we can ensure they get end users going in the right direction.

Social media and marketing analysis are also very important areas nowadays; for some cases it may be important to create custom dashboards where each one is different from the others. In those cases, we can always use CTools dashboards.

The first steps in creating a dashboard

There are a few steps to take before starting to develop the dashboard itself. First, we need to gather the requirements, then we need to see what the best visualizations are or the best way to display the information, then create a mock-up or dashboard design, next do a breakdown of the components and data sources to use, and later start the development of the dashboard. It's not the purpose of this book to go into detail about all of these points, but we can give you some insights.

Getting the right requirements

One of the first steps, and it's a really important one, is to collect the requirements. Gathering the requirements can be the difference between just doing a project and really delivering a valuable project that can have an impact and push companies forward. The following questions need to be answered:

- Who is going to use the dashboard?

  When designing a dashboard, we should consider the audience and what they need most. Different people in a company will want different information. Executives might want at-a-glance statistics and trending, whereas a department manager might want to get just an overview of some global results of the company (but will certainly need more details about what he is managing). A technician may need more detailed information.

- What expectations do the end users have?

  A dashboard is useful and users are happy when we provide the information that they need. It's important to know what expectations users have for the dashboard. This is an open question that may give you some ideas and help you really get to know the goals or the motivations behind wanting the dashboard.

- Is this dashboard replacing any other system/reports? Can you get a copy of them?

  If there are some reports we can use to get a clearer idea what needs to be displayed and what format the data should be in, that would be great. We could make a copy of a report/dashboard that is already being used, as it's much easier to understand the requirements if we can see the current report, and it may be useful when explaining the advantages of the change.

- Should we respect the existing **User Interface (UI)** guidelines (colors, fonts, layout, elements, and so on)?

  Usually, companies already have some UI elements, colors, and so on that are UI-related, and we may use them. This will also make it easier for end users to focus on the real information and not get distracted by colors that are different to what they are used to. Of course, this should not break the rules of creating proper UIs.

- What information should be displayed?

  A dashboard is a quick way to display KPIs, insights, and trends, so we need to discover what the dashboard should show to the end user. Users need to be able to quickly access the information.

- What granularity will the data have and what level should be displayed?

  It's also important to understand what the granularity of the data is to be displayed, as the filters will depend on this. The level of detail that we have on the dashboard can dramatically change the way we display each one of the sections or the way they interact with each other. Having details about one KPI, to see why sales are going down, can reduce the time needed to take action. Just by clicking on top of the KPI to get details is one of best ways to go. This can also be important because of performance reasons.

- How is the data being filtered? What filters will we need, and for what sections?

  What data levels we should be able to filter within the dashboard is also important. Filters are one of the most commonly used components when sifting through data on a dashboard, however any other component can also be used. We can have filters for particular sections of the dashboard, but it is usual to have common filters applied all over the dashboard.

  Having a way to filter the time range and frame for the available KPIs, charts, and tables, will give the user valuable information, for instance, providing the ability to filter data for the last 30 days, last seven days, or the last hour.

- What are the best visualizations for achieving the intended results?

  Just by looking at the dashboard, the user should be able to understand the results without spending too much time on understanding how to read the information. The information displayed should be intuitive to read, and if there is too much data, an update to a section may be required. The value and the quantity of the data will also determine the best visualization.

- Will the data be displayed to users with different roles?

  Different roles have different responsibilities and access to different levels of information. While many KPIs are shared, different ones may also be required for different roles.

Creating a mock-up or dashboard design

After getting the requirements, we should create a mock-up or a dashboard design of the dashboard. With the answers/requirements determined in advance, we now start by creating some kind of wireframe containing all the sections and each one of the components. Here, the wireframe can be seen as a two-dimensional illustration that specifically focuses on space allocation, prioritization of content, the functionalities available, and the intended behaviors.

Whenever possible, this should be done by UI/UX experts, and should provide the necessary details that are important not only for visualizations, but also for navigation. No one wants to learn how to navigate a dashboard, or have training just to understand the dashboard, so just keep it simple. We should never undervalue the user's visual experience. Use visual elements, colors, and styles, but not too much. Apply alignments and layering to deliver information and increase the appeal. Use images if absolutely necessary, and be consistent when creating multiple dashboards. Usually, a clean dashboard is better than a full dashboard where users have to look around and may have trouble finding what they need. Start with a simple and clean dashboard that has the essential information, and provide a way for users to drill down.

The interaction with, and feedback from, the users is very important in this phase, because what we agree to do in this phase may become difficult to change after starting the actual development of the dashboard. Of course, we may need to make some adjustments, but it should not be more than that.

There are many tools to do this with, and if you are not a designer, you can use simple tools that provide an easy way to build wireframe mock-ups, and can guide you during development. But if you can have a pixel perfect design, don't hesitate to get it, as it will make a big difference to the final result.

Of course, interaction with the developer is also important, because the designer may end up creating something that may become time-expensive to develop, and all the teams working together will certainly find a way that works for everyone.

Don't forget that a dashboard should be fast to load. Having the best-looking dashboard is not always enough if it's slow to get results to the user. Also, it's easier for a user to understand waiting for drilled-down data than for main KPIs. Anyhow, you should ensure fast responses to keep your users engaged, so the project team should bear this in mind.

Team and project management

When working on medium-to-large projects, we often end up having a team working on the project. The team can be divided into two or more groups, for example, the back end and the front end. When working on the front end, it may be useful to have more than one developer working on a single dashboard. When that happens, it's always a good idea to have a project manager that can lead the project and team, and sync with the client's project manager, without the need for developer interaction, so everyone can focus on their own tasks and responsibilities. Even when working as a solitary person on a project, you will get better results if you can make a plan of the work to be done and the time window.

Developing a dashboard

Having already completed the dashboard design, we need to start work on the dashboard itself. Here, we should do what's called a functional breakdown of the dashboard. This is a document where you can specify the components to be used on each section of the dashboard, and the queries and parameters to be set on each of the components.

It's also very useful if you add the estimated time that will be spent on each task so you can have a good idea of how much time will be needed to develop the dashboard. This is a great help in managing not only the work that was planned versus the work that has been completed, but also to give you an overall idea of the components, parameters, listeners, and queries to use. For each one of the queries, the breakdown should include the resulting columns and types.

You will spend some time creating the functional breakdown, but you will save time when developing the dashboard, as ideas will become clearer, you'll anticipate some problems, and some questions will be raised that need answers. You will also gain massive advantages from this if you are working on a team, as each team member will know what has to be done and how to achieve the goals.

Doing this breakdown will also give you an advantage when building the documentation for the project/dashboard, and also for the knowledge transfer at the end of the project. When doing the knowledge transfer to the customers, we need to ensure this information is the best, is complete, and is easy to understand. When delivering to a customer technical team, we should be able to do this in a complete and understandable way. The functional breakdown will help them understand how the dashboard works. So, everyone can take advantage of this document.

Once all the tasks are delivered to the team's different elements, the team should start the development of the back end and the front end of the dashboard. But they should always look back to the dashboard design and the functional breakdown and take these into account.

Don't forget the version control

Create or request a version control repository, and make sure that the team's elements have the proper access and rights to it. We will come back to version control later on in the book.

The time has come when you need to start creating your dashboard, but for this you need to install the CTools.

Installing CTools

One of the first steps when developing a custom dashboard is to install the CTools. It's required that you already have Pentaho installed and well set up. There are three ways of installing the CTools:

- Using Pentaho Marketplace
- Using the `ctools-installer` (this is only for earlier versions of Pentaho such as 4.5 and 4.8; it might work on Pentaho 5.x, but it is not recommended, and it will not work for 6.x)
- Manually

Starting from version 5.2, CTools comes already installed, so you can skip the installation process; however, it's important to know the process because sooner or later you may want to upgrade. The standard CTools, the ones that come installed with Pentaho and that were used during the writing of this book, do not allow you to edit or create a new CDE dashboard. But you can perform a few changes to make this possible. You just need to uncomment the `<operation>` and `<overlays>` code lines in the following files for the CDE and CDA plugins:

- `/cda/plugin.xml`
- `/pentaho-cdf-dd/plugin.xml`

The plugins can be found in the `pentaho-solutions/system` folder of your Pentaho installation.

Installing the CTools using Pentaho Marketplace

The first way, and definitely the easiest, is using Pentaho Marketplace. To follow this process, you need to make sure you have a Pentaho version that already includes Marketplace; otherwise you should download the files and install it first.

Pentaho **Community Edition** (**CE**) already comes with Pentaho Marketplace installed by default, which may not happen in EE. Starting from Pentaho 6.1 and above, the Marketplace should come already installed by default.

The first step is to check whether Marketplace is available in your Pentaho version. In the **Pentaho User Console** (**PUC**), you can click on the operational menu and check that you have an option available to execute Marketplace. If you have it already installed, you can skip the installation of Pentaho Marketplace; otherwise you will need to install it.

If I had to provide a definition of Pentaho Marketplace, I would say this: Marketplace is a graphical interface running on Pentaho itself that allows users to know what plugins are available and to install/uninstall them, at the same time giving developers the ability to publish their work and make solutions or utilities available to others that may solve a problem or add a new functionality.

Marketplace can be downloaded from `http://community.pentaho.com/marketplace/plugins/`. Depending on the version of Pentaho you are using, check it using PUC menu under **Help** | **About**, and download Marketplace for the version of Pentaho you are using. You will get a zip file, so unzip the file and, after stopping the Pentaho Server, copy the unzipped folder into your `pentaho-solution/system` folder. You will end up with a folder named `marketplace` in your system folder. Start the BA Server and you should have Marketplace already available to be used.

Upon launching Pentaho Marketplace, you should get an image like the following figure:

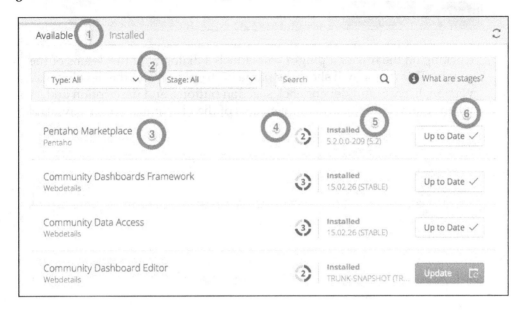

The numbers in the preceding screenshot are explained as follows:

1. The tabs on the top area of the frame let you filter the plugins by status. They are available in Marketplace (will show all plugins), or can be installed on your Pentaho server.

2. The drop-down selectors allows you to filter the plugins.

    Each one of the rows represents a plugin. You can identify the plugin by its name and developer. You can get more information, or search for plugins online, at the Marketplace website (http://www.pentaho.com/marketplace/).

3. You can also identify the development stage of the plugin. The number and color identify the development stage. Depending on whether it's in a Customer Lane or Community Lane, there will be a blue or green color, where the number represents the stage in each group. To get more details on this, please visit the Marketplace page at http://www.pentaho.com/marketplace/.

4. The status can be one of two options, **Installed** and **Available**. A plugin that is already installed can then be updated.

5. Depending on the available actions, you will get different buttons such as:

Clicking on the row of a plugin will launch a dialog with the details of the plugin. This dialog will show the name of the plugin and the developer, version, license, and dependencies, action buttons, and description and, when scrolling down, some screenshots of the plugin may also be available:

It's important to know what version of the plugin we should install. This may be a standard version, a stable version, or a trunk version. The standard version is the version that comes installed with Pentaho 5.2 and above. This version lets you open dashboards or use each of the CTools, but with some limitations. For example, you will be able to open CDE dashboards, but you will not be able to create or edit them. To create or edit dashboards you need to install the stable version.

From the drop-down menu, you should select which version you want to install. Then, you should click on the action, which is **Install** or **Uninstall**. After clicking on **Install/Uninstall**, you will get a confirmation dialog and if you proceed, you will also get some feedback about the success of the request made as a number shown in previous screenshot:

1. From the dropdown, it will be possible to select the version.
2. From the buttons, it will be possible to install/uninstall it.

By selecting and installing another version, the files will be overwritten, so there is no need to uninstall the previous version. Note that after the process is completed, you need to restart the BA server.

Check the plugin dependencies and don't forget to install them
When installing a plugin, you need to take a look at the dependencies, as they are not installed automatically when you install a plugin. No order is required but all the dependencies must be installed.

Installing the CTools using the CTools installer

The CTools installer, which should only be used for Pentaho versions earlier than 5.x, is a script that will download the proper version of the selected plugins, unzip the folder, and copy the files into the right folders. You can download it from `https://github.com/pmalves/ctools-installer`. When executed, the script will check whether there is a new version and will inform you about it. I advise you to always install the updates, as depending on the version of Pentaho you are using, you may need an upgrade, and it can make a big difference.

To make use of the script, you need to run it from the command line, and if you're running just the script with no options, you will get a list of changes in the script, as well as the usage. When running `./ctools-installer.sh`, you will get something like:

```
Usage: ctools-installer.sh -s solutionPath [-w pentahoWebapPath] [-b branch]


-s    Solution path (eg: /biserver/pentaho-solutions)

-w    Pentaho webapp server path (required for cgg on versions before
4.5. eg: /biserver-ce/tomcat/webapps/pentaho)

-b    Branch from where to get ctools, stable for release, dev for trunk.
Default is stable

-c    Comma-separated list of CTools to install (Supported module-names:
marketplace,cdf,cda,cde,cgg,cfr,sparkl,cdc,cdv,saiku,saikuadhoc)

-y    Assume yes to all prompts

--no-update Skip update of the ctools-installer.sh

-n    Add newline to end of prompts (for integration with CBF)

-r    Directory for storing offline files

-h    This help screen
```

To successfully run the installer and install the plugins, you will need to provide the solution path using the -s options and specify the absolute path to your `Pentaho Solutions` folder or the path where you are running the script from.

`Pentaho Web App` folder is optional, and is only mandatory when installing the CGG plugin on versions previous to Pentaho 4.5. You will not need to specify this option otherwise.

You may also specify the branch to install CTools from. For that option, you may use a value of `stable` or `dev`, depending on what you want to install.

The stable version is the one to use

In some cases, you can use the development version. For example, if you need a bug fix or just to make use of new functionality, then you might want use the dev version; otherwise you should avoid it.

You will be asked something like:

```
Install CDF? This will delete everything in pentaho-solutions/system/
pentaho-cdf. you sure? (y/N)
```

You should answer `y` when you want to install the referred plugin, or `N` if you don't want to install it. But you can also avoid this if you want to confirm the installation of all plugins. For this, add the option `-y` to the `ctools-installer` script. This will confirm the installation of all the plugins available for the selected branch.

Depending on the branch, the number of CTools to be installed will also vary

When using the `Assume yes to all prompts` option, make sure you know which ones are installed for the branch you are selecting. The number of plugins will be different depending on the branch you are selecting. When using `dev` on the branch option, it will include more plugins compared to the `stable` branch.

Sometimes, you don't want to install all the Ctools at once. For this, `-c` is available. This should be used followed by the abbreviation of each of the CTools names that you want to install without a prompt, separated by a comma. This gives you a way to automate the install of the CTools.

When you are behind a proxy, you may have some difficulties using the script. This blog post from Pedro Alves can help you overcome the problem: `http://pedroalves-bi.blogspot.de/2014/07/using-pentaho-marketplace-over-proxy-or.html`.

There is a new option that lets you use the installer to download the plugin, and later install the CTools in offline mode. To achieve this, you should use the option `-r` and specify the folder to use. If no folder exists, the script will create it and download the folders to it, but will not install them. When the folder you are pointing to with the `-r` option exists, then it will install the CTools using the files inside, without the need to download them. Note that you can copy the downloaded folder to another location/machine, and when pointing to the existing folder, the installer will use them. So the first time, you will need to run the script from a machine that is able to successfully download the CTools `.zip` files from the Internet. You can see what the options are by running the command:

```
./ctools-installer.sh
```

Here is an example of the syntax of a complete command to install the CTools:

```
./ctools-installer.sh -s pentaho-solutions/ -b stable -c cdf,cda,cde,cgg
-r offlineCToolsFiles
```

This will create a folder and subfolders with the CTools files, or you can just install them from the specified location.

Manually installing the CTools

A manual installation of the CTools is also possible. For this, you should download the plugins yourself. Go to the Marketplace web page (`http://www.pentaho.com/marketplace`) where you can select your version of Pentaho and the plugin, and download it. Unzip the folders and copy them into the `pentaho-solutions/system` folder. When restarting the server, the plugins will be working properly. Just make sure you are downloading the version of the plugin that corresponds to your Pentaho version. Be careful with the versions you are installing, and make sure that all the dependencies are also installed, because some plugins are dependent on each other. For example, when installing CDE you also need CDF to be installed.

Concepts and frameworks used

You should already know that the CTools work on the back end using Java, and make use of the Pentaho API, and on the client side, work on top of HTML, CSS, and JavaScript.

CDF and implicitly CDE are HTML pages that employ JavaScript to make dashboards more interactive and dynamic. These tools also make use of CSS to make the user interface the most astounding it can be.

To leverage the code and work on the CTools side, but also to make it possible to use the most recent and advanced technology, they include some frameworks/libraries that you can take a look at. The most used ones and the ones you should take a look at are as follows:

Utilities:

- jQuery (https://jquery.com/)
- jQueryUI (http://jqueryui.com/)
- jQuery i18n (https://plugins.jquery.com/i18n/)
- Mustache (https://github.com/janl/mustache.js)
- Backbone (http://backbonejs.org/)
- Underscore (http://underscorejs.org/)
- Moment (http://momentjs.com/)
- Require (http://requirejs.org/)

Layout-related:

- Modernizr (http://modernizr.com/)
- Bootstrap (http://getbootstrap.com/)
- Blueprint (http://www.blueprintcss.org/)
- Font-awesome (http://fortawesome.github.io/Font-Awesome/)

Components:

- Raphael (http://raphaeljs.com/)
- Protovis (http://mbostock.github.io/protovis/)
- DataTables (https://www.datatables.net/)
- Community Charts Components – CCC (www.webdetails.pt/ccc)
- Select2 (https://select2.github.io/)
- Chosen (http://harvesthq.github.io/chosen/)
- Sparkline (http://omnipotent.net/jquery.sparkline/#s-about)
- Fancybox (http://fancybox.net/)

Some of these frameworks and libraries are covered in the book, at least a part of the libraries and frameworks. To make the most out of them, you should read their documentation. It's not the purpose of this book to teach you how to work with them.

Summary

By now, you should have learned what the most common uses of the CTools are. You got to know a summary of the CTools, a little bit of history, and how they were born. You also now know how to install them using the different processes that exist. We talked about the frameworks/libraries that are used with them, but you should gain some more knowledge on how they work, because that will make all the difference when building your dashboards. For that you can refer to the provided links, the official webpages and at least get an idea of how they work.

You won't have a full understanding about the process of building CTools dashboards just yet, but you have an idea, and it's just a matter of adjusting process to the way you work and to provide the best services to your clients. You saw that an important part of this process is to ask the right questions and get a full and accurate knowledge of the business and its goals.

To be able to build a dashboard we need to get data, so in the next chapter, you will learn how to use CDA, and find out how to get the most out of it.

2
Acquiring Data with CDA

When we want to display data on a dashboard, we need to get this data from anywhere and display it in the easiest way possible, without having to write code to parse the results in a way that components can make use of these results. Using Pentaho, you have many ways to access data. If you are calling a report built with Pentaho plugins or client tools, you will be able to select one kind of data source, but if you want to use your own application and make use of Pentaho data, it would be possible for you to use XMLA, Kettle transformations as web services, and the **Community Data Access (CDA)** plugin.

The purpose of this book is to cover Community Tools, so this chapter is focused on the use of CDA. You will learn about the available data sources, how to create a new data source, how to pass some parameters to the query to get the right results, and then how to preview the results. You can write your own customized queries but if this is not enough, then you will learn how to manipulate the output that will be exposed to the dashboards or to the exports.

CDA also makes it possible to export the results of your queries to various standard types as a result, so this chapter will also explain how to make use of that endpoint. There is also a chance to combine data from different data sources to make a join or union, so this is also covered in this chapter.

This chapter focuses on teaching you how CDA works, so we will get deep and write some code. You may not even need to write it, however, you will get a better and deeper understanding of how CDA works by doing so. Don't be scared, because it's really simple to create CDA data sources without writing code or editing XML files manually.

This chapter covers the following topics:

- Available Pentaho data sources using CDA
- Defining a new data source
- Testing and displaying the results of a query
- Using parameters to get the expected results
- Available endpoints and how to export results
- Creating compound queries
- Making use of the cache to improve performance
- Sorting and pagination on server side

Introduction to CDA

CDA was one of the first CTools. Its main purpose is to provide data abstraction for multiple kinds of data sources wrapped as web services. It was first created to be used as an interface between the data connections and the **Community Dashboard Framework (CDF)**, but nowadays it can also be used in Report Designer to embed data in third-party applications.

CDA includes many different output types that we can configure, and also includes some configurable cache options to optimize performance, which you will have the chance to learn about. Another great feature in CDA that is somehow related to performance, is to sort and paginate on the server side.

The following diagram is an example of how CDA can be used to acquire data from. CDA is able to provide data to a CDF and/or CDE dashboards. However, an external application can get data directly from CDA using its endpoints. When requested for data, CDA will check whether the cache is enabled and whether there are results already cached. It will only query the final data sources when no values for that query (that includes the parameters used) have been cached, values in the cache have already expired, or the cache keys do not match:

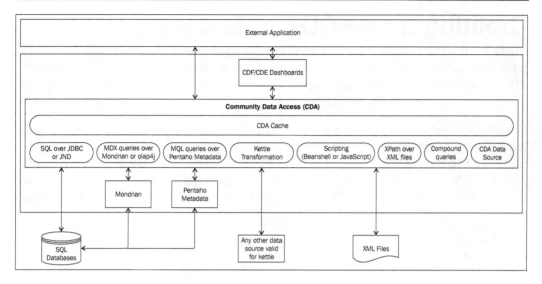

To enable the cache, we need to set some options when defining the CDA data source, but let's focus on the general functionality and leave these details to be explained later on in this chapter.

As we can see in the diagram, the available data sources for CDA are:

- SQL over JDBC or JNDI.
- MDX queries over Mondrian or olap4j.
- MQL queries over a Pentaho metadata connection.
- Kettle transformations.
- Scripting (only Beanshell and JavaScript are currently supported).
- XPath over XML files.
- Compound queries.

CDA files are a definition of the different sources to get data from. As you can have multiple data sources defined inside a single CDA file, you need to specify an **identifier (ID)**. ID: the identifier of the connection. This child element is the unique identifier for that same CDA data source. Setting this child element would allow you to identify a particular query to be executed and get the data from it. It can also be seen as or called **Data AccessID**. It is mandatory and unique — the opposite of some other properties that are common to all data sources, which we will cover later in this chapter.

Creating a new CDA data source

There are multiple ways to create CDA data sources. One of the ways is to use CDE, where no code or XML is needed, and we will cover this later in the CDE chapter. There is another way, which is using the CDA editor, or just editing the file by hand using the Pentaho Text Editor plugin.

For now, I want you to understand the internals of CDA, so we need to start with the hardest way to create a CDA file—by creating/editing an XML file. The CDA files that are XML files will define the Pentaho repository and will have a `.cda` extension. This way, Pentaho will recognize the file extension and will provide the capability to preview the results or edit the file. The main structure of a CDA file is the following:

```
<?xml version="1.0" encoding="UTF-8"?>
<CDADescriptor>
   <DataSources>
      <!-- HERE LIVES EACH ONE OF <Connection>-->
   </DataSources>
   <!-- HERE LIVES EACH ONE OF <DataAccess> -->
</CDADescriptor>
```

As a `.cda` file is written using XML syntax, let's consider the concepts behind XML. XML files have elements and attributes.

The first line dictates that the file is written using the XML format type and the following lines will define all the connections and data access. We do it using the CDADescriptor element. Inside it, we will have a data source element with the definition of the data sources that can be used by different queries. It does not make sense to define the connections to the database when defining a query. Most of the time, queries that we want to execute share the same connections settings, so we can define the settings for the connections.

When defining the properties for each data access, we need to set some attributes like in the following example:

```
<Connection id="1" type="sql.jdbc">
...
</Connection>
```

Downloading the example code

You can download the example code files for this book from your account at `http://www.packtpub.com`. If you purchased this book elsewhere, you can visit `http://www.packtpub.com/support` and register to have the files e-mailed directly to you.

You can download the code files by following these steps:

- Log in or register to our website using your e-mail address and password.
- Hover the mouse pointer on the **SUPPORT** tab at the top.
- Click on **Code Downloads & Errata**.
- Enter the name of the book in the **Search** box.
- Select the book for which you're looking to download the code files.
- Choose from the drop-down menu where you purchased this book from.
- Click on **Code Download**.

You can also download the code files by clicking on the **Code Files** button on the book's webpage at the Packt Publishing website. This page can be accessed by entering the book's name in the **Search** box. Please note that you need to be logged in to your Packt account.

Once the file is downloaded, please make sure that you unzip or extract the folder using the latest version of:

- WinRAR / 7-Zip for Windows
- Zipeg / iZip / UnRarX for Mac
- 7-Zip / PeaZip for Linux

The code bundle for the book is also hosted on GitHub at `https://github.com/PacktPublishing/Learning-Pentaho-CTools`. We also have other code bundles from our rich catalog of books and videos available at `https://github.com/PacktPublishing/`. Check them out!

The following attributes are mandatory:

- **ID**: This is used to define a unique name that will later be used to identify the connections that the queries will be using.

- **Type**: This is used to define the type of connection, and this will set the elements that we need to have inside. When using CDE, this type will be set automatically when selecting the data source type to create.

  After having all the connections defined, you will need to jump and start creating the data access. For each one of the queries, create an element like the following example:

  ```
  <DataAccess id="1" connection="1" type="sql" access="private"
              cache="true" cacheDuration="300">
      . . .
  </DataAccess>
  ```

The following attributes should be set:

- `id`: This is used to define the data access identifier that will be used in the components.

- `connection`: This is the identifier of the connection created previously. Different `DataAccess id` can share the same `connection id`.

- `access`: This defines whether the data access is visible. Here we can have one of two values: private or public. Private will say that the data access will not be visible, and public says the opposite. You may want to define that a data source is private when it is just to be used inside compound queries to create unions or joins between queries.

- `cache`: This defines whether the results of the query will be cached. Possible values are true and false. You should set it to true if you want your query to be cached. The default value is true.

- `cacheDuration`: This defines the cache duration in seconds. The query will be executed again after the specified seconds have passed. The query will be executed and the results cached again. This attribute will be ignored when the cache is set to false. The default value is 3600, the same as one hour expressed in seconds.

- `type`: We have the same goal when defining a connection and a Data Access, but they have different purposes, so we also need to specify the query type.

You can take a look at the following example to see how your `.cda` file should look after defining all the connections and Data Access. The example used is to define a query in a new type, and it uses the JSON syntax:

```xml
<?xml version="1.0" encoding="UTF-8"?>
<CDADescriptor>
    <DataSources>
        <Connection id="query" type="scripting.scripting">
            <Initscript></Initscript>
            <Language>beanshell</Language>
        </Connection>
    </DataSources>
    <DataAccess access="public" connection="query"
                id="query" type="jsonScriptable">
        <Cache duration="3600" enabled="true"/>
        <Columns/>
        <Parameters/>
        <Query>{
            "resultset":[["row1", 0]],
            "metadata":[
                {"colIndex":0,"colType":"String","colName":"value"},
                {"colIndex":1,"colType":"Integer","colName":"name2"}
            ]}
        </Query>
    </DataAccess>
</CDADescriptor>
```

Once you have the file uploaded/saved and available inside the Pentaho repository, you will get the ability to use a CDA editor/previewer.

There is an easy way to create CDA data sources

Like I already told before, there are easier ways to define a CDA data source. Later, you will see that you can also use CDE to create/edit data sources in a CDA file in a simpler way, using an intuitive **Graphical User Interface (GUI)**. Don't get scared.

You should now be able to create a new CDA file. To do so, you should use your preferred code editor. Start by creating a new file in your file system with the name `myFistQuery.cda` and add the XML we just mentioned. Upload the file into the Pentaho repository and then open the file by clicking on **Open** in the right section of the **Pentaho User Console**. Select the **Data Access identifier**.

Available types of CDA data sources

The data sources covered in this book are the ones already pointed out previously, but we need to see them in detail. To create a new data source, you should also specify the attribute type that will be used to distinguish the method to be called on the server side to get the data and return the results. Depending on the data source that you are creating, you should also specify some properties that may be different depending on the kind of data source. Let's look at each one of the available options.

Each one of the following distinguished subsections will give you a brief overview and inform you about the properties that should be defined for the connections and also for the Data Access types. There are some common properties, such as the columns, that we will cover later in this chapter. For now, we will only focus on the different ones.

SQL databases

You can use this type of connection to get data from any source that uses **Structured Query Language (SQL)** and that can be reached using a JNDI connection or a JDBC driver. You can use one of these two kinds:

- sql.jdbc: To be utilized when using SQL over JDBC
- sql.jndi: To be utilized when using SQL over JNDI

    When creating a connection of the sql.jdbc type, we should also specify the following properties:

    ○ Driver: The Java class name to use (for example, org.postgresql. Driver)

    ○ URL: The URL to connect to (for example, jdbc:postgresql:// localhost:5432/database)

    ○ User: The username to use

    ○ Pass: The user's password

    When defining the connection for a sql.jndi connection, you would need to set the following properties:

    ○ jndi: The connection's name as defined in the context.xml file

JNDI autocomplete filed when using CDE
When setting this child element using CDE editor, a list of the JNDI connections available will be presented to you.

When specifying the Data Access properties, there is one that is mandatory:

- `Query`: Provides the SQL query to be executed

Mondrian cubes

When specifying the type for an MDX connection, we have the following available types:

- `mondrian.jdbc`: To be utilized when using MDX over JDBC
- `mondrian.jndi`: To be utilized when using MDX over JNDI
- `olap4j.defaultolap4j`: To be utilized when using MDX over olap4j

To set a connection of a `mondrian.jdbc` type, the following properties must be defined:

- **Driver**: The Java class name to use (for example, `org.postgresql.Driver`)
- **URL**: The URL to connect to (for example, `jdbc:postgresql://localhost:5432/database`)
- **User**: The username to use
- **Pass**: The user's password
- **Catalog**: The Mondrian schema to use

When creating a connection of the `mondrian.jndi` type, use the following properties:

- **jndi**: The jndi identifier
- **Catalog**: The Mondrian schema to use

And when creating a connection of the `olap4j.defaultolap4j` type, you should use:

- **Driver**: The Java class name to use (for example, `mondrian.olap4j.MondrianOlap4jDriver`)
- **URL**: The URL used to get call the driver class (for example, `jdbc:mondrian:`)

- **JDBCUser**: The username for the connection to the database (for example, `pentaho_user`)

- **JDBCPassword**: The password to verify authentication on the database (for example, `password`)

- **JDBCDriver**: The driver for the connection to the database (for example, `org.hsqldb.jdbcDriver`)

- **JDBC**: The URL to connect to the database (for example, `jdbc:hsqldb:hsql://localhost:9001/Sampledata`)

- **Catalog**: The path to the Mondrian schema (for example, `mondrian:/SteelWheels`)

To define the Data Access for a Mondrian data source, we should start discussing the difference between normalized and denormalized output. It's out of the scope of this book to explain data normalization/denormalization in detail, but it's important that you know the difference between them.

Normalized queries will have an output as expected, with the same number of columns as defined, but for denormalized queries—regardless of the number of selected measures—CDA will only display the name of the column and the value. Looking at the examples provided by the CDA samples, you would see the difference between them. With the normalized queries, we will get the result as provided in the query:

[Time].[(All)]	[Time].[Years]	[Measures].[Sales]	[Measures].[Quantity]
All Years	2004	4750205.89	47151
All Years	2005	1513074.46	14607

The denormalized queries will have a different output format, as referred to before, and will only have two columns representing the measures. All the selected measures in columns will be denormalized to appear as levels and value, where each level represents the measure name, followed by the value. Each one of the measures names will appear as a value of the column representing the level:

[Time].[(All)]	[Time].[Years]	[Measures].[MeasuresLevel]	Measure
All Years	2004	Quantity	47151
All Years	2005	Quantity	14607
All Years	2005	Sales	1513074.46
All Years	2004	Sales	4750205.89

Looking at both tables, it is easy to understand the big difference between them. This definition should be specified in the type attribute when creating the Data Access element. Depending on connection type and the output format, you should choose one of the following types: MDX, denormalizedMDX, olap4j, and denormalizedOlap4j.

So when defining the Data Access for an MDX data source inside a .cda file, you should also specify the following properties:

- **Banded**: This is only used and valid for normalized queries, and it also defines how the output is. If a classic mode is used, the result will be like we showed previously. When using a compact mode, only one column will be presented for each one of the dimensions used, corresponding to the lowest selected level.

- **Query**: This is the query to be executed.

Pentaho metadata

The Pentaho metadata data sources are used when acquiring data using a **Pentaho Metadata Schema**. When specifying a metadata query, we need to set the metadata. metadata type. This allows Pentaho metadata to be accessed from a dashboard through an MQL query. To do this, and when defining the connection, we should provide the following properties:

- **DomainId**: The domain used when creating the metadata schema
- **XmiFile**: The path and name of the file of the metadata schema

When creating the Data Access, we also need to specify:

- **Query**: A valid metadata query to be used to get data to the dashboard

Kettle transformations

This kind of data source, kettle transformations, allows you to get data from a kettle transformation. Besides the fact that it delivers powerful **Extract**, **Transform**, and **Load** (ETL) capabilities, it allows us to have many input sources. It provides a GUI with zero coding required, and the great ability to connect, combine, and transform data from multiple sources, making it easier when we have to deal with a hybrid data ecosystem. It also makes it possible to use predictive analytics.

Whatever you do with kettle, you will then be able to get data from a particular step in the transformation. Some time ago, it was only possible to call a transformation, but now we have the ability to run jobs from inside a transformation, which makes it even more powerful. Let's suppose you need some information from MongoDB. Well, you will be able to acquire data from MongoDB using a kettle transformation that will be called from the dashboard.

Also, let's suppose you want to apply some data mining algorithms using Weka or R. You can achieve your goals with kettle and get the results in your dashboard.

It's very simple to use — you just need to create a data source, and you should use an attribute type of `kettle.TransFromFile`. Also, when setting the connection, you will need to specify the following properties:

- **KtrFile**: This is used to specify the path and name of your transformation.
- **Variables**: This is used to specify the mapping between kettle parameters and the parameters used in the dashboard. You know how to use parameters in kettle transformations, you already know that you might specify parameters in your kettle transformations in a way you can run those kettle transformation with values that can be specified when executing them. The dashboard can also make use of parameters, which we will cover later in this chapter.

You should make use of the element "variables", to create a relationship between the parameters used inside the dashboard and the parameters you have defined inside your dashboard. To make use of this, you should specify as many variables as you need, the `datarow-name`, and the `variable-name` attributes.

If you look at the `.cda` samples, you will find a `kettle.cda` transformation that is defining parameters to be sent to the transformation. Let's look at the sample:

```
<Connection id="1" type="kettle.TransFromFile">
  <KtrFile>sample-trans.ktr</KtrFile>
  <variables datarow-name="myRadius"/>
  <variables datarow-name="zipCode" variable-name="myDashZipCode"/>
</Connection>
```

The first variable defines a `datarow-name`, but it does not define a variable name, and that's because the parameter inside the transformation has the same name as the parameter defined to be used in the data source. The second one defines both `datarow-name` and `variable-name`, and that's because the names are not similar, so we need to create the map between them.

When defining the Data Access, we also need to define the kettle step name that we want to retrieve the data from. This is done using the query child element:

- **Query**: This defines the name of the step to get data from

Scripting data sources

Scriptable data sources are very useful when you start to build your dashboard, but you still do not have a query to start with. Sometimes, when working in a team, this may happen. If two teams start to work on the same project at the same time, with the same goal, the back-end team may not have the ability to provide a query to be used to start building the dashboards.

Let's suppose that we will have MDX queries. To have MDX queries, we need to have a Mondrian schema that works on top of a data warehouse. For this, it's necessary to build some ETL that will later be translated in a data warehouse. On top of what we are also building, we need a Mondrian schema to make MDX queries. All of this takes some time, so to start developing your dashboard, you have been provided with the ability to create some *dummy data sources*.

CDA started with one scriptable query, but has recently added a new one.

For both types of scripting when creating a scriptable data source, we need to create a similar connection. We need to specify the attribute type, that should have a value of `scripting.scripting`, but also the following child element:

- **Language**: For both kinds of scriptable queries, we should set the value `beanshell` or `overJavaScript`.

The definition of this data source should look something like this:

```
<Connection id="scriptable" type="scripting.scripting">
   <Language>beanshell</Language>
</Connection>
```

When defining the Data Access, it's different, so for the first case, when setting the language to `Beanshell`, we should end up with something like the following:

```
<DataAccess id="overBeanshell" type="scriptable"
connection="scriptable" access="public">
   <Name>Sample query on SteelWheelsSales</Name>
      <Query>
import org.pentaho.reporting.engine.classic.core.util.TypedTableModel;
String[] columnNames = new String[5];
columnNames[0] = "Region";
columnNames[1] = "Q1";
```

```
columnNames[2] = "Q2";
Class[] columnTypes = new Class[5];
columnTypes[0] = String.class;
columnTypes[1] = Integer.class;
columnTypes[2] = Integer.class;
TypedTableModel model = new TypedTableModel(columnNames, columnTypes);
model.addRow(new Object[]{ new String("East"), new Integer(10), new
Integer(10) });
model.addRow(new Object[]{ new String("West"), new Integer(14), new
Integer(34) });
return model;
        </Query>
</DataAccess>
```

Scripting using JavaScript is a new type of data source that will simplify your life, but has the same drawbacks as when setting the language to `overJavaScript`:

```
<DataAccess id="overJavaScript" type="jsonScriptable" access="public"
connection="scriptable" >
        <Cache duration="3600" enabled="true"/>
        <Columns/>
        <Parameters/>
        <Query>{
            "resultset":[["row1", 0]],
            "metadata":[
                {"colIndex":0,"colType":"String","colName":"value"},
                {"colIndex":1,"colType":"Integer","colName":"name2"}
            ]}
        </Query>
    </DataAccess>
```

Be careful using scripting data sources

You should be careful when using a scripting data source, and there are two reasons for this. The first one is that this type of query is very fast to execute, so you should always try to use a real data source, otherwise you will not know if your dashboard is having performance issues. There are some tricks that you can apply to the queries and to the dashboard to make them work faster, and we will cover them later.

The second reason is that you would always get the same result, because almost certainly you are not creating scriptable code that can deliver different results when changing parameters. Since you will get different results when you apply real queries, it's important that you keep looking at your dashboards using real data.

XPath over XML

Another type of data source is XPath over XML. This will allow you to grab specific nodes from a specified XML file. When defining the connection, the type should be `xpath.xPath`, and the mandatory property for the connection is:

- **DataFile**: The path and name of the XML file to extract data from. This will be something like the following:

```
<Connection id="xpath" type="xpath.xPath">
<DataFile>region.xml</DataFile>
</Connection>
```

When defining the Data Access, we also should specify the XPath string query in the query element:

```
<DataAccess access="public" connection="xpath" id="xpath"
type="xPath">
    <Query>/*/*[REGION=9]</Query>
</DataAccess>
```

More complex queries using XPath can also be done using a kettle transformation

The query specified in the last example would extract all the nodes where a region is equal to 9 from the file with the name `region.xml`. This example is very similar to what can be done using a kettle step. If you are trying to achieve some other results that are not achievable only using this data source, you can create a more complex kettle transformation and then call the transformations as you've already seen.

Compound queries

You can use compound queries to make a join or union of the results of two queries. There are two types of compound queries: join and union. For both of these types, we don't need to define a connection, because in reality we will be using the Data Access that is already defined. Since we are using another data source already created, and that which can only be created with the purpose to be used here, then as referred to earlier, they can be defined with an attribute `access` set to `private`. This way, they will not be seen in the previewer, but can be used inside the compound queries.

When creating a Data Access, we need to specify the attribute as being of the type `joins` or `union`, depending on the case. For the first case, when defining a join, we should define the following properties:

- **JoinType**: The join type will have the kind of join that you may know from the following SQL queries: Inner, Left Outer, Right Outer, and Full Outer

- **Left**: Here, we need to define two attributes: the `id` of the data source to be used and also the keys that should be used for the right side of the join

- **Right**: This is similar to the previous property but for the data source to be used on the left side of the join.

The other type, union, should include the following properties:

- **Up**: Identifies the query to be used on the top of the union

- **Bottom**: This identifies the query that will be placed on the bottom part of the union

Note that when defining the union, the number of columns should be the same.

You can use compound queries to make the join or union of the results of two queries, but you can also use a kettle transformation to get data from different data sources, do a lot of operations such as joining the results, and then returning the results to CDA so that they can be delivered to you in the format you have chosen. Kettle, or Pentaho Data Integration, as you prefer, is used for these operations.

You can find examples for all these types of data sources inside CDA plugin samples. You can access the samples using PUC and open them from the folder: `/public/plugin-samples/CDA/cdafiles`.

Common properties

There are some common properties that should or can be used when defining a Data Access. These properties are:

- **Cache**: The cache can also be defined as an attribute when defining a Data Access. When defining the cache as an element, we should also specify the two attributes, `duration` and `enabled`. The first attribute is used to define the time that the query will be cached since the last execution. The `enabled` attribute will be set to true or false depending on whether you want to enable it or disable it.

- **Name**: This is the friendly name of the data access being defined.

- **Columns**: This is an element that can create a different output by changing the name of a column or just by adding new ones using calculated columns. To change the name of columns, you would just need to specify the columns' idx, starting from 0, and the desired name, as shown in the following example:

```
<Column idx="0">
    <Name> Region </Name>
</Column>
<Column idx="1">
    <Name> Quantity </Name>
</Column>
<Column idx="2">
    <Name> TotalPrice </Name>
</Column>
```

  To create a calculated column, we need to specify the name of the new column and the formula to be used. The formulas should match the **open formula** specification. Please refer to http://wiki.pentaho.com/display/Reporting/Formula+Expressions to find out more information about this:

```
<CalculatedColumnidx="0">
    <Name> Unit Price </Name>
    <Formula>= [TotalPrice] / [Quantity] </Formula>
</CalculatedColumn >
```

- **Query**: Almost all Data Access makes use of this element. Refer to each one of the the data sources types referred earlier to get more information.

- **Parameters**: These are the parameters to be sent/used in the query. They is covered in the next subsection.

- **Output**: This element lets us define a different output than the one defined in the queries. Please refer to the *Manipulating the output of a data source* subsection.

Making use of parameters

We definitely do not want our queries to be static. If you can use a criterion in a query to restrict the set of records that the query returns, you also want that criterion to be changed dynamically without always having the same static value. This allows you to create a query that can be easily updated without needing to change the query itself.

Parameters on SQL queries

Having a parameter is like having a variable that can change over time. Each time the query runs, the parameter will be replaced by the value that the parameter is holding, returning data based on a criterion. The way to build a parameter is to use the following syntax: `${parameterName}`. When setting a query to grab the customer for a particular country like:

```
select * from customers where country in ('USA');
```

You can change the static value by the parameter that you want to use:

```
select * from customers where country in (${country});
```

If the country is equal to USA, then the result from both queries is exactly the same. The advantage of using this parameter is that you would not need to change the query to grab the customers from another country. Just by changing the value of the parameter when running the query again, the results will also change with respect to the selected country. This is very useful when used inside dashboards, because dashboards are meant to be dynamic and respond to changes or interaction from the user.

When using parameters in CDA, you should also set a child element, `Parameters`. You should create your parameters like the following XML syntax:

```
<Parameters>
  <Parameter default="USA" name="country" type="String"/>
</Parameters>
```

In one single query, you can define more than one parameter. So, inside the `Parameters` tag, you will have a `Parameter` element for each one of the parameters that you want to define. The attributes to define are the name of the parameter that should match to the one used in the query, the default value to be used when no other value is used, and the type of the parameter. For the type, you can use one of the following:

- `String`, `Integer`, `Numeric`, or `Date`: This depends on the type of value that you will use. Just to be clear, the Integer type can contain only whole numbers, such as 10 or 365. The Numeric type can contain decimal numbers such as 15.39.

- `StringArray`, `IntegerArray`, `NumericArray`, or `DateArray`: These are used when you have multiple values to be included in an IN condition.

As an example, your CDA file would look like the following:

```xml
<?xml version="1.0" encoding="UTF-8"?>
<CDADescriptor>
   <DataSources>
      <Connection id="sqlSample" type="sql.jndi">
         <Jndi>SampleData</Jndi>
      </Connection>
   </DataSources>
   <DataAccess access="public" connection="sqlSample" id="sqlSample"
type="sql">
      <Cache duration="3600" enabled="true"/>
      <Columns/>
      <Parameters>
         <Parameter default="USA" name="country" type="StringArray"/>
      </Parameters>
      <Query>select * from customers where country in (${country})</
Query>
   </DataAccess>
</CDADescriptor>
```

When using SQL queries, CDA replaces the parameters as prepared statements. SQL queries passed to this method go to the database for precompilation if the JDBC driver supports it. If it does not, then precompilation occurs when you execute prepared queries. They are precompiled in the database and their access plan will be reused to execute further queries, which allows them to be executed much quicker than normal queries generated by a statement object. Another advantage of using them is that it will disable the ability to prevent SQL injection attacks.

Parameters in MDX queries

Parameterizing in MDX queries is much simpler than in SQL. It's not possible to perform SQL injection attacks, so CDA lets you have a parameter that is part of the query or the full query. You can use whatever tool you need/want and pass the query as a parameter to be executed by Mondrian. You might think that this would cause a security-related problem by passing a query that a user could not execute. When security in Mondrian is well implemented, even if you create a query to grab a part of data that you are not allowed to, you will not get the results back.

Using parameters in a Mondrian query is very similar, except for the fact that you can use the parameter anywhere in the query.

It's not the purpose of this book to teach you how MDX works or how to build MDX queries, so we will just stick with some sample queries. Creating the following query will show the sales by quantity for each one of the members of a particular level of a territory:

```xml
<?xml version="1.0" encoding="UTF-8"?>
<CDADescriptor>
<DataSources>
<Connection id="mk" type="mondrian.jndi">
        <Catalog>mondrian:/SteelWheels</Catalog>
        <Jndi>SampleData</Jndi>
    </Connection>
</DataSources>
<DataAccess access="public" connection="mk" id="mk" type="mdx">
<BandedMode>compact</BandedMode>
<Cache duration="3600" enabled="true"/>
<Columns/>
<Parameters>
    <Parameter name="markets" default="Territory" type="String"/>
</Parameters>
<Query>
SELECT
NON EMPTY {[Measures].[Quantity]} ON COLUMNS,
NON EMPTY {[Markets].[${markets}].Members} ON ROWS
FROM [SteelWheelsSales]
</Query>
</DataAccess>
</CDADescriptor>
```

You can see the query is defined with a parameter ${markets}. The parameter has a default value of Territory, so if no other value is set, the resulting query will show the quantities that were sold for each one of the territory's members. If a value of Country, State, Province, or City is set, then the quantities shown have numbers that correspond to each one of the levels of the selected level of the dimension territory.

As we referred to before, you can pass a parameter anywhere in the query, or just have the query as a parameter. Here is an example:

```xml
<DataAccess access="public" connection="mk" id="mk" type="mdx">
<BandedMode>compact</BandedMode>
<Parameters>
        <Parameter name="myQuery" default="SELECT {[Measures].[Sales]}
ON COLUMNS FROM [SteelWheelsSales]" type="String"/>
```

```
    </Parameters>
    <Query>
        ${myQuery}
    </Query>
</DataAccess>
```

Parameters on kettle queries

When grabbing data from a kettle query, we don't need to define a query to be executed by kettle. Well, you may need to define one inside the transformation, but not in CDA. What you can do is pass the parameters to the kettle transformation. As we may have parameters in a dashboard that have a different parameter name in the kettle transformation, we will need to map them. Looking at the example provided by the CDA samples, we can see the variables that are used by the transformation inside the definition of the connection:

```
<?xml version="1.0" encoding="utf-8"?>
<CDADescriptor>
<DataSources>
        <Connection id="1" type="kettle.TransformFile">
          <KtrFile>sample-trans.ktr</KtrFile>
          <variables datarow-name="myRadius"/>
          <variables datarow-name="ZipCode" variable-name="myZip"/>
        </Connection>
    </DataSources>
<DataAccess id="1" connection="1" type="kettle" access="public"
cache="true">
    <Name>Sample query on SteelWheelsSales</Name>
        <Query>Report Columns</Query>
        <Parameters>
          <Parameter name="myRadius" type="Integer" default="30"/>
          <Parameter name="ZipCode" type="Integer" default="32771"/>
        </Parameters>
    </DataAccess>
</CDADescriptor>
```

myZip and myRadius are the names of the parameters defined inside the transformation, but we can see that the parameters ZipCode and myRadius are used inside CDA. That's the reason why the example sets a variable datarow-name=ZipCode and variable-name=myZip. These two, names and variable name need to be related to each other.

As the other parameter has the same name inside CDA and the kettle transformation, there is no need to establish the mapping—just set it so that CDA needs to pass the parameters to the transformation. You can also see that the CDA parameters are similar, as defined inside the definition of the Data Access.

Private parameters

Parameters can also be defined as private. When you define a parameter as private, the value is set on the server side, so even when you try to pass a parameter value from the client side, the value will be the value that is set by default. That's why the access can be set to private.

A use case of this is when you want to pass the username or tenant to a SQL query, and you want the username to be able to send a value that would compromise the real identity. So if you're setting the value of ${[security:principalName]}, on the server side, this parameter will be evaluated and replaced by the username of the user's login, no matter what value the user is sending from the client side to overwrite the default parameter value. For this, the parameter and SQL query should be set like the following:

```
<Parameters>
    <Parameter default="${[security:principalName]}" name="username"
type="String" access="private"/>
</Parameters>
<Query>SELECT * from Employee where id=${username}</Query>
```

Using session variables

You can also get values from a session variable to be used in CDA parameters' values using ${[session:sessionVariableName]}. Don't forget that to do this, you will need to have it defined on the server. You have multiple ways to set a session variable: using xActions, through Java code, using the Set session variables step available in the new BA Server Utils plugin for kettle, and through the Startup Rule Engine plugin for BA Server.

By default, a value is set as public; otherwise, you will need to specify that the parameter access level is private.

Editing and previewing

Once you have created a file and uploaded it to BA Server, the `.cda` extension will tell Pentaho how to handle this file. When clicking on a `.cda` file, in the context menu that becomes available on the right side of **Pentaho User Console (PUC)**, you will be able to edit and open the previewer. When selecting edit, you will see a screen like the following:

You can see the editor on the center of the page, and three buttons on the right-hand side, above the editor. We are able to change the XML file and use the buttons to trigger some actions. The available actions are:

- **Save**: To save the changes we can make in the editor
- **Reload**: To reload the content of the file
- **Preview**: This will open the previewer so that we can see the results of the execution of the data source

There are two ways to preview a query result when using CDA. The first one is using the CDA previewer, a GUI that will let you select the Data Access that you would like to execute. To open the previewer, you can select the `.cda` file in the PUC browser and click **Select Edit** or double-click on the file, click on the **Preview** button of the editor, or call the previewer in the browser:

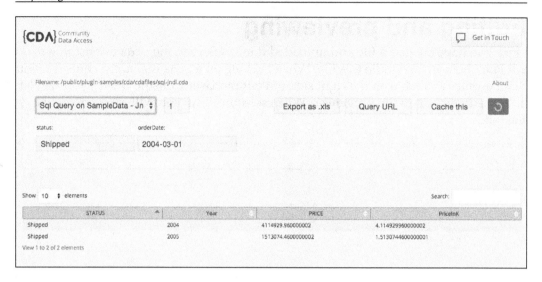

The first step to get results is to select the data access using the dropdown. Next, set the values of the parameters, if they exist, and then click the refresh button. On the bottom of the page, you will get the results of the execution of the query.

There are also three available buttons: from left to right, the first one gives you the ability to export the results to an .xls file. The second one presents a dialog window with the URL you can use to call the query using an HTTP request. The last one gives you the ability to schedule the execution of the report so that the results can be cached.

When clicking on the **Cache this** button, you get a dialog where you can choose the time interval to execute the query and cache the results.

Advanced options for cache scheduler

There is also an advanced option so that you can schedule it by using a *Cron Expression*. More information about Cron can be found at: https://en.wikipedia.org/wiki/Cron

There is another way to get and check the results which is not so user-friendly. This is by calling the endpoint in your browser to get the results from the execution of a query. The URL is provided to you when you click the **Query URL** button. You can also pass the parameters, and as a bonus, you can test the pagination on the server side and select the output type that you want to get results with. We will briefly cover this option later.

Manipulating the output of a data source

Manipulating the result of a data source is really simple. You can use the child element Output when setting the Data Access. Let's suppose we are performing a query that is returning 10 columns, but we only want to display the first two. If that's the case, then you should set the following child element in the Data Access definition:

```
<Output indexes="0,1" mode="include"/>
```

This child element tells CDA that it should use the first and second columns, identified by index 0 and 1. The mode will tell CDA that these are the columns to be included; otherwise, if you use exclude, you will get all the columns except the first two.

When accessing a query through a URL, another way to manipulate the output is to have a different output format. This can be achieved by calling the URL and adding a parameter outputType of one of the following formats: JSON, XML, CSV, XLS, or HTML.

For example, if you want to manipulate the output of the data source, you can use something like the following URL example can be used in your browser:

```
http://localhost:8080/pentaho/plugin/cda/api/doQuery?path=/public/
plugin-samples/cda/cdafiles/sql-jndi.cda&dataAccessId=1&paramstatus=S
hipped&paramorderDate=2004-03-01&outputType=csv
```

This request will download a .csv file and depending on the chosen format, it will be displayed in the browser or will just download a file (by default, if the file recognizes the format, the content will be rendered on the browser, otherwise the content will be download). The default format is JSON.

CDA cache

CDA is able to cache the queries that have been executed. Every query that runs will be cached or not cached, and by the time defined in the *Cache* property element when defining the Data Access. You can also set the interval of time to grab results from the cache, avoiding new requests to the server.

Managing the cache and the scheduler

In the PUC menu, click on **Tools | Refresh | CDA Cache Manager**, and you will have the ability to clean the CDA cache. When choosing this option, every single cache will be flushed.

It's also possible to manage what has been cached or is scheduled to be cached. By clicking on the PUC menu and going to **Tools | CDA Cache Manager**, it will open a new tab with the scheduled/cached queries manager. When opening the manager, you have the ability to choose between two modes by using the **Scheduled Queries** or **Cached Queries** buttons, respectively:

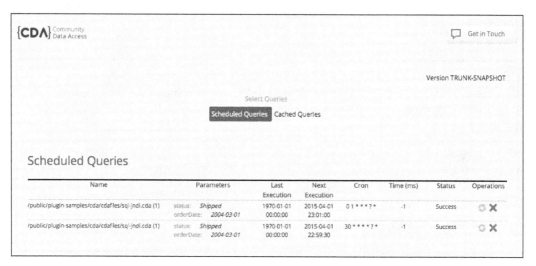

The previous image is an example of the **Scheduled Queries** manager, and it will display all the queries that have been cached. For each query, you have some information about the last execution, the next execution, the Cron expression, the status, and also two buttons, **Execute** or **Remove**, from the scheduler:

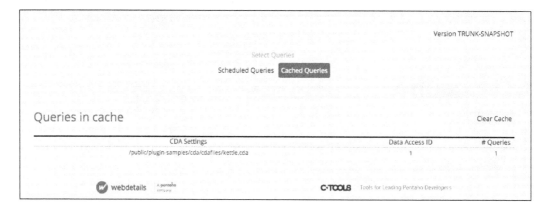

In the **Cached Queries** screen, you will see the queries that have been cached. When clicking on each row, you will get details about cached query, such as the executed query, the parameters used, the number of rows, how many hits, and also some actions buttons. The actions buttons are used to display the results below the query, and make it possible to remove a particular item from the cache. You also have a button that can empty the cache by removing all the items from the cache.

Cache keys

When using a **Dynamic Schema Processor** (**DSP**) to be used on Mondrian and MDX queries on top of CDA, we may face some problems with cached results. To optimize the cached results, CDA will use the query, the parameter values, and the role of the user as keys to manage/control the cached queries and the results. In a multi-tenant environment, it's important that the user or some other key can be set. More information about multi-tenancy is available at: `https://help.pentaho.com/Documentation/6.0/0R0/070/Multi-Tenancy`.

Configuring local cache keys

We can define cache keys in two different ways, The first way can be set when defining the data access, inside the Cache element, where we may also define the keys to use like the following:

```
<DataAccess>
  <Cache enabled="true" duration="500">
    <Key name="tenantId" value="${[session:org.pentaho.tenantId]}"
default="/pentaho/tenant0"/>
    </Cache>
</DataAccess>
```

This will make CDA add a key when managing the cache, and the cache will be segmented, also taking into account the `tenantId` value that will be acquired from the session variable `org.pentaho.tenantId`. The default value will be used if the used session variable is not defined at the time.

Some other valid examples provided by Webdetails are as follows:

```
<Key name="data-access-roles" value="${[system:data-access/settings.
xml{data-access-roles}]}" default="data-access-roles"/>

<Key name="user-in-session" value="${[security:principalName]}"
default="user-in-session"/>

<Key name="tenantId" value="${[session:org.pentaho.tenantId]}"
default="default-tenant"/>
```

Configuring system-wide cache keys

The other way to define cache keys, configuring it to be used system-wide, has a drawback, all defined data accesses would need to define their cache keys. There is a way to make these keys system-wide. To do this, you need to edit the file `cda.properties`. You can find the file at `pentaho-solutions/system/cda/`.

At the end of the file, you have a commented example on how to set the keys, which is very simple. They keys are defined like the following:

```
pt.webdetails.cda.cache.extraCacheKeys.key=value
```

An example of how to use `tenantId` is as follows:

```
pt.webdetails.cda.cache.extraCacheKeys.tenantId=${[session:org.
pentaho.tenantId]}
```

Save the file, restart BA Server, and CDA will start using the configured keys. These settings will be valid for all the queries.

Web API reference

One of the interesting things in knowing how to work with the API is that we can use CDA to get data into an external application. This is interesting if we're not using CDE or CDF to build the dashboard. Anyhow, a good reason for you to know about the API is so you can go further when using CTools.

You can make requests to CDA using Web API. The base URL to use is `$BASE_URL/$WEBAPP/plugin/cda/api/`, where `$BASE_URL` is the protocol, hostname, and port, and `$WEBAPP` is the web application name used on Apache Tomcat, and the default webapp is defined as pentaho.

For example, the following URL is referring the `pentaho` webapp: `http://localhost:8080/pentaho/plugin/cda/api/doQuery?path=/public/plugin-samples/cda/cdafiles/mondrian-jndi.cda&dataAccessId=1&paramstatus=Shipped`

Next we will cover the available endpoint. An endpoint, defines the particulars of a specific endpoint at which a given service is available.

getCdaList

The `getCdaList` endpoint will get a list of all the CDA files available inside the repository. There is no need to specify the parameters for this endpoint.

For example: `http://localhost:8080/pentaho/plugin/cda/api/getCdaList`

listQueries

The `listQueries` endpoint will list all the queries available in a CDA file. There is one mandatory parameter that needs to be used: `path`, to specify the path to the CDA file where we want to get the queries from. There is an optional parameter that we can specify, `outputType`, which defines a different output format for the results. The default value is `json` and the other option is `xml`.

Example of the call to list queries: `http://localhost:8080/pentaho/plugin/cda/api/listQueries?path=/public/plugin-samples/cda/cdafiles/mondrian-jndi.cda`

listParameters

The `listParameter` endpoint will list all the parameters that are defined in a particular query. There are two mandatory parameters that need to be used: `path`, to specify the path to the CDA file where the queries are defined, and `dataAccessId`, to specify the query we want to use. There is an optional parameter that we can specify, `outputType`, which defines a different output format for the results, where the default value is `json` and option is `xml`.

Example on how to list parameters: `http://localhost:8080/pentaho/plugin/cda/api/listParameters?path=/public/plugin-samples/cda/cdafiles/mondrian-jndi.cda&dataAccessId=1`

doQuery

This method makes a call to a query and returns the result. There are two mandatory parameters that need to be used: `path` and `dataAccessId`. The first one will inform the method which file should be used to get the connection and the query to be used. The second one informs which one of the data accesses that were defined in the CDA file are to be used. You should remember that in the last chapter, we needed to define connections, and that data access would point to a defined connection.

When using parameters, you should also specify the values of those parameters. To do this, it should be passed to the URL `paramParameter`, where `Parameter` corresponds to the name of the parameter.

There are other options that are optional, such as `outputType`, to specify a different output format for the results, where the default value is `json` and options are `xml`, `csv`, `xls`, or `html`.

If there is a need to have pagination, we can also define `paginateQuery`, which should have a Boolean value, and if we are setting a value of true, we should also specify `pageStart` to define which to start with and `pageSize` to define the numbers of rows we want to get.

Another parameter, `bypassCache`, can be used with a value of true if we need to bypass the cache and make CDA raise a new request to the database. To sort the query using a particular column or groups of columns, we should use `sortBy` and specify the list of columns.

Example on how to execute query: `http://localhost:8080/pentaho/plugin/ cda/api/doQuery?path=/public/plugin-samples/cda/cdafiles/mondrian- jndi.cda&dataAccessId=1&paramstatus=Shipped`

Let's suppose you want to get data to your web application that is not built with CDE or CDF. You can do this by calling the same requests that CDF and CDE do. To get data, you need to specify which CDA to use and which data access identifier should be used. You can also specify the parameters to paste to the query, and then the URL will be as follows:

`http://localhost:8080/pentaho/plugin/cda/api/doQuery?path=/public/ plugin-samples/cda/cdafiles/mondrian-jndi.cda&dataAccessId=1&paramsta tus=Shipped`

This request is calling `dataAccessId 1`, which is available in the `Mondrian-jndi. cda file` located at: `/public/plugin-samples/cda/cdafiles`. It passes `Shipped` as the status parameter value. You will get the result in the `json` format as explained previously, and it will contain the metadata, `queryInfo`, and the `resultset`. It will provide you with information on the columns' names and the type being returned, how many rows were returned, and also a multidimensional array that represents the results.

clearCache

The `clearCache` will clear the CDA cache. Example: `http://localhost:8080/ pentaho/plugin/cda/api/clearCache`

previewQuery

This method will open the CDA previewer. Example: `http://localhost:8080/ pentaho/plugin/cda/api/previewQuery?path=/public/plugin-samples/cda/ cdafiles/mondrian-jndi.cda`

editFile

This method will open the CDA editor for a particular query. We should define a parameter with the path to the CDA file. The parameter is path. Example: `http://localhost:8080/pentaho/plugin/cda/api/editFile?path=/public/plugin-samples/cda/cdafiles/mondrian-jndi.cda`

manageCache

This method will open the cache manager, which we already covered previously in this chapter. Examples: `http://localhost:8080/pentaho/plugin/cda/api/manageCache`

Let's suppose you want to get data to your web application that is not built with CDE or CDF. You can do this by calling the same requests as CDF and CDE do. You can also specify the parameters to paste to the query, and then the URL will be as follows:

`http://localhost:8080/pentaho/plugin/cda/api/doQuery?path=/public/plugin-samples/cda/cdafiles/mondrian-jndi.cda&dataAccessId=1&paramstatus=Shipped`

Hands-on dashboards

Now it's time for you to create your data sources. In order to display the results from the queries, in the next chapter, you should create a CDA file with the following content:

```xml
<?xml version="1.0" encoding="utf-8"?>
<CDADescriptor>
<!--Data source for the dashboard, a unique data source is used for
all connections-->
    <DataSources>
        <Connection id="SampleData" type="mondrian.jndi">
            <Jndi>SampleData</Jndi>
```

```
            <Catalog>mondrian:/SteelWheels</Catalog>
            <Cube>SteelWheelsSales</Cube>
        </Connection>
    </DataSources>
 <!--Data Access to get the territories values-->
    <DataAccess id="territories" connection="SampleData" type="mdx"
access="public">
        <Name>territories</Name>
        <BandedMode>compact</BandedMode>
        <Query>
            WITH
                MEMBER [Measures].[UID] AS [Markets].CURRENTMEMBER.
UNIQUENAME
            SELECT
                UNION([Markets].[All Markets], DESCENDANTS([Markets].
[All Markets], [Markets].[Territory])) on ROWS,
                {[Measures].[UID]} on COLUMNS
            FROM [SteelWheelsSales]
        </Query>
        <Output indexes="1,0" mode="include"/>
    </DataAccess>
 <!--Data Access to get the countries values-->
    <DataAccess id="countries" connection="SampleData" type="mdx"
access="public">
        <Name>countries</Name>
        <BandedMode>compact</BandedMode>
        <Query>
            WITH
                MEMBER [Measures].[UID] AS [Markets].CURRENTMEMBER.
UNIQUENAME
            SELECT
                UNION([Markets].[All Markets], DESCENDANTS(${marketQue
ryParam}, [Markets].[Country])) on ROWS,
                {[Measures].[UID]} on COLUMNS
            FROM [SteelWheelsSales]
        </Query>
<!--Parameters and default values to be used on the query. -->

        <Parameters>
            <Parameter name="marketQueryParam" type="String"
default="[Markets].[All Markets]"/>
        </Parameters>
        <Output indexes="1,0" mode="include"/>
```

```
            </DataAccess>
    <!--Data Access to get the top 50 customers -->
        <DataAccess id="top50Customers" connection="SampleData" type="mdx"
access="public">
            <Name>top50Customers</Name>
            <BandedMode>compact</BandedMode>
            <Query>
                WITH
                    SET CUSTOMERS AS TopCount([Customers].Children, 50.0,
[Measures].[Sales])
                SELECT
                    NON EMPTY {[Measures].[Sales]} ON COLUMNS,
                    NON EMPTY CUSTOMERS ON ROWS
                FROM [SteelWheelsSales]
                WHERE ${marketQueryParam}
            </Query>
    <!--Parameters and default values to be used on the query.-->
            <Parameters>
                <Parameter name="marketQueryParam" type="String"
default="[Markets].[All Markets]"/>
            </Parameters>
        </DataAccess>
    </CDADescriptor>
```

We are creating a data source that points to the sample data source that is created during the Pentaho installation. We also have two MDX queries, the first one to get the territories and the unique name for each one, but filtering the undesired values. We are also changing the order of the columns from 0, 1 to 1, 0. The second one gets the customers that belong to a particular market. This query is created using a parameter for the markets, which has a default value to select all the customers available. When firing the query with a different value, we will get different results by filtering the customers based on the market they belong to.

This example will be used in some samples during the next chapter. Don't forget to preview the results and confirm that you are able to return the results for both queries.

Summary

Now you know how to create data sources that can bring data to your reports/dashboards. You should now understand how to create different types of queries by defining all the XML elements. There is an important part of the chapter on how to send parameters to the queries. One of the query types is a Kettle query, where you need to specify the mapping between the parameters that come from the dashboard and the variables defined inside the kettle transformation. If necessary, we can blend data, just by creating queries for different data sources that will later be combined using a join or union in a compound query.

We also covered how to preview the queries, how to edit a CDA file, and how to manage or clean segments of the CDA cache. You should now be able to schedule the queries so that they can be cached and give shorter response times to the users who are accessing the same query.

This chapter showed you how to create or edit a CDA file manually; however, you don't always need to do so.

Now that you know how to get data into the dashboard, we can start creating a dashboard, or at least getting to know the basic concepts of how to build a dashboard. In the next chapter, you will learn about CDF.

3
Building the Dashboard Using CDF

There are two ways to build the community dashboards: using the **Community Dashboards Framework (CDF)** or the **Community Dashboard Editor (CDE)**. You could leverage some of the work and do it faster when you are using the second option, but behind it, we will still be using CDF. You could choose not to read this chapter, but to have proper knowledge of how the CDE works, and to achieve better results, you should be able to understand the concepts behind the CDF API. In this chapter, you will get the chance to see the lifecycle of the dashboard and its components. Pentaho uses the CDF framework on the platform, so acquiring knowledge about how to use CDF can be an advantage when using other tools than CDE.

While covering CDF, we will present to you some of the most important and commonly used methods/functions available for this tool. Of course, we need to start covering the components and get them working. Sending parameters to the queries is an important part of the process, as you will definitely want to create interactive, and not static, dashboards. We will also cover how to work with filters and make components react to changes that the user makes to the dashboard.

To have a dashboard that could be rendered by any user in any part of the world, we should also provide our dashboards with the ability to change language, and the formatting of numbers and dates depending on the user's settings, which we can grab from the browser or from the Pentaho platform.

The main purpose of this chapter is for you to understand the lifecycle of dashboards and their components, to know what methods are available on the CDF API, and to see how to use them.

Understanding the basics of a CDF dashboard

We have already mentioned that CDF will work on the browser as a HTML page that will make use of the JavaScript and CSS languages, frameworks, and libraries.

But how does CDF really work? When we are making a request to the Pentaho platform to get a dashboard, we make a request to a Pentaho plugin. That request is done through the Web API that the plugin is providing on the server side. This server-side code is written in Java, and by reading the dashboard's files, will send the HTML and JavaScript code to the browser for the execution of the dashboard on the client side (the browser). This code will include some scripts that are mandatory so that the plugins can execute themselves in the browser. The number of libraries may vary depending on the components included. The following image is a really simple diagram that should give you a clear understanding of how the requests to get the dashboards are handled:

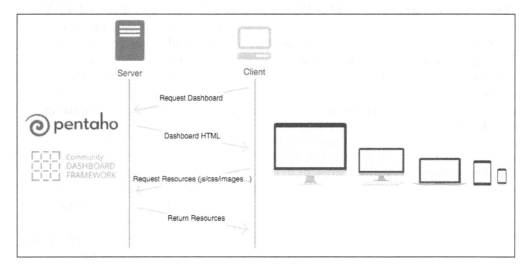

Lifecycle of dashboards and components

The start of the lifecycle begins with the execution of the dashboard, when the request is made to the CDE or CDF. As we saw earlier, and to be more precise, the dashboard starts when the browser gets all the resources and starts executing the JavaScript code inside the dashboard. To start the execution of the dashboards, there is a function that needs be called, `[dashboard].init()`. This will make the browser start the execution of all the code that may be defined. For now, let's consider `[dashboard]` as just the name of a variable that we may use when creating the code for our dashboard.

In the following diagram, you will see two different areas:

- The dashboard lifecycle, which refers to the lifecycle itself

- The component lifecycle, which refers to each of the components on the dashboard

The dashboard will start, and during the execution of the dashboard, one or more components will be executed, so the diagram shows the lifecycle from the start of the dashboard until it finishes its execution, including the components themselves:

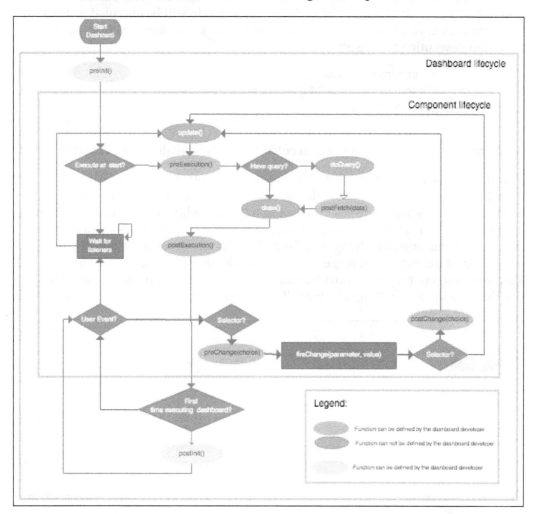

Looking at the legend section of the diagram, you will find some colors that identify the functions which can be defined by the developer, as part of the lifecycle, to extend the behavior of the dashboard and components. By looking at the diagram, you can identify whether they belong to the lifecycle of the dashboard or to the components.

To get a better understanding of the preceding diagram, we need to split it into two diagrams, so you can understand the lifecycle of the dashboard and the components themselves, and later on how they work together.

The `preInit` function will be called by CDF and may include some custom code. If you define the function with some code inside, the code will be executed just before the initialization of the dashboard. So, you will execute the lines inside just before CDF starts executing the dashboard:

```
[dashboard].preInit = function() {
// Code to execute before CDF starts the execution of the
// dashboard, goes here.
}
```

As the name suggests, code is to be executed before the initialization of the dashboard.

You should also have noticed that there is a function called `[dashboard].postInit()`, which works exactly the same way as the previous function, but will only be executed after it finishes the execution of the dashboard, just before delivering control to the user. These two functions are not executed again, unless you refresh the page. At this time, the changes in the dashboard will only be executed by the interaction of the user, or by some custom code. Of course, the dashboard will keep working, but no pre- or post-execution will be called. So, the lifecycle of the dashboard will be something like the following diagram:

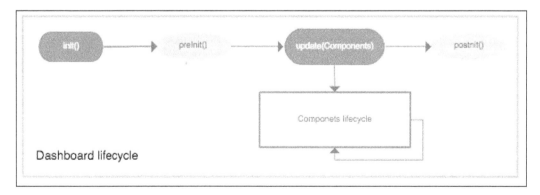

Let's see how the lifecycle of the dashboard works. First, the dashboard's init() function is called and starts the execution of the custom code that can be placed inside preInit(). The next step is to start the execution of all the components, ordered by the grouped priority of execution, and when CDF finishing the execution of the task, CDF will execute the code inside postInit(). When the components are executed, the lifecycle of the components will keep running and changes in the dashboard will depend on listeners (these are parameters/variables that the components can listen to in order to be notified about changes). These listeners will update the components based on a user's, or a predefined action.

On the complete diagram, the one that includes both the dashboard and components lifecycle, we can see that components are executed on the initialization of the dashboard when the executeAtStart property is set to true; otherwise the component will be started and will only be executed when fired by a listener. When a component is executed, its lifecycle will be as shown in the following diagram:

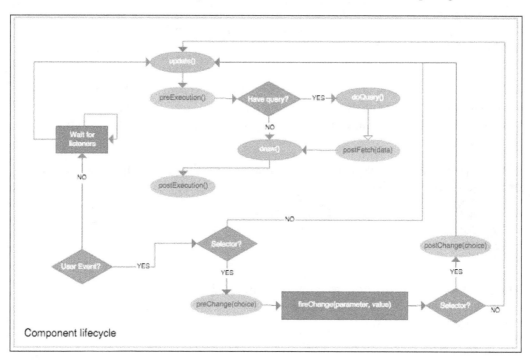

Component lifecycle

When executing a component, the first function to be called is preExecution, and as an option, the developer can place some code to be executed inside the function.

From there, if there is a query to execute, CDF will call a function that is responsible for the execution of the query and, after getting the results, will call postFetch with an argument that is the result set of the execution of the query. The user can also specify the code to be executed, which can be used to make necessary changes to the results.

From there, or just if there is no query to be executed, CDF will call the draw function for the component and start rendering the elements on the page. After that, postExecution will be called, which is a function that can also be defined by the developer to run some custom code. This can be used to perform some actions after the components have been rendered on the page, so we can use it to make some change on the **Document Object Model (DOM)** of the web page.

The preExecution function should be defined as shown in the following example, to prepare the components and specify some options:

```
[component].preExec = function() {
// Code to execute before CDF starts the execution of the
// dashboard, goes here.
}
```

If for some reason we need to cancel the execution of a component, there is the chance to return a value of False inside the pre-execution function. This makes it possible to make some validations before proceeding with the execution of the component(s).

The postFetch function is where we can manipulate the results from the execution of the query. It can be defined as:

```
[component].postFetch = function(data) {
// Code to manipulate data. Should always return a valid result.
return data;
}
```

The postExecution function, as already mentioned, can be used after the components, and elements that belong to it are rendered on the DOM, and can be specified as follows:

```
[component].postExec = function() {
// Code to execute before CDF starts the execution of the
// dashboard, goes here.
}
```

This ends the first cycle of the execution of the component and delivers the next execution to the events listener. The main function of the listeners is to keep listening for changes to a specific parameter or parameters. The listeners will be pointing to a parameter on the dashboard that will be kept under observation, in order to request the update of a component every time CDF gets notified about a change to that parameter.

The change of parameter values may be dependent on, or associated with, user interaction. When the user interacts with the dashboard, this will fire a change in the values of a parameter that is being observed, initiating the execution of the components that are listening to it, or to them.

User interaction can be made by the click of a button, selecting from a dropdown, or even clicking on a radio button. Filters and/or selectors are particular cases of components that also have two more functions that can be defined by the user. When applying a change to the selector, the components will fire a change in a parameter.

One of the functions will be triggered before that, preChange, and another one after the parameter is already changed, postChange. Both functions can receive one argument that is the new choice made by the user. The preChange function can be used to make validations, and postChange can be used to perform some actions after the changes are confirmed in the parameter:

```
[component].preChange = function(usersChoice) {
// Code to execute before the fireChange() of the parameter
return usersChoice;
}
```

The difference between a selector and a filter is that in a selector, at least one value should be selected, while in a filter, when you don't select a value you are selecting everything. That's because on a filter if you don't do a selection, you are not filtering.

The postChange function is pretty much the same syntax, except the name of the function and of course the code inside to be executed. Here, you will not need to return a value.

This is the hardest part of CDF to understand, but when you understand the workflow of the lifecycle, you will get better dashboards than before. Don't worry if you didn't fully understand it, as we will go back to some of the concepts during the rest of the book.

Creating a CDF dashboard

Nowadays, CDF can make use of **Asynchronous Module Definition (AMD)**. AMD is a JavaScript specification that defines an API on top of which we are able to create code modules and their dependencies. Modules can be loaded asynchronously, even if they depend on each other. AMD concepts also allow the developer to encapsulate code in smaller, more logically-organized files.

RequireJS is a JavaScript file and module loader that implements the AMD specification that CDF is using. One of the advantages is that you can create and reuse modules without polluting the global namespace. The more polluted your global namespace is, the bigger the chance of a function/variable collision. Another advantage is that you can structure your code into separate folders and files, and RequireJS will load them asynchronously when needed, in a way that ensures everything works just fine.

The sample code that we are using in this book is already based on the use of RequireJS inside CDF. These changes will also leverage the process of embedding a dashboard or part of a dashboard. We will cover how to embed a dashboard or part of it in third-party applications later in the book. For now, you should just focus on learning how to create a dashboard.

To build a CDF dashboard, you need to create two main files that are mandatory:

- **XCDF**: This is the main file that identifies the dashboard as a CDF dashboard type inside Pentaho. This is the file that identifies the dashboards inside Pentaho, and where the general settings are. For instance, we can set the name, template, and style for our dashboards. This file is written using the XML syntax.

- **HTML**: This is the template file with HTML content where the components will be rendered.

XCDF is the main file, where the root element `<cdf>` and the following child elements are:

- `<title>`: This corresponds to the title displayed in the **Pentaho User Console (PUC)**.

- `<author>`: This is the author of the file that will be displayed inside the user console.

- `<description>`: This is the description displayed in the PUC and on the browser.

- `<icon>`: This is the icon to be displayed.

- `<template>`: This is the HTML template file to render. This is the second mandatory element.
- `<style>`: This is the name of the style to use to render the dashboard.
- `<require>`: This is set to true or false to define whether or not we're using the RequireJS dashboard. We can load a different `style` file with the `require` suffix.

The content of the XCDF file should be something like:

```xml
<?xml version="1.0" encoding="UTF-8"?>
<cdf>
  <title>My first dashboard!</title>
  <author>My Name</author>
  <description>My first dashboard!</description>
  <icon></icon>
  <template>myFirstDashboard.html</template>
  <style>clean</style>
  <require>true</require>
</cdf>
```

But what's the difference between the properties style and the template? Well, the difference between them is that the style will have the HTML of the full page and can be used for multiple dashboards. Let's say that the style will have the content that is similar from dashboard to dashboard. On the other hand, the template is the file that has the HTML and JavaScript code to render the dashboard.

The template or the HTML and JavaScript would be something like:

```html
<style>
</style>
<div class="container-fluid">
    <h1>My first dashboard!</h1>
</div>
<script language="javascript" type="text/javascript">
    var dashboard;
    require(['cdf/Dashboard.Clean'],
        function(Dashboard) {
            dashboard = new Dashboard();
            dashboard.init();
        }
    );
</script>
```

We can see that there is the `<style>` element where we can add some CSS to be applied to our dashboard. Here, we can also have references to external files and extend the dashboard, including CSS or JavaScript code. This is pure HTML, so here you can do what you would usually do when on a web page.

You can also see some HTML tags where all the content will be placed, so here you should have the layout needed for your dashboard. At the end, there is the `<script>` tag with the JavaScript code to execute the dashboard. On the last sample code, you can also see that we are calling the required modules that we need for our dashboard.

To be able to have the core code of the dashboards available to use, we must include a module that specifies the dashboard type. In the previous example, we did not specify any other component or module.

At least one of the following modules that correspond to a dashboard type should be included:

- `[cdf/Dashboard.Clean]`: This will load its main dependencies, and will load the base code for the dashboard. It will not load any framework to be used in the layout, and you can use one of your own preferences.

- `[cdf/Dashboard.Bootstrap]`: This will load the same libraries and code as the previous one, plus the Bootstrap framework. This way you have the code for the dashboard, but can also make use of this great framework to build responsive dashboards. We will cover a little bit more on this framework later.

- `[cdf/Dashboard.Blueprint]`: This will load the same libraries and code as the first one, plus the Blueprint framework.

Use Bootstrap to build responsive dashboards

During this book, we will just cover the Bootstrap framework by including a call to `cdf/Dashboard.Bootstrap`. We will only use a Bootstrap dashboard type in our examples. This is a more advanced framework that allows us to build responsive dashboards, which it is also possible to use in CDE dashboards. You should use the `cdf/Dashboard.Clean` module if you want a clean dashboard. That way you can use another framework.

You can see the dashboard style as a file that will have the common code to apply to multiple dashboards. When you are creating dashboards for multiple customers, you can create/adapt a template for each customer and create dashboards that will make use of the code inside the style page file. Inside your `[baserver]/pentaho-solutions/system/pentaho-cdf` file, you will find some HTML pages that can be used by defining the style element. The options for them are as follows:

- Clean: This will make use of the code defined in the files `template-dashboard-clean-require.html` and `template-dashboard-clean.html`. Selecting one or the other will depend on the flag on the `<require>` element. If the value is true, then `template-dashboard-clean-require.html` will be used, and `template-dashboard-clean.html` otherwise.

- Mantle: This will make use of the code defined in the files `template-dashboard-mantle-require.html` and `template-dashboard-mantle.html`. Like the previous options, we will need to set the `<require>` element with a value of true or false.

The difference between them is that they will apply different styles/wrappers to the dashboard. The first one will not apply any style at all, while the second will apply a style that is related to the new Pentaho theme.

Defining an empty or invalid style for a dashboard

If we do not set a valid option or available style when creating a new CDF dashboard, the CDF API will make use of the default one. It will use the `dashboard-template.html` file.

In the last example code we presented, you can also see functions that are called when the modules are loaded, and these functions will receive as an argument the module that we have included. In the previous example, we just included the dashboard type, and we are using an argument with the name `dashboard`. This variable will make reference to the dashboard object that contains the functions to add components, add parameters, start the execution of the dashboard, and so on.

In this chapter, we will cover some of the available functions. For now, you need to understand that to create a dashboard, we need to create a new instance of the `dashboard` object, and later make a call to the `init()` function. This will create the dashboard and trigger its execution.

Hands-on dashboards

At this point, you should be able to understand the basic concepts to create a really simple page showing just the text `My first Dashboard!`. To do so, you just need to follow these steps:

- Inside your file system, create a file with the name `myFirstDashboard.xcdf`. You should use the code that we previously used for the XCDF file, in the *Creating a CDF dashboard* section.

- Create another file with the name `myFirstDashboard.html` in the same folder as the previous file, and write the code that we previously used for the template files (HTML), in the *Creating a CDF dashboard* section.

Compress the folder with the two files using the ZIP file format, and upload the file to the Pentaho repository. Once uploaded, you need to double-click the `myFirstDashboard.xcdf` file to open the dashboard. You should get a simple page, showing the text `My first Dashboard!`.

Using the Community Text Editor (CTE) to edit files inside Pentaho

CTE is a Pentaho plugin that you may install using Marketplace. The plugin provides the ability to edit the contents of a file within the JCR repository, directly from the PUC. You will not be able to create the files with it, but will be able to change the content and save the changes, which will immediately be recognized by Pentaho. This is very useful if you want to edit `.xcdf`, `.html`, `.css`, `.js`, and other file formats. More information can be found at: `https://github.com/webdetails/cte`.

You will find the sample code inside the book samples in the `/CtoolsBookSamples/myFirstDashboard` folder.

Using components inside the dashboards

We have not really covered the concept of a dashboard if we do not show any **Key Performance Indicators** (**KPIs**), charts, tables, and so on. CDF provides many components we can use to create the dashboard. To use them, we just need to extend the code we used previously. You saw that we need to include the modules we will need. Each component is a module that has its own dependencies that will be loaded automatically when we include the component.

The previous example shows the code that should be placed inside the XCDF file. This code creates a dashboard with a simple text component that returns a simple `Hello World!` message.

If you look at the code, you will find that we are including the dashboard module and also the component module. You will see that we are already using the Bootstrap framework. For this case, we are also including `cdf/components/TextComponent`, the module that makes it possible to use a text component, one of the simplest components that exists within CDF. To make it possible to use the component, we also need to specify an argument in the function that will represent the object of the component being called.

To define a new component, we should make a call to the dashboard function `addComponent` with an argument that will be a new instance of the text component, and we can create as many instances as we would like. When creating instances of a component, we need to set some properties and/or functions, and this will depend on the component that we are including in the dashboard:

```
<style>
    .msgContainer {
        background-color: #4682B4;
        color: white;
    }
</style>
<div class="container-fluid">
    <div id="container" class="container">
        <div id="row" class="row">
            <div id="col" class="col-sx-12">
                <div id="msgContainer" class="msgContainer"></div>
            </div>
        </div>
    </div>
</div>
<script language="javascript" type="text/javascript">
    var dashboard;
    require(['cdf/Dashboard.Bootstrap', 'cdf/components/
TextComponent'],
        function(Dashboard, TextComponent) {
            dashboard = new Dashboard();
            dashboard.addComponent(new TextComponent({
                name: "myTextComponent",
                type: "textComponent",
                htmlObject: "msgContainer",
                executeAtStart: true,
```

```
            priority: 5,
            expression: function() {
                return "Hello World!";
            }
        }));
        dashboard.init();
        return dashboard;
    }
);
</script>
```

The next step, after creating all the instances of the components to use and setting all the necessary properties and/or functions for each component, is to initialize the dashboard by calling the init() function of the dashboard instance.

You should have noticed that we are creating a variable outside the dashboard module, which we then make use of inside the dashboard and assign to the dashboard instance. This will make it possible to interact with the dashboard later. We will have a dashboard variable available in the global scope, so we will be able to create interactions between dashboards, but we will cover that later on in the book.

If you create a .xcdf file with a template tag that is pointing to the previous code, and execute by making a call to Pentaho, you will get a dashboard with your first component already working.

You should have noticed a property called htmlObject. This property is used to specify where on the dashboard the components should be rendered. It needs to point to the name of an element of your HTML. This will make the component create all its elements as children of the element specified in the htmlObject property.

Defining data sources for components

We don't want static dashboards, we want to query data to be shown in them. There are two ways to set queries in components. The data sources can be of one of two types, CDA and non-CDA:

- Going the CDA way, you need to define it using the query it's defining, inside the component, an object such as queryDefinition or chartDefiniton depending on the component, with a set of properties:
    - **path**: This is the path that points to a CDA file. You can make use of the CDA files created as explained in the chapter dedicated to CDA.
    - **dataAccessId**: This should set the ID of an available data source, also covered in the CDA chapter, that is set in the file we are pointing at.

- Going the non-CDA way, by just using a simple SQL or MDX query, we can define, inside the component, an object `queryDefinition` or `chartDefiniton`, depending on the component, with a set of properties:

  - **queryType**: This is the type of the query selecting one of the two values available, `mdx` or `sql`.

  - **jndi**: This is the name of the JNDI defined in Pentaho.

  - **catalog**: The catalog can be seen as the Mondrian schema to be used. When using mdx, we should also specify the schema name to use. No need when using a SQL query.

  - **query**: This is the function that returns the SQL or MDX query to get the data.

In the following two samples, we have two dashboards with a table component each. We used a table component to be able to present the results that come from the query. Let's look at the first example, where we are using a query defined in a CDA file, and grab the results from a query that is set in the CDA file.

The first step will be to set a query like we covered in the last chapter, after which we need to point to the CDA by setting the name and location of the file, and the data access source that we want to use. You can see that `path` and `dataAccessId` are defined in `chartDefiniton`.

The sample query that we are using is the one we created at the end of the last chapter:

```
require(['cdf/Dashboard.Bootstrap', 'cdf/components/TableComponent'],
    function(Dashboard, TableComponent) {
        dashboard = new Dashboard();
        var dashboardPath = dashboard.context.path.match(/^(\/
([^/]+\/)*)(.*)$/)[1];
        dashboard.addComponent(new TableComponent ({
            name: "top50Customers",
            type: "tableComponent",
            parameters:[],
            listeners: [],
            chartDefinition: {
            path: dashboardPath+"customers.cda",
            dataAccessId: "top50Customers"
        },
            htmlObject: "table",
            executeAtStart: true,
            priority: 5
        }));
        dashboard.init();
        return dashboard;
    }
);
```

You should be asking why use `chartDefiniton`? Well, I really don't know why, maybe some mistake that cannot be undone. The main idea you need to be aware of is that the components that are able to represent data coming from a query will do this by defining `chartDefinition` or `queryDefiniton`, depending on the component that we are using. By the end of this chapter, you will know what to use in what components, so let's proceed and you can learn something else before we cover that part.

The second example depicts how to directly call an MDX query without the need for a CDA file:

```
require(['cdf/Dashboard.Bootstrap', 'cdf/components/TableComponent'],
        function(Dashboard, TableComponent) {
            dashboard = new Dashboard();
            dashboard.addComponent(new TableComponent ({
                name: "top50Customers",
                type: "tableComponent",
                parameters:[],
                listeners: [],
                chartDefinition: {
                queryType: "mdx",
                jndi: "SampleData",
                catalog: "mondrian:/SteelWheels",
                query: function(){
                    return "select NON EMPTY {[Measures].[Sales]} ON
COLUMNS,"+
                            " NON EMPTY TopCount([Customers].[All
Customers].Children, 50.0, [Measures].[Sales])" +
                            " ON ROWS from [SteelWheelsSales]";
                }
            },
                htmlObject: "table",
                executeAtStart: true,
                priority: 5
            }));
            dashboard.init();
            return dashboard;
        }
    );
```

You should know that when grabbing results this way from a query, you are making a POST request to the CDF Web API, calling `viewAction`, which will execute `xAction`, and you'll get the result in an appropriate format that can be understood by the table component. This call will execute `xAction`, located inside the Pentaho repository at `/public/plugin-samples/pentaho-cdf/actions/jtable.xaction`, and pass some of the parameters we have specified, such as the query type, JNDI, the catalog, and query. The result is then processed by the component, which will finally render the results in the browser.

What's the best option? For many reasons, such as security, options, query abstraction, and cache among others, I would advise that you always use CDA. CDA allows you to abstract from the queries, and will let you work as a team. While one of your team is building the queries and all the related tasks, you can just focus on the dashboard, but using the data sources defined within, you have the ability to query for data. When using CDA, you will have your query results cached, so you will have better response times than using the other option.

As we saw earlier, when using SQL queries you could allow SQL injection, but CDA will avoid those malicious requests. Another reason is to have private parameters without the need to make changes to your `xAction`, change that would affect all other requests that are being executed through that same `xAction`. There are many more options and data sources you can create using CDA, and I would even risk saying that there is no data source from which you are not able to get data. I believe that these reasons are enough to justify executing queries through CDA.

To get more information about them, please refer to: `http://wiki.pentaho.com/display/ServerDoc2x/03.+Action+Sequences`.

Pentaho Action Sequence, also known as xActions

The `xActions` have a lot of utility inside Pentaho, but they can be replaced by Kettle transformations in some cases. If you have the ability to install a new plugin, you can leverage your work and use Kettle transformations, and replace some `xActions`. There is a plugin called Startup Rule Engine, which you can find in Marketplace, that allows you to execute Kettle transformations during the start up, login, or logout from Pentaho. To be honest, I don't dislike `xActions`, even if it's hard to debug and takes some time to create; `xActions` are fast to execute.

Creating and using parameters in data sources

You can see a parameter as a variable which is storing some value. In the last example, we created a parameter, and now we want to make use of it so we can send it to the query and have queries that can give back different results, depending on the input. To achieve this, we need to have a parameter inside the query in a way that we can later pass some value through the parameter. You already saw how to create parameters in the queries and how to set default values. Now we want to send a value to the query that can change depending on the user interaction, so the user can get the intended results, and have a proper visualization with the correct information in it:

```
require(['cdf/Dashboard.Bootstrap', 'cdf/components/TableComponent'],
    function(Dashboard, TableComponent) {
        dashboard = new Dashboard();
        dashboard.addParameter('marketDashParam','[Markets].[All
Markets]');
        var path = dashboard.context.path;
        var dashPath = path.substring(0,path.lastIndexOf('/'));
            dashboard.addComponent(new TableComponent({
                name: "top50Customers",
                type: "tableComponent",
                parameters:[['marketQueryParam', 'marketDashParam']],
                listeners: [],
                chartDefinition: {
                    path: dashPath+"/customers.cda",
                    dataAccessId: "top50Customers"
                },
                htmlObject: "table",
                executeAtStart: true,
                priority: 5
            }));
            dashboard.init();
            return dashboard;
        }
    );
```

After creating a new instance of the dashboard, we are creating a parameter using the line of code: `dashboard.addParameter('marketDashParam', '[Markets].[All Markets]')`. This will create a parameter in the dashboard that can be used by components or used on custom code. In the previous code example we are creating a variable with the name `marketParam` that will have a default value of `[Markets].[All Markets]`.

We are also finding the dashboard path by getting it from `dashboard.context.path`, so that we can point the dashboard to the CDA file. When creating a new instance of the table component, we are also setting the property parameters. When triggering a query, this property will be used to find out which parameters and value should be sent to the queries.

What CDF needs to do is request a query and say, *Hey these are the parameters you have here, and they should be replaced with these values*. The parameters property needs to be defined with an array of arrays, and each array will be a pair of a query parameter name and a dashboard parameter name. In each pair, the first value is used to identify the name of the parameter used inside the query, and it will be replaced before sending the query. The second value of each pair is the name of the parameter of the dashboard from where we want to grab the value to be sent. So we need to set as many values pairs as parameters names and values we want the query to use.

When defining a parameter/variable, we should have a default value, and once sent to the query, we will overwrite the default values that we have set in the CDA file. If you change the value of the parameter in the dashboard later and fire the query again, it will use the value that the dashboard parameter is storing. If you don't specify a default value, no value will be passed to the query, and a default value that may be specified in the query might be used. Neither of these are mandatory, but it might break your query or make the query not return the results.

We have started to cover listeners, and we will be talking about them in this and the next chapter. The listeners will give us a way to receive a notification when there is a change in a parameter. A listener points to a parameter, so if the value of that parameter is changed, the component is notified and updated.

As we covered in the lifecycle, when a component executes/updates, this will trigger a new query. In the component, we need to define the parameters that should be sent to the query. So, if you set the parameters to be on the list of listeners, and if you also set the parameter on the parameters to be sent to the query, every time a change is fired in the parameter, the parameter is sent to be used in the query. The request can be processed using, for instance, the value of the parameter as part of a where clause of a query.

If you create a new dashboard with the previous code, you will get a table showing all the customers. If you change the value to [Markets].[APAC], you will get only the customers that belong to the territory identified by APAC. It's not the intention of this book to teach you MDX, MQL, SQL, or how to apply filters, so if you don't know any MDX, you should try to understand it a little bit, as this could save you a lot of time and work. Just for the users that are not familiar with MDX, when applying [Markets].[All Markets], we are applying a filter that will display customers for all the markets. That way we are not applying any filter.

Most of the examples that will be shown here use MDX. Building a dashboard usually works better with MDX, and has other big advantages such as security. It's not mandatory for you to build a dashboard with MDX, but you should really consider it.

Take a look at the following diagram showing **Pentaho CDF Dashboard**:

To get a better understanding of how to use parameters and how they work with queries:

1. First, you need to set the connection and create the queries. You need to specify the connection and the data access identifier, where you need to specify the query and the query parameter to be replaced just before the request sends.

2. The second step is to create the `territoryDashParam` parameter on the dashboard.

3. Next add the component and define the path to the CDA file, which data access identifier to use, and the parameter mapping between what you have in the query and in the dashboard.

4. Last, initialize the dashboard, which will trigger the query passing the value of the dashboard parameter you have at that particular point in time, to execute the query. The results will then be rendered in the dashboard using the component you have set.

The importance of listeners inside the components

We do not want our users to be executing code and making the changes. What we want is to have a way to let the components know that they need to update themselves when a change happens in the dashboard. That's the purpose of the listeners. You could say that a component should be listening for the changes in the parameter(s) that exist in the dashboard. Components have a property called listeners, which you should define as an array. When creating a dashboard, what do you think provides the user with the ability to interact with the dashboard during runtime? The answer is, mostly the listeners.

In the console of your browser, run the following lines:

```
dashboard.setParameter('marketDashParam', '[Markets].[EMEA]');
var component = dashboard.getComponentByName('top50Customers');
component.update();
```

The first line of the code is used to change the value of the dashboard parameter, the second is to get the component instance, and the last one is to update the component. You will see that the dashboard now shows the customer data of another market territory.

The developer tools in your browser

Each browser has their own developer tools, which can have some differences from browser to browser, but the concept and main functionality are the same. Even if every browser, has its own developer tools, you might be able to install Firebug.

The array that should be defined on the listeners will have all the parameters that the component should be listening for to know about changes. So, let's suppose we set the table component to listen to `marketDashParam`. Later, when the user changes the parameter value, they can also notify the components that are listening to it. This will automatically trigger the update of the component.

The following code shows you how to set the listeners. You will see in the example that a listener is being set on the market parameter:

```
require(['cdf/Dashboard.Bootstrap', 'cdf/components/TableComponent',
'cdf/components/SelectComponent'],
        function(Dashboard, TableComponent) {
            dashboard = new Dashboard();
            dashboard.addParameter('marketDashParam', '[Markets].[All
Markets]');
            var path = dashboard.context.path;
            var dashPath = path.substring(0,path.lastIndexOf('/'));

            dashboard.addComponent(new TableComponent({
                name: "top50Customers",
                type: "tableComponent",
                parameters:[['marketQueryParam', 'marketDashParam']],
                listeners: ['marketDashParam'],
                chartDefinition: {
                path: dashPath+"/customers.cda",
                dataAccessId: "top50Customers"
              },
                htmlObject: "table",
                executeAtStart: true,
                priority: 5
            }));
            dashboard.init();
            return dashboard;
        }
    );
```

In CDF, we have a way to change the value of a parameter and send a notification, in order to update other components. This can be done through the execution of the following line of code:

```
dashboard.fireChange('marketDashParam', '[Markets].[EMEA]');
```

As soon as you execute the preceding code line, you will see an update in the dashboard.

Interaction between components

However, this is not enough—you need something more, because we still need to execute a line of code to make changes happen. If you make a filter available to the user, a dropdown for instance, which makes them able to apply changes to the table, they will not hesitate to use it. I am pretty sure you will want to do this, if not with a dropdown, then with a date selector, a button, a radio button, a checkbox, a simple text box, or whatever you can think of where the user can make a change or selection.

The first step is to add some kind of component that can provide interaction with the user. For our purposes, let's use a simple dropdown. The following code is an example of how to create a new instance of a `select` component:

```
new SelectComponent({
        name: "marketFilter",
        type: "selectComponent",
        parameter: "marketDashParam",
        valueAsId: false,
        queryDefinition: {
          path: dashPath+"/customers.cda",
           dataAccessId: "territories"
        },
        htmlObject: "selector",
        executeAtStart: true,
        priority: 5
    }));
```

Defining a component means simply applying settings to properties. We do this by setting properties and/or functions to the components. You can see in the previous code that the first two properties are the type and name of the component. Next, we set a parameter that states which parameter the selector should write the user selection with when a new value is selected. At the beginning, the selector will display the option that corresponds to the value inside the parameter, but once the user selects a new option, the component will trigger a change in the parameter, changing the values and notifying the other components about the changes.

Please note that we are now talking about a parameter and not the parameters of the component:

- Parameters is the property that allows us to specify the parameter/variable that will be sent to the query.

- Parameter is the variable where to set/get values.

You can see the parameter of a select component as the variable where the value of the selection will be stored, while the parameters are the variables that will be passed to the query on its request.

They can both be set on a single component, but why? Let's imagine the case where you have a selector that is dependent on another selector, and it gets the values for the dropdown from a query. In this case, we need to specify the parameters that should be used on the query. Anyhow, we also need to define the parameter/variable where we can store the selected value when the user makes a selection.

You also need to set datasource, sometimes referred to as the query to use, and htmlObject, the element name, where the component will be rendered in the layout. Should the component be executed at the beginning of the dashboard? If yes, we need to set the executeAtStart property to true, and also the priority of execution.

You will see later that is possible to set parameters and listeners on the selectors, in case you want to have cascading filters, where the value of a filter will be used in the query of another filter. Just don't forget that the big difference between parameter and parameters is that in a parameter you are setting the name of the variable that will store the selection, and in parameters you are saying which parameters should be used to execute the query and populate the dropdown or whatever.

Populating a selector with data can be done using a query or a values array

Usually, you would set a query to populate a selector, but when a small amount of static values are required, we can use the valuesArray option.

Let's look at an example of how to set the properties, have a selector making changes to a parameter, and notify the table component about changes:

```
require(['cdf/Dashboard.Bootstrap', 'cdf/components/TableComponent',
'cdf/components/SelectComponent'],
        function(Dashboard, TableComponent, SelectComponent) {
            dashboard = new Dashboard();
            dashboard.addParameter('marketDashParam', '[Markets].[All
Markets]');
```

```
var path = dashboard.context.path;
var dashPath = path.substring(0,path.lastIndexOf('/'));
dashboard.addComponent(new SelectComponent({
    name: "marketFilter",
    type: "selectComponent",
    parameter: "marketDashParam",
    valueAsId: false,
    queryDefinition: {
    path: dashPath+"/customers.cda",
    dataAccessId: "territories"
  },
    htmlObject: "selector",
    executeAtStart: true,
    priority: 5
}));
dashboard.addComponent(new TableComponent({
    name: "top50Customers",
    type: "tableComponent",
    parameters:[['marketQueryParam', 'marketDashParam']],
    listeners: ['marketDashParam'],
    chartDefinition: {
    path: dashPath+"/customers.cda",
    dataAccessId: "top50Customers"
  },
    htmlObject: "table",
    executeAtStart: true,
    priority: 5
}));
dashboard.init();
return dashboard;
    }
);
```

You are now starting to have a dashboard that is able to provide interaction to the user, where the user can select a market to filter the customers that get to the table. It works without the need to execute any other line of code; interaction will be enough.

The following example dashboard is illustrated with two selectors, one for the territory and another one for the country. You will see that when selecting a particular territory, only the countries for that territory are showing:

```
<div class="container-fluid">
    <div class="container">
        <div class="row">
```

```html
        <div class="col-xs-12">
            <h1>CTools Book Samples!</h1>
        </div>
    </div>
    <div class="row">
        <div class="col-xs-12 col-md-6">
            <div id="territorySelector" class="selector"></div>
        </div>
        <div class="col-xs-12 col-md-6">
            <div id="countrySelector" class="selector"></div>
        </div>
        <div class="col-xs-12">
            <div id="table" class="table"></div>
        </div>
    </div>
</div>
</div>
<script language="javascript" type="text/javascript">
    var dashboard;
    require(['cdf/Dashboard.Bootstrap', 'cdf/components/
TableComponent', 'cdf/components/SelectComponent'],
        function(Dashboard, TableComponent, SelectComponent) {
            dashboard = new Dashboard();
            dashboard.addParameter('territoryDashParam', '[Markets].
[All Markets]');
            dashboard.addParameter('countryDashParam', '[Markets].
[Country].Members');
            var path = dashboard.context.path;
            var dashPath = path.substring(0,path.lastIndexOf('/'));
            dashboard.addComponent(new SelectComponent({
                name: "territoryFilter",
                type: "selectComponent",
                parameter: "territoryDashParam",
                valueAsId: false,
                queryDefinition: {
                path: dashPath+"/customers.cda",
                dataAccessId: "territories"
              },
                htmlObject: "territorySelector",
                executeAtStart: true,
                priority: 5
            }));
            dashboard.addComponent(new SelectComponent({
                name: "countryFilter",
```

```
                    type: "selectComponent",
                    parameter: "countryDashParam",
                    valueAsId: false,
                    parameters:[['marketQueryParam',
'territoryDashParam']],
                    listeners: ['territoryDashParam'],
                    queryDefinition: {
                    path: dashPath+"/customers.cda",
                    dataAccessId: "countries"
                },
                    htmlObject: "countrySelector",
                    executeAtStart: true,
                    priority: 5
            }));
            dashboard.addComponent(new TableComponent({
                name: "top50Customers",
                type: "tableComponent",
                parameters:[['marketQueryParam', 'countryDashParam']],
                listeners: ['countryDashParam'],
                chartDefinition: {
                path: dashPath+"/customers.cda",
                dataAccessId: "top50Customers"
            },
                htmlObject: "table",
                executeAtStart: true,
                priority: 5
        }));
        dashboard.init();
        return dashboard;
    }
  );
</script>
```

When selecting a new country, changes will happen in the tables. To make it possible, we should define two parameters in the dashboards. One parameter for the territories that the country selector will be listening. Another parameter for the countries, which the table will be listening to. A very important note is that the territory component will store the selection in the territory parameter and the country selector in the country parameters.

Just by using two parameters and setting some properties such as a parameter, listeners, parameters, and queries, we can have an interactive dashboard. Wait until you get to know how to create interaction from table and charts components, you will learn how to create much more interactive dashboards. We will cover this in *Chapter 6, Tables, Templates, Exports, and Text Components*.

Using preExecution and postExecution

The preExecution and postExecution functions are very similar concerning their usage, but different in their purposes.

The first one, preExecution, you can see as preparing the execution of the component. One really good example is to point to another data source, or even to a different CDA file. Let's suppose you have multiple queries that are used in multiple dashboards, and you want to have a simple file where all the common queries are placed. This is possible to change with just a couple of lines of code in the PreExecution function.

Another good example is when you want to have cascading parameters. Let's suppose you want to have a selector where you can choose between the market level (country or city), and the second filter will show you countries or cities depending on what you have selected for the first one. The first will drive the query for your second filter, and so the values to select will vary between country or city. The following code will help you understand how we can make cascading parameters work using the pre- and post- execution functions:

```
require(['cdf/Dashboard.Bootstrap', 'cdf/components/TableComponent',
  'cdf/components/SelectComponent', "cdf/Logger", "cdf/lib/jquery"],
    function(Dashboard, TableComponent, SelectComponent, Logger, $) {
        dashboard = new Dashboard();
        dashboard.addParameter('marketLevelDashParam', 'territories');
        dashboard.addParameter('marketDashParam', '[Markets].[All
Markets]');
        var path = dashboard.context.path;
        var dashPath = path.substring(0,path.lastIndexOf('/'));
        dashboard.addComponent(new SelectComponent({
            name: "marketLevelFilter",
            type: "selectComponent",
            parameter: "marketLevelDashParam",
            valueAsId: false,
            valuesArray: [["territories","Territory"],["countries","Co
untry"],["cities","City"]],
            htmlObject: "marketLevelSelector",
            executeAtStart: true,
            priority: 5,
            postExecution: function(){
                $('#marketLevelSelectorLabel').text('Select market
level:');
            },
        }));
        dashboard.addComponent(new SelectComponent({
```

```
            name: "marketFilter",
            type: "selectComponent",
            parameter: "marketDashParam",
            valueAsId: false,
            parameters:[],
            listeners: ["marketLevelDashParam"],
            queryDefinition: {
            path: dashPath+"/customers-selection-change.cda"
        },
            htmlObject: "marketSelector",
            executeAtStart: true,
            priority: 5,
            preExecution: function(){
                var level = dashboard.getParameterValue("marketLevelD
ashParam");
                this.queryDefinition.dataAccessId = level;
            },
            postExecution: function(){
                var level = dashboard.getParameterValue("marketLevelD
ashParam");
                $('#marketSelectorLabel').text('Select from
'+level+':');
            }
        }));
        dashboard.addComponent(new TableComponent({
            name: "top50Customers",
            type: "tableComponent",
            parameters:[["marketQueryParam", 'marketDashParam']],
            listeners: ['marketDashParam'],
            chartDefinition: {
            path: dashPath+"/customers-selection-change.cda",
            dataAccessId: "top50Customers"
        },
            htmlObject: "table",
            executeAtStart: true,
            priority: 5
        }));
        dashboard.init();
        return dashboard;
    }
);
```

The trick here is to have two parameters: `marketLevelDashParam` and `marketDashParam`. The first one is used to store countries or cities, depending on the user's selection in the first selector. The second will be used to store what country or city the final user selects, so that we can then use it in the parameters of the table in order to be sent as part of the query and to get only the customers for that particular selection. The first selector does not have any tricks, just a `postExecution` function, similar to the one in the second selector, which we will explain next.

The real magic is in the listeners and `preExecution` of the second selector. This selector will be listening for changes in `marketLevelDashParam` and will use the value of the parameter to know which query to use and run. The query that will be executed will be a new query based on the value for the level, where the level is the value that was selected.

On this line, and in all other functions inside components, `this` refers to the component itself, followed by changing `dataAccessId` in the `queryDefinition` object. You saw in previous examples that we can use `this` to define which CDA file and which data access ID the component should use to get the data.

Similar to this case, you can also change the path and point to another CDA file. To get the stored value(s) in a dashboard parameter, we can use the following line of code:

```
var level=dashboard.getParameterValue("marketLevelDashParam")
```

This way, we are pointing to a query `countries` or `cities` that are defined on the CDA file.

In front of each selector, you can see a label. The `postExecution` function is being used to change the label for the selector. Take a look at the post execution function of the second selector and you will see that we are grabbing the value of the parameter that identifies the level of the filter, and this value will be used as part of the label.

The code `$('#marketSelectorLabel').text('Select from '+level+':')` is used to change the text inside the label before the selector. This could be done, and would be even better, in the pre execution function, but you would not see how to use post execution. Usually, post execution is used to manipulate the HTML generated during the rendering of the component, and this is only available in post execution. A good example is applying a jQuery plugin, which we will cover in the CDE chapters. Another example is to attach an event to some elements that the component made available on the page. There are a lot of use cases, and we just don't have the space to cover them all.

Just keep in mind that you should use preExecution to execute code to prepare the execution of the component, and postExecution to execute code to manipulate the DOM that the component has created in the dashboard.

In our example, just add a new option (Territory) to the values array of the first selector. Set the values array as:

```
valuesArray: [
["territories","Territory"],
["countries","Country"],
["cities","City"]]
```

If you now execute the sample code of your dashboard, you will automatically be able to choose the customers, with the option to select all of those who are in a particular territory level.

Understanding how to work with postFetch

In the Steel Wheels sample data, which we have been using in our examples and is available with the standard installation of Pentaho, we have one territory showing in the selector as having a #null value. This description is not friendly to the end user, so we may make a change, thereby manipulating the result set that we get from the execution of the query. With this, we can change the description of #null to something like NA.

The following code is for the territory selector component, where we just added a function to define the code to be executed on the postFetch function:

```
dashboard.addComponent(new SelectComponent({
            name: "territoryFilter",
            type: "selectComponent",
            parameter: "territoryDashParam",
            valueAsId: false,
            queryDefinition: {
            path: dashPath+"/customers.cda",
            dataAccessId: "territories"
        },
            htmlObject: "territorySelector",
            executeAtStart: true,
            priority: 5,
            postFetch: function(data) {
                // manipulate result from query
```

```
                    for (var i=0; i<data.resultset.length; i++) {
                          if (data.resultset[i][1]=="#null")
                                data.resultset[i][1]="NA";
                    }
                    return data;
              }
        }));
```

You can see the postFetch function being defined and passing the result of the execution of the query as an argument. This result can be manipulated by changing the values inside the data variable.

First let's just quickly review something we covered in the last chapter. When creating a query through CDA, the results are by default returned in a JSON format, something like:

```
{
"metadata":[
   {"colIndex":0,"colType":"String","colName":"UID"},
   {"colIndex":1,"colType":"String","colName":"Markets"}
],
"resultset":[
     ["[Markets].[All Markets]","All Markets"],
     ["[Markets].[#null]","#null"],
     ["[Markets].[APAC]","APAC"],
     ["[Markets].[EMEA]","EMEA"],
     ["[Markets].[Japan]","Japan"],
     ["[Markets].[NA]","NA"]
],
"queryInfo":{"totalRows":"6"},

}
```

The result is a JSON object composed of:

- metadata: This is an array of objects where the metadata is described. Each column will be an element of the array, so we will have as many elements on the array as columns returned from the query. For each element of the array, you will get an object with:
    - colIndex: The index of the column
    - colType: The data type contained in the columns
    - colName: The name of the column

- **resultset**: Here you will get the result of the execution of the query. The result set is a multidimensional array. Each element of the array will contain the result of a row and each row will be an array with as many elements as columns. In our example, we will have an array of six rows and two columns.

- **queryInfo**: This is an object with a unique element, totalRows, which contains the number of rows in the result set.

You now understand the JSON returned from the execution of the CDA queries, so let's return to our example on how to manipulate the result set. Don't forget that this is the default format, but when using the CDA Web API, you can change the format type of the result, as already covered in the last chapter.

So in the sample code, you can see that we are using a for loop to iterate over all the rows contained in data.resultSet, and use the if condition to check whether the second column, the one with the description, will be shown in the selector. If we have a #null value, we will just change the value to be NA in the same position with in the array. Note that we are just changing the description and not the ID, because the ID will be used to filter the results for the country selector.

A very important step is to return the object that you need to be used in your component. In our sample, we are just returning the same object that with a changed value. That same value will be used by the component when being rendered.

It's also important for you to know that you can use postFetch not only to manipulate data, but also to manipulate parameters, or another component on the dashboard, or even manipulate elements on the DOM. Let's suppose that you want to change some behavior or settings on the component based on the result of the execution of the query. An example would be changing the column type, headers, and format based on the results, and the number of columns based on the result set. This kind of operation is what will make all the difference when developing the dashboard, but will also produce outstanding results. Here again, imagination is the only limit.

Using preChange and postChange

Now it's time to cover preChange and postChange. These two functions will only be available in components whose main purpose is to be used as filters. Examples of this are select, input, date range, radio button, button, multi button, and so on.

Every component where we can set a parameter to store the selections and the lifecycle of the component will trigger `fireChange` to that parameter. We have the option to specify the function that will be executed both before this happens and after applying the changes to the parameter, `preChange` and `postChange`. Take a look at following image:

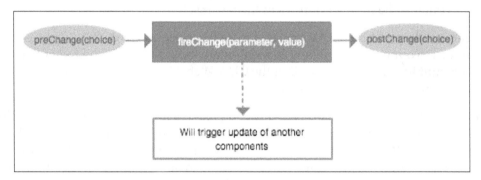

As you can figure out, that the first function, the `preChange` function, can be used to execute the code that can validate the options and take some actions before changing the parameter value. Can be used to prepare something before other components starts to execute because they are listening to that same parameter. The other `postExecution` function, can be used to perform operations that need to be extended just after the changes on the parameter are confirmed.

In the next sample code, the options that we have in our selector are different to the name of the query, so we can make use of `preChange` to control what the value to use on `fireChange` will be. To achieve this, we just need to return the value that we need for the `fireChange` function, and this value will then be passed to the `postChange` function:

```
dashboard.addComponent(new SelectComponent({
    name: "marketLevelFilter",
    type: "selectComponent",
    parameter: "marketLevelDashParam",
    valueAsId: false,
    valuesArray: [["1","Territory"],["2","Country"],["3","City"]],
    htmlObject: "marketLevelSelector",
    executeAtStart: true,
    priority: 5,
    postExecution: function(){
        $('#marketLevelSelectorLabel').text('Select market level:');
    },
    preChange: function(choice) {
        var selection = "";
```

```
        switch (choice) {
          case "2":  selection = "countries";
                     break;
          case "3":  selection = "cities";
                     break;
          default: selection = "territories";
          }
          return selection;
      },
      postChange: function(choice) {
          Logger.log("You choose the value: "+choice+" for parameter
     "+this.parameter);
          }
      }));
```

A very common use case for `preChange` is to apply validations and return an appropriate value or propagate changes to more parameters that are dependent on the selections made by the user, per instance, in a drop-down. Common use cases for `postChange` is to take some actions after the parameter changes have started to be propagated to the other components, to display some information about the selection made by the user in another element of the dashboard, or just to execute some custom code.

Priority of component execution

The order of the execution of the components will depend on another property for each component. The `priority` property should be set using integer values. Lower values as higher priorities. The default value of the property is 5. The components with the same priority are executed at almost the same time and they are executed in an arbitrary order, but during the same routine. If a different and higher priority is set for a component, it will only be executed after the ones with a lower priority are executed. Each similar priority will correspond to a cycle, where it will start with the execution of the components, and will end after the last component that has the same priority finishes.

Inside a dashboard, to change the order of execution of the components, you just need to change the `priority` property and set another value.

Let's look at the following example where we have five components:

- Components 1 and 2: priority 5
- Components 3: priority 10
- Components 4 and 5: priority 15

In the following image the X-axis is the time and the Y-axis is the priority:

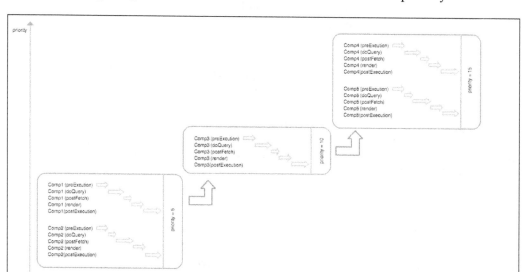

In the preceding image we can look at the components with the same priority as being in the same group, and because the execution of components in the same group will be asynchronous, they will be executed at the same time, and only when all the components of that group have finished will the components with the nearest priority up be executed.

So, in the preceding image, you can see that components 1 and 2 start the execution at the same time, and only after they're finished will the execution of component 3 start. The order of execution for components of the same priority is arbitrary, and you should not expect any sequence that you can guess. Also, components 4 and 5, which have the highest priority, will start the execution only after the component with priority 10 has finished executing.

Available components and properties

When defining new components, you need to define a set of properties that define the object and/or the behavior. The generic and mandatory properties of all/almost all the components are:

- `type`: This property assumes a variety of values such as `tableComponent`, `buttonComponent`, `selectComponent`, and so on, depending on the component that is used.

- `name`: This is the unique identifier of the component inside the dashboard.

- `listeners`: Will accept an array of a strings with the name of the parameters. If a value on each one of those parameters changes, the component will be updated. This array is crucial to create interaction among components.

- `parameters`: This accepts an array of arrays, where each array will have the name of the parameters of the query and the parameters of the dashboard with the value to be used.

- `parameter`: For components where user input is required, this is where the input is stored to be used later.

- `htmlObject`: This is the ID of the HTML object that will be replaced by the component's content result and be reached by calling a method from inside the component using `this.placeholder()`.

- `priority`: This is the priority of the component's execution, defaulting to 5. The lowest priorities have the highest priority of execution. Components with the same priority will be executed simultaneously.

- `executeAtStart`: If set to false, the component will not execute at the start of the dashboard, but it can be updated as soon as one of its listeners has changed.

Some other properties have already been covered, such as `preChange/postChange` or `preExec/postExec`, and we will cover others in the remaining chapters.

There are a lot of components available in CDF, and more in CDE. When you install the CTools, you also get some samples that you can find under `/public/plugin-samples/CDF/Require samples/Documentation/Components Reference`. These samples are very useful for getting knowledge about each of the available components and how they work. For each component, you will find a CDF dashboard that will provide you with a description of the component, the available methods, and the options. Also available is sample code and a previewer of the components, where you can also understand how to use the component inside a dashboard.

If you know how the lifecycle works and how you can define and use a component, you are now able to create a dashboard on your own.

It would not make sense to waste a bunch of pages just providing almost the same information as you have seen in the previous examples, but you don't yet have a summary where you can see which properties are available for which components. We will show you how to work with the most important components in the next chapter, where we will cover a great deal of the available properties.

Adding resources – JavaScript and CSS

You already saw how to create a new dashboard, and add components, but you haven't yet seen how to include JavaScript and CSS code, which is available in CDF. I always like to add my JavaScript files with the code for the project/dashboard. Regardless of whether we are creating a dashboard or multiple dashboards in a project, we should always develop it while bearing in mind that we may need to have multiple dashboards, and some of the code and style could be reused for these multiple dashboards.

If you are building dashboards that are similar to each other, you should rethink the way you are creating or designing your dashboards. A dashboard can be flexible in a way that will let you change the behavior and the data to be displayed in an easy way, without too many components and or too much logic.

Let's suppose we are creating four dashboards and all the dashboards will share the style, but also will have different components. Some of the components will share some properties, but will have some specific properties for their case. What we can do is have some files that contain JavaScript code and CSS rules that are applied to all the dashboards, and some other files that can be applied for a specific dashboard. The files that are specific to a particular dashboard will just extend or overwrite the existing code.

JavaScript code is easy to extend and overwrite, and when using CSS you should write rules, or just load the files in a different order to define which rules are extending or overwriting the remaining ones.

Using internal modules

The way to add JavaScript code in a file to a dashboard is by including a module when creating the dashboard. RequireJS provides a way to do this, you just need to follow the rules and be able to use modules that are already defined, or just point to a file by its relative path. There are a lot of modules in CDF that you can use, and if not you can include your own.

The modules that are available by default in CDF are the following:

cdf/Dashboard. Clean	cdf/Dashboard. Bootstrap	cdf/Dashboard. Blueprint	cdf/Logger
cdf/Addin	cfd/dashboard/ Utils	cfd/dashboard/ RefreshEngine	cdf/lib/ modernizr
cdf/lib/jquery	amd!cdf/lib/ jquery.ui	cdf/lib/jquery. blockUI	cdf/lib/jquery. impromptu

cdf/lib/jquery. fancybox	cdf/lib/mustache	cdf/lib/ datatables	cdf/lib/jquery. ui.autobox
cdf/lib/jquery. templating	cdf/lib/ bootstrap	cdf/lib/jquery. bgiframe	cdf/lib/jquery. jdMenu
cdf/lib/cdf. jquery.i18n	cdf/lib/ OpenLayers	cdf/lib/ queryParser	cdf/lib/jquery. corner
cdf/lib/jquery. select2	cdf/lib/jquery. chosen	cdf/lib/jquery. multiselect	cdf/lib/Raphael
cdf/lib/base64	cdf/lib/moment	amd!cdf/lib/ underscore	amd!cdf/lib/ jquery. ui.autobox
amd!cdf/lib/ backbone	amd!cdf/lib/ daterangepicker. jQuery		

The way to add a resource is just to use the module ID, in the require instruction, like in the following example:

```
require(['cdf/Dashboard.Clean',
        'cfd/dashboard/Utils',
        'cdf/Logger'],
            function(Dashboard, Utils, Logger) {
                dashboard = new Dashboard();
                Looger.log(Utils.numberFormat(0.2, '0.00%'));
                dashboard.init();
            }
    );
```

We included three modules in the previous example. The first one for the dashboard type will include the dashboard's core functionality, the second one will include the utilities functions, in our case to format a number as a percentage, and the last one to make it possible to send log messages to the console. You can also see in the dashboard's code that we are just sending a log message to the console with a number formatted as a percentage with two decimal places.

Defining and including new modules

We may also want to include our own code so that we can also create a module of our own by using the define function of require.

The syntax is as follows: define([[id,] dependencies,] factory). First, two arguments, ID and dependencies, are optional and consist of an ID for the module and the dependencies for your module. You can avoid defining the ID, and if that's the case, the file name and path will be used as ID for the module. Third, factory is a function that is executed to instantiate a module. If the dependencies argument is not specified, this means that the module has no dependencies. You can get more detailed information from the RequireJS website (http://requirejs.org/docs/api.html). The following code is an example of how to define a module to be used in a dashboard:

```
define(function() {
        var myModule = {
            sayHello: function(user) {return 'Hello '+user+'!'}
        };
        return myModule;
    }
);
```

The module is defined in a JavaScript file with the name myModule in the same folder as the dashboard.

Next, you can see how we can include a custom module in a dashboard and make it possible to use the unique function sayHello. The module function is called inside the expression function of the component:

```
require(['cdf/Dashboard.Bootstrap', 'cdf/components/TextComponent',
'myModule', 'css!myDashboardStyle'],
        function(Dashboard, TextComponent, myModule) {
        dashboard = new Dashboard();
        dashboard.addComponent(new TextComponent({
            name: "showText",
            type: "textComponent",
            parameters:[],
            listeners: ["inputParam"],
            htmlObject: "showMessage",
            executeAtStart: true,
            priority: 5,
            expression: function(){
```

```
                             return myModule.sayHello(dashboard.context.user ||
        'world');
                    }
            }));
            dashboard.init();
            return dashboard;
        });
```

Including CSS files

But that's not all, because when defining a dashboard, we definitely want to make it unique and outstanding, and we also want to include CSS in our dashboard. The way to do this is very similar to what we saw earlier with the modules, but we need to prepend the path/file name with `css!`. This will load the CSS file when the dashboard is also being loaded, and all the styling will be applied as intended.

If we have a file called `myDashboardStyle.css` on the same level as the dashboard HTML file, then we should have the file included as `css!myDashboardStyle`, which was also included in the last example.

Dashboards utilities

There was once a time when we needed to add libraries as external resources to leverage the process of formatting dates and numbers. Nowadays, it is possible to do the formatting without the need to include external files. We can do the formatting just by including the `cfd/dashboard/Utils` module. This will make `require` load all the dependencies without any more effort.

Formatting numbers

Numbers can be formatted to look like currency, percentages with decimal places, thousands, and abbreviations. To format numbers, you should use the function `numberFormat`, available in the dashboard object. In our examples, you could do this by calling `Utils.numberFormat(value[, format[, langCode]])`. The function accepts the arguments; the first one is the value to format, the second one is the format mask, and the last is the language and locale to use when formatting the number.

The mask or format argument is a string made up of symbols that shows how to format the number. The most commonly used symbols are listed in the next table. There is always the need to enclose the format in quotes or double quote marks. The number formatting is based on `cdo.NumberFormat`, code that is built in CCC and Protovis. CCC, which was covered in the first chapter, is the chart library that brings a lot of flexibility to represent data using charts/graphs, while Protovis is the JavaScript library that CCC uses:

Symbol	Description
0	This is the digit placeholder, which prints a trailing or a leading zero in this position, if appropriate
#	This is a digit placeholder, which will never print trailing or leading zeros
.	This is a decimal placeholder
,	This is a thousands separator
−, +, $, ( ), space	This is a literal character, that is, a character that is displayed exactly as typed into the format string

We also have the ability to use several standard formats with the format function. Instead of specifying symbols in the format argument, you will denote these formats by using a name in the format argument of the format function. These names should be enclosed inside the quotes that define the format mask:

Symbol	Description
Currency, or C	This displays a number with thousands separators, if appropriate. It displays two digits to the right of the decimal separator. The output is based on settings and/or language and locale specified.
Abbreviation, or A	This will abbreviate the number, if appropriate, and include a symbol that indicates the number of zeros that the user should consider when evaluating the number. You can also specify abbreviations by using only the letter A.

Let's look at some examples on how to use the masks to format numbers with the `numberFormat` function (first you can see the number being formatted, in the middle you can see the format mask being applied, and on the right side you can see the result):

Numbers

Number	Format mask	Resulting string
1250	0.##	1250
1250	0.00	1250.00
1250	00000.0	01250.0
1250	#####.00	1250.00
1250.45	#.0	1250.5
1250.45	#,#.00	1,250.45
1250.45	#,#.000	1,250.450
12349867450.45	#,#.0	12,349,867,450.5

Currency

Number	Format mask	Resulting string
1250	#,#.0 €	1,250.0 €
1250	#,#.0€	1,250.0€
1250	$1,250.0 €	$1,250.0
1250	#,#.0Currency	1,250.0$
1250	C#,#.0	$1,250.0
1250	#,#.0\u00a4	1,250.0$

Abbreviation

Number	Format mask	Resulting string
12568	'0.00 Abbreviation'	12.6k
12568	'0.00 A'	12.6k
1250	0.000A	1.250k
1250	0.###A	1.25k
1250000	0.#A	1.3m

Number	Format mask	Resulting string
1250000	0.##A	1.25m
125873987343	0.##A	125.87b

Percentages

Number	Format mask	Resulting string
0.2	0.00%	20.00%
0.96	0.00%	96.00%
0.9636	0.0%	96.4%

There are ways to change the general settings and the language/locale settings, so let's cover that now.

Languages and locales

For the third argument, you should set the language-locale to use so that the format knows what the default masks are and/or the currency symbol to use. When using currency and defining the language and locale, you should not specify the symbol to use, and just use C, letting the formatter apply the defined settings:

Number	Format mask	Language	Resulting string
323636	0.0C	pt-pt	323636.0€
323636	C0.0	en-us	$323636.0
323636	C0.0	en-gb	£323636.0

Multiple formats

You also may want to specify format masks for positive and negative numbers, and you are able to do so just by separating the formats with semicolons. It should be used by specifying [positive_mask]; [negative_mask]; [zero_mask]; [null_mask]:

Number	Format mask	Resulting string
-323636	$#,##0;($#,##0)	($323,636)
0	$#,##0;($#,##0);zero	zero
null	$#,##0;($#,##0);zero	
null	$#,##0;($#,##0);zero;nil	nil

Formatting and manipulating dates

We can also use a function to format dates and time. When using the CDF Utils to format the date and time, in reality we are making use of MomentJS, a JavaScript library that is automatically included when using the CDF Utils module in our dashboard. We can format dates by using the dateFormat function, and similar to what you saw earlier, you should use the following function: Utils. dateFormat(date[, format[, langCode]]). The first argument is the date, which can be a string or a moment call with the input format of the specified date:

```
dashboards.dateFormat('2014-12-20', 'DD/MM/YY')
dashboards.dateFormat(moment('20/12/2014','DD/MM/YYYY'), 'DD/MM/YY')
```

The previous examples will return the same result, but are specifying the input date in different formats. The second example would not recognize '20/12/2014' as a valid date, so we need to use MomentJS to specify the input format as 'DD/MM/YYYY'.

The first argument of the function is the date to format, where you can specify a string or a MomentJS object. It's good practice to do it as in the second example, due to compatibility reasons when rendering the dashboard in different browsers.

The second argument of the function is the format mask to be used by the formatter, and it's based on the format masks provided by MomentJS. You can get more information at: http://momentjs.com/docs/#/displaying/format/.

It's not the purpose of this book to explain how to work with MomentJS, you just need to know that is a really great library that also allows you to manipulate dates. It's very easy and intuitive to use, and you will find detailed documentation, with a lot of examples, on their website at http://momentjs.com/docs/. Usually, dates are very important in all projects, so we really advise you to get to know how to work with this library.

When using a date like new Date() on the date argument of the function, we could end up getting the following results:

Date	Format mask	Resulting string
new Date()	dddd, MMMM Do YYYY, h:mm:ss a	Friday, May 29th 2015, 9:27:37 am
moment('20/12/2014','DD/MM/YYYY')	DD-MMM-YY, hh:mm	20-Dec-14, 12:00
moment()	DD/MM/YYYY	29/05/2015
moment()	ddd, hA	Fri, 9PM

Internationalization of numbers and dates

When talking about the internationalization of numbers and dates, there is a function that you can use to add or change the settings. The function to use is `Utils.configLanguage(langCode, config)`, which will receive two arguments, one of which is the language/locale code and another is the settings object. The language code is just a string with an identifier and the configuration is an object that can contain one or both keys with the settings to format numbers and dates. The keys are:

- `number`: This configures the number's format language
- `dateLocale`: This configures the date's format language

In the following example, we can see the usage for both options, and both options will expect an object with the settings to use:

```
Utils.configLanguage('myLangCode', {
    number: {
        mask:               '#,0.##',
        style: {
            integerPad:     '0',
            fractionPad:    '0',
            decimal:        ',',
            group:          ' ',
            groupSizes:     [3],
            abbreviations:  ['k','m', 'b', 't'],
            negativeSign:   '-',
            currency:       'F'
        }
    },
    dateLocale: {
        months: [
            "January", "February", "March", "April", "May", "June",
            "July", "August", "September", "October", "November",
"December"
        ],
        monthsShort: [
            "Jan", "Feb", "Mar", "Apr", "May", "Jun",
            "Jul", "Aug", "Sep", "Oct", "Nov", "Dec"
        ],

    }
})
```

After these settings are defined, we may use them using `langCode` defined. In our example, we have set our own language code as `myLangCode` in the following function:

- `Utils.numberFormat(value[, format[, langCode]])`

- `Utils.dateFormat(value[, format[, langCode]])`

The last argument of each function is the language code, and if we apply `myLangCode` string in there, we will be using the setting we have set for this specific language as:

```
Utils.numberFormat(254179)
```

The function will return the number formatted with the default format mask `'#,0.##'` and return the number formatted accordingly.

In the example, you can see that we are setting definitions for `number` and `dateLocale`, but you define just one of them. It's not mandatory to define both.

For the `dateLocale` settings, there are more options that we could customize, so you can find the complete reference at `http://momentjs.com/docs/#/customization/`.

Dashboard storage

It's now possible to maintain parameter states between different sessions. Instead of using simple parameters, objects inside the special namespace `storage` can be saved and restored.

Dashboards can store values as per the user preferences. Let's suppose you have a dashboard where you want to persist the status next time you get on the dashboard. It's possible to do this with the storage functionality of CDF. Each time that the function `dashboard.saveStorage()` is called, CDF will store the content of the `dashboard.storage` object. When the dashboard is loaded for that user, the dashboard will have access to the object `dashboard.storage` where all the collections (objects and arrays) or functions are defined.

Don't forget to save the storage:

Storage will only be saved on the server side after running the `dashboard.saveStorage()` function; otherwise if you refresh the dashboard before saving it, you will notice that you have lost the last changes before the last save.

You can also force the load of the storage, by calling `dashboard.loadStorage()` function, or if you want to clean the storage, you just need to run `dashboard. cleanStorage()`. You can also just clean part of the storage by deleting it:

```
require(['cdf/Dashboard.Bootstrap', 'cdf/components/
TextInputComponent', 'cdf/components/TextComponent', "cdf/Logger"],
        function(Dashboard, TextInputComponent, TextComponent, Logger)
{
            dashboard = new Dashboard();
            dashboard.addParameter('inputParam', dashboard.storage.
inputParam || "");
            dashboard.addComponent(new TextInputComponent({
                name: "inputTextComponent",
                type: "textInputComponent",
                parameters:[],
                parameter: "inputParam",
                htmlObject: "inputComponent",
                executeAtStart: true,
                priority: 5,
                postChange: function() {
                    dashboard.storage.inputParam = dashboard.
getParameterValue(this.parameter);
                    dashboard.saveStorage();
                }
            }));
            dashboard.addComponent(new TextComponent({
                name: "showTextComponent",
                type: "textComponent",
                parameters:[],
                listeners: ["inputParam"],
                htmlObject: "textComponent",
                executeAtStart: true,
                priority: 5,
                expression: function(){
                    return dashboard.getParameterValue('inputParam');
                }
            }));
            dashboard.init();
            return dashboard;
        });
```

The previous example shows that we can make use of storage in CDF. In the dashboard, we have two components and one parameter. The parameter created has, as a default value, `dashboard.storage.inputParam || ""`, meaning that it will grab the value from a previously saved parameter in the storage object. If it is not defined, it will return an empty string, which is the case when executing the dashboard for a user for the first time.

> **Take caution when storing a huge amount of information in the storage**
>
> This works on a per user basis, and the developer needs to be aware that everything saved will be loaded for every dashboard for that same user, so if too much is stored, one may have a performance penalty.

The first defined component is an input component that will let you enter text in the input box, and, once the value is confirmed, it will write the value for the parameter. But, at that time, only the parameter has the value entered, so we also need to write value to the storage object and save it.

That is what we can see in the `postChange` function, where we are just writing a variable inside the context with the value to store. Once we have created or overwritten the variable value, we need to save it with the instruction `dashboard.saveStorage()`. We could also have another component, such as a button component that would clean the storage by executing the instruction `dashboard.cleanStorage()`. You should try it.

> **Loading the storage object**
>
> If for some reason you need to update the value of the storage object, you can do this by calling `dashboard.loadStorage()`, but only if that's the case. You don't need to do this at the beginning of the dashboard because the storage object will be automatically filled out when the dashboard starts.

Dashboard context

When the dashboard loads, there is also an object that will be available to get some information about the context where the dashboard is running. This object can be accessed using the variable that is instantiating the dashboard. Let's check the content of the object:

- `user`: This is the ID of the user that is logged in
- `roles`: This is an array of strings that contains the roles associated with the user
- `serverLocalDate`: This is the timestamp of the server
- `serverUTCDate`: This is the UTC timestamp on the server
- `sessionTimeout`: This is the time timeout interval for the session
- `path`: This is the dashboard path in the Pentaho repository
- `locale`: This is the language and locale that is set on the Pentaho server for the logged in user

Sometimes there is the need to add some more information when generating the dashboard, so CDF gives you the capability to add that information, and you are able to do this in two ways: using values from session variables directly in Pentaho, or using values from queries. Session variables are variables that can store values in the user session in Pentaho. There are two steps in Kettle that can be used to get/set session variable values. For more information, please refer to: `http://wiki.pentaho.com/display/EAI/Get+Session+Variables` and `http://wiki.pentaho.com/display/EAI/Set+Session+Variables`.

The configuration should be set using a solution file `cdf/dashboardContext.xml`, and you can take a peek at the default configuration file that is available in the `/system/pentaho-cdf/dashboardContext.xml` file.

To include the session variable key/value pair in the context of the dashboard, you should change the configuration file to include the settings, so that CDF knows what variables should be included. You should add the `<sessionattributes>` element, which contains as many `<attribute>` elements as variables we want to include. This should be placed inside the `<context>` root element. Let's suppose you have a session variable with the name `myTerritory`, where you have some information about the territory of the user that is logged in. You will end up with a file like this:

```
<context>
  <!-- Query auto-includes -->
  <autoincludes>
    <autoinclude>
```

```
    <cda><![CDATA[/public/cdf/includes/(.*)/(.*?)\.cda]]></cda>
    <ids>.*</ids>
    <dashboards>
      <include><![CDATA[.*/$1/.*\.wcdf]]></include>
      <include><![CDATA[.*/$1/.*\.xcdf]]></include>
      <include><![CDATA[.*/$1/.*\.cdfde]]></include>
    </dashboards>
  </autoinclude>
 </autoincludes>
 <sessionattributes>
   <attribute name="myTerritory">myTerritory</attribute>
 </sessionattributes>
</context>
```

You can see that the file is pretty similar to the default one, and the only difference is that we are including the `sessionatrributes` elements to include the value of the session variable `myTerritory` in the dashboard context.

Including multiple session variables

If you have more than one variable you want to include, you just need to add as many attribute elements as the variables you need.

As previously mentioned, we can also include some values resulting from queries; as we can understand by its name, `autoincludes` provides you that ability. At the beginning of the configuration file of the last sample code, we can see the `autoincludes` elements that contain the rules to define which files will be included or excluded.

You can imagine how you could achieve the same results by adding queries and changing the priority of execution of the components so that you have some results loaded before any other query is triggered. But you would need to add this logic to the dashboard by yourself, and it is even more time expensive when you need those results to be included on multiple dashboards. So the `autoincludes` can save you some time and avoid unnecessary logic and complexity.

Looking at the previous example, you will see the `include/exclude` elements where we need to set the regular expressions rules to include or exclude dashboard files that will have the auto-includes in the context. The CDA XML element is where the pattern is defined for the CDA files with the queries, whose results will be included in the context of the dashboard. You can also specify the pattern for the data access ID of the CDA files to be included.

The way this works is by placing the CDA files with the queries and default parameters inside the `public/cdf/inludes` hierarchy folder, and every dashboard with the same relative path to the root folder will include the results in the context. Let's suppose you have a CDA file inside `public/cdf/includes/public/myfolder` and a dashboard inside `public/myfolder`. The dashboard's results of the queries will be included in the context of the dashboard. On the other hand, if you have a dashboard that is under `public/myotherfolder`, it will not include the results in the context. This is done using the default configuration, but you can change the default behavior. By changing, adding, or removing rules you will be including or excluding files.

The syntax would be set like:

```
<autoinclude>
      <cda>cda_pattern</cda>
      <ids>id_pattern</ids>
      <dashboards>
        <include>includePattern_1</include>
        <include>includePattern_2</include>
        <exclude>excludePattern_1</include>
        . . .
        <include>includePattern_n</include>
        <exclude>excludePattern_n</include>
      </dashboards>
    </autoinclude>
```

In the preceding block of code, CDF will include all the results of the data access identifiers in the context object, from the CDA files whose IDs match `id_ pattern` and the path of the file matches `cda_pattern`, if all include rules are true and the exclude rules are false. This leads us to the dashboards element, where we may have any number of include and exclude elements.

These elements should be ordered by importance, from the least to the most important, and we can also include back references to capture groups from the CDA pattern. In the default configuration, we can see `/$1/`, which references the path capture group, meaning that the path begins with the previously matched CDA files. The path for the dashboard that is being executed will be checked against the include/exclude patterns in order of importance, and the dashboard will automatically include CDAs queries if it matches at least:

* One `include` rule
* Unless it matches a subsequent `exclude` rule
* Unless it matches a further include rule

Getting back to the session variables, you can also achieve the same results by creating a query auto included that uses a Kettle transformation in combination with the `BA Server Utils` plugin to read the values of the session variables. This way, the values of the session's variable will also be included. The step to use would be `getVariable`.

To access the results in the dashboard, you just need to access the dashboard context object such as `Dashboards.context.sessionAttributes` and `Dashboards.context.queryData` to get access to the session variables or query results, respectively.

Both dashboard storage and context can be used in CDE. To be more precise, all the functionality available in CDF is also available in CDE, but not the other way around.

Useful functions of the CDF API

CDF provides a list of methods/functions that you can and should use when building the dashboards. Next, you will find some of the most used functions.

Functions from the dashboards module:

- `init(components)`: This function is used to start the execution of the dashboard. You have seen this function in our examples. It receives an argument and an array of the components to execute. This function can be called without any argument, but in this context we need to add the components to the dashboard using the `addComponents` function.

- `addComponents(components)`: This function accepts an array with the components to add to the dashboard.

- `addComponent(component)`: This is the same as the previous function, but will just add one component.

- `removeComponent(component)`: This will remove a component from the list of the components of the dashboard.

- `getComponentByName(component)`: This returns the component with the name specified as an argument.

- `update(component)`: This will update the component. The function receives an argument, that is, the name of the component to update.

- `updateAll(components)`: This updates a set of components. The argument is an array of strings with the name of the components to update.

- `isBookmarkable(parameter)`: This verifies whether a parameter is bookmarkable and returns the Boolean value of the condition.

- `setBookmarkable(parameter, value)`: This sets a parameter as bookmarkable and also sets its default value.

- `getQueryParameter(parameter)`: This gets the value of a parameter that was passed through the URL used to call the dashboard in the browser.

- `setParameterValue(parameter, value)`: This sets the value of a parameter. This is the first argument of the parameter name, and the second argument is the value to set. This function does not notify the listeners.

- `fireChange(parameter, value)`: This is the same as the previous function, but will notify the listeners.

- `getParemeterValue(parameter)`: This returns the value of a parameter.

- `preInit()`: This can be defined to be executed before the dashboard starts the execution.

- `postInit()`: This can be defined to be executed after the dashboard finishes the first render of the dashboard.

- `saveStorage()`: This saves the contents of the object.

- `loadStorage()`: This reloads the object (this is done automatically at the dashboard rendering time, and is useful only to undo certain operations).

- `cleanStorage()`: This empties the entire storage of that user.

- `storage`: This is the object where the storage will be loaded, and where the developer should store the values of the persistent parameters.

- `context`: This is an object that contains a set of properties that define the context where the dashboard is executed. It has some properties such as the user, roles, path to the dashboard, and more.

- `on(event_name, callback, context)`: This allows the developer to attaching the event to the events fired by the CDF dashboards.

- `off(event_name)`: This allows the developer to remove the event.

- `trigger(event_name)`: This triggers an event.

- `objectToPropertiesArray(object)`: This returns an array from an object of properties and can be used to define some of the properties of a component. This function accepts an argument, that is, the object to be translated to an array.

- `propertiesArrayToObject(array)`: This returns an object from an array. This function has an argument that is an array.

Functions from the logger module:

- `log(message, type)`: This writes a message to the console with one of the following types: `log`, `error`, `warn`, `info`, or `debug`.

Functions from the components module:

- `update()`: This function will update the component, but is called from the update function of the component itself.

- `getValue()`: The function is then used by the `processChange` function, getting a value to be used later.

- `processChange('component_name')`: When creating custom components that require the input of the user, this function should be called to make changes to the parameter and notify the listeners. If it exists, `preChange` will be called by executing `fireChange` using the defined parameter, and also if defined, `postChange` will be called for execution.

Summary

CDF is the API to create dashboards and reports. By this point, you should understand the concepts behind the lifecycle of the dashboard and components. You should also know how to create a dashboard using the CDF API, and know the most part of the available methods, which are very important when creating advanced dashboards. We also covered a very important topic related to the use of parameters and listeners to create interaction among components.

Of course, you have a lot more to learn, and there are some more advanced concepts that we will cover in the following chapters.

In the next chapter, we will start covering CDE, and how to build a dashboard in an easier and faster way than by just using CDF.

4
Leverage the
Process with CDE

In the previous chapter, you saw how to create custom dashboards at the code level, and now you will see how to build them in an easier and faster way. Creating a custom dashboard should not be difficult and time-consuming, and CDE is a Pentaho server plugin that allows you to create, edit, and render a dashboard easily. CDE can build all the code for you, and you just need to use the graphical interface that CDE will make available to you to create or edit your dashboards.

The topics covered in this chapter are based on how to create a dashboard using a **graphical user interface (GUI)**. You will gain knowledge on how to build a responsive layout for the dashboard, add components, add some custom code, and add resources (both JavaScript and CSS) to the dashboard to create and use data sources without the need to create the CDA file by hand. What you learn here will help you to leverage the process and decrease the development time of the dashboards.

In the previous chapter, we already covered a major part of the core concepts that you need to build a dashboard using CDF/CDE. When you are building a CDE dashboard, you are creating CDF content, even if you are using CDE only components, as at the end they are also using and working on top of CDF. You are not required to build a dashboard by writing code using CDF, so you can skip writing CDF code, but it is important to know how it works and have a good understanding of it. Only this way will you be able to make the most out of CDE when building your dashboards. Make sure you really understand the lifecycle of the dashboard and components, as this is very important, even if you don't want to create your dashboards by writing your own code using CDF.

During this chapter, we will cover the following topics:

- Including resources in the dashboard
- Creating responsive dashboards
- Creating and customizing the layout of the dashboard
- Defining and using data sources
- Making use of parameters and listeners
- Making use of components
- Changing the order of execution of the components
- Previewing the dashboard

A brief introduction to CDE

CDE is a graphical interface tool where you can create your dashboard. Using CDE, you are able to decrease the development time, because CDE will generate the CDF code for you. But how does this work? The dashboard file is created on the client side and saved to the server side. When we later request that dashboard, we are making the request to the server which will deliver to the client side as an HTML page. This HTML page will not only include all the libraries needed for the execution of the dashboard, but will also provide the code for the dashboard. As soon as the browser, on the client side, has the HTML page, it will make the request to get all the libraries or JavaScript and CSS files that are needed or included by the developer in the dashboard. The server will return the files to the browser, and the web page that in turn is the dashboard, can begin executing.

When rendering the components, the dashboard, or to be more precise, the components, will make the requests for the queries to get the data to be displayed on the page. After getting the results and executing the remaining code, the dashboard is finally ready, and the user now has the ability to start interacting with the dashboard.

As we saw in previous chapters, the interaction of the user will generate changes on the parameters that in turn will trigger the update of the components, which will trigger new queries to get new data to the dashboard.

You should not expect CDE to have direct properties or options that you can directly set for everything you can do on the web or in a business analytics solution, but CDE will definitely provide a way to do these things; you just need to have an open mind and a good understanding of how CDE works. CDE works on top of CDF and CDA, and uses CCC. This way, you will find a solution for all your goals and build amazing, stunning dashboards that can go much further and build prescriptive solutions.

Working with the editor

One of the first things you need to learn to do is save and edit a particular dashboard. Usually, when using the term *open the dashboard*, we are referring to the operation of calling the dashboard using the generatedContent endpoint, which will execute the dashboard in the browser. This way, you will execute the dashboard and be able to interact with the dashboard. This is the operation that the final user will perform when requesting a dashboard.

There is another term that is frequently used, *open the dashboard using the edit mode*, which refers to the process of editing the dashboard in a way that you can make changes to the dashboard or just look at its layout, components, and data sources. This operation can be done using both wcdf.edit and the edit endpoints.

From now on, just let's use open and edit, the first when referring to the call to the dashboard to render the dashboard, and the second to make changes to the layout, components, or data sources.

The ability to create a new dashboard in a Pentaho standard installation

By default from version 5.3 and above, CTools comes with the Pentaho standard installation, but with a disabled flag that would not provide an option to create a new dashboard. You can overcome this by installing the last stable version of CTools (CDE, CDF, CDA, and CGG), by following the procedures in the second chapter.

To create a new dashboard, go to **Pentaho User Console (PUC)** and select from the menu: **File | New | CDE Dashboard**, and you will get a new tab with CDE Editor. What Pentaho is doing here is calling an endpoint that you can also call directly in your browser using the following URL: http://<server>:<port>/pentaho/api/repos/wcdf/new.

To open or edit a dashboard, you should select the dashboard from the repository using the PUC browser and click the open or edit button on the rightmost panel. Depending on the operation you are doing, you will get a new tab in the PUC, which uses one of the following URLs:

- To edit: http://<server>:<port>/pentaho/api/repos/<path>/wcdf.edit
- To open: http://<server>:<port>/pentaho/api/repos/<path>/generatedContent

Here, path would the path and filename of the dashboard and something similar to :public:Steel Wheels:CTools_dashboard.wcdf, which would redirect you to the Steel Wheels sample CDE dashboard. This will lead you to a good example that you later should edit and take a look at to recap what you have learned by reading this book. This is also a way to learn a few more tricks.

When creating a new dashboard or editing an existing one, you will get something like the following image, that we can divide into six sections:

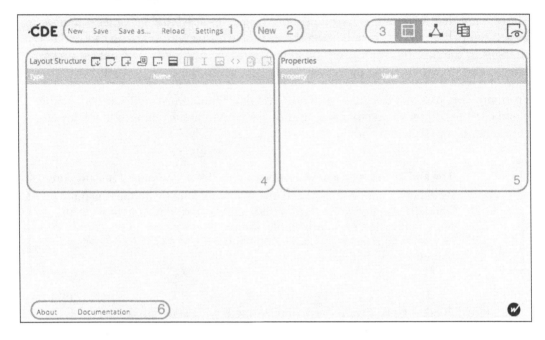

The sections shown in the previous image are explained as follows:

1. **Main toolbar**: Here you will find some functional buttons such as **New**, **Save**, **Save as...**, **Reload**, and **Settings**. This is where you select where to save a file, the name, and description of the dashboard, and also the style and the dashboard type or the framework to use when creating the layout.

2. **Title of the dashboard**: This is the title given to the dashboard when saving it. When creating a new dashboard, you will see the name as New Dashboard. This means that you haven't saved your dashboard or you just gave it the title of New Dashboard, and let me tell you, that's not the most creative title or name to give to a dashboard.

3. **Perspectives toolbar**: You can select which panel you want to display in the perspective panel area.

4. **Perspective panel area**: Depending on the selection you make in the **Perspective** toolbar, you will get the layout, components, or data sources panels.

5. **Properties panel area**: For each one of the selections in the elements of the perspectives panels, you will have at least 2 panels, one for the existing elements and another with the **Properties** available for the existing elements.

6. **Help and documentation toolbar**: Here you have two options: the first one will display a brief description of the tool, with information about the installed version. Selecting the second option will give you the same dialog, but it contains documentation and some buttons where you can find some basic documentation and links to the CDE tutorial and sample demos you can buy from Webdetails/Pentaho.

Let's now start to look each of the sections. There are two sections that are really simple to explain and understand, so let's start with those two.

Operational toolbar

The main toolbar will show you the options in the following image:

```
New    Save    Save as...    Reload    Settings
```

New

This allows you to create a new dashboard. It will do the same operation as the **New** option in PUC.

Save and Save as

The behavior of **Save** and **Save as...** is the same as you get in all other applications. When clicking on **Save** for the first time, you will get a dialog where you need to specify the folder where you want to save the dashboard, and also specify the following:

- **Name**: The name of the files in the dashboard. This is the name to use when saving the file in the repository.

- **Title**: The name that identifies the dashboard. This is the name that will be displayed when browsing the Pentaho repository and the name that will be displayed in the browser when editing or rendering the dashboard.

- **Description**: This is just some more information that will be added to the metadata of the dashboard.

- **Dashboard/Widget**: You can select between a dashboard or a widget, but let's just focus on saving the files as dashboards. Nowadays, we will see better alternatives to widgets, but anyhow, we will cover widgets later on in this book.

After selecting the folder in which you want to save the file, and adding the file name, you are able to click on the **OK** button, and save the file successfully.

When clicking **Save** for a dashboard that has already been saved, this will overwrite the existing files. **Save as...** will have the same behavior as saving a new dashboard for the first time. The following image shows the dialog you will get:

When saving a CDE dashboard, three files are written to the repository, all of them with the same name but with different extensions:

- **WCDF**: This is saved as an XML file, containing the main information about the dashboard such as the title, description, author, style, layout type, and a flag for RequireJS.

- **CDFDE**: This is saved using the JSON syntax and will have all the information, keys, and values for all the properties and elements that have been used or are just needed for the rendering. Layout, components, custom code, and query definitions are part of the file.

- **CDA**: This is also saved as XML with the structure explained in the second chapter. It will have data sources that are defined using the editor. You will see later that we can make the components use the queries that are in another CDA file, which is useful when we are creating multiple dashboards where we have some common queries, or just have a centralized file with all the queries. We can use the editor to create CDA files and define data sources in an easy way, just using the editor to create a new dashboard, but not defining layouts or components. This file is only saved when data sources are defined, otherwise, only the first two files are saved.

Reload

Reload will load the dashboard files again, and all the changes made since the last saved change will be discarded.

Settings

Using the **Settings** operational button, you will be prompted with a dialog box where you are able to set/change the following options, as shown in the following image:

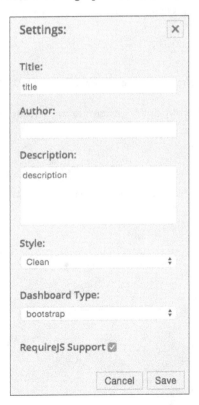

The options shown in the previous image are as follows:

- **Title**: This is the title of the dashboard, as defined when saving it.

- **Author**: This is the name of the author of the dashboard. The only way to change the author is by changing it here in the settings dialog, or changing the WCDF extension file by hand.

- **Description**: This is the description of the dashboard, as defined when saving it.

- **Style**: As explained in the CDF chapter, the style is where we can choose from an existing HTML page that will provide similar content for multiple dashboards. When in CDE, there is a dropdown where we can choose from the styles that are available. The one selected by default is the **Clean** template, but you have three more templates that can be applied, and they are used in the web details documentation and for the Pentaho App Builder dashboard/plugin.

  There is also the chance to create new styles, by creating your own templates with similar content that dashboards can have, which is very simple to do. We just need to create an HTML page with content to be presented in all the dashboards using the style. This should be similar to the following example:

```
<!DOCTYPE HTML>
<html>
  <head>
    <meta http-equiv="Content-Type" content="text/html;
charset=utf-8">
    <meta name="viewport" content="width=device-width, initial-
scale=1">
    @HEADER@
  </head>
  <body>
      <div class="dashboardWrapper">Your dashboard will be wrapped
by this element
    @CONTENT@
    </div>
    @FOOTER@
  </body>
</html>
```

Defining a new style is just creating an HTML page where we need to add the following strings, which will be replaced by the HTML and JavaScript code needed for the dashboard:

- ° @HEADER@: This will be replaced by the scripts to include the JavaScript and CSS needed for the execution of the dashboard.

- ° @CONTENT@: This will be replaced by the HMTL with the structure defined in the Layout panel and the JavaScript code generated by CDE to run the dashboard, using as a base the components and data sources defined and the components panels.

- ° @FOOTER@: This will be replaced by some supplementary code to render some content that may be needed for the dashboard.

The styles should be uploaded to the repository and should be placed inside the folder /public/cde/styles. The styles inside the dropdown will have the name of the file, but two files should exist. One when creating legacy dashboards, not using RequireJS, and another when using RequireJS. The file name containing the style to be applied when using RequireJS should be appended by the text Require. For instance, create an HTML page with the name customStyleRequire.html containing the previous code and upload it to the folder /public/cde/styles folder. By creating your own styles, you can add content that will be used in all the dashboards where the style is applied.

Refresh the CDE plugin

When uploading files into the folder /public/cde/*, we should refresh the CDE, and to do this, you need to make a call to the following URL: http://<server>:<port>/pentaho/plugin/pentaho-cdf-dd/api/renderer/refresh. This call will refresh the CDE, and all the content added to that folder will now be included in the CDE editor and will be available when rendering the dashboards.

- **Dashboard Type**: This will specify which framework to use when creating the layout. There are three options available:

  - ° **Blueprint**: This creates a dashboard using the Blueprint CSS framework. You can get some more knowledge on their website: http://www.blueprintcss.org.

  - ° **Mobile**: This creates a dashboard using the JQuery Mobile framework. If you pretend to use it, you can get some more knowledge at their website by using the following URL: https://jquerymobile.com/.

- ° **Bootstrap**: This creates a dashboard using the Twitter Bootstrap framework. You could go through all the documentation, but you can just start by reading about the grid system, the concept that you really need to know to create the layout for the dashboards.

  The following URLs are a good start: `http://getbootstrap.com/css/#grid` and `http://getbootstrap.com/css/#responsive-utilities-classes`

  In this book, we only cover Bootstrap, which is selected by default. This is the right one to use when building responsive dashboards. Just by looking at the names, you could think that to build a mobile dashboard, you should use the Mobile option, but that's not really true. You can use Bootstrap to build a desktop and/or mobile dashboard, something that would not be fully true when using the mobile framework. If you build a dashboard with the mobile framework, it won't become a desktop dashboard.

- **RequireJS Support**: This checkbox will be used by CDE to know whether the code should make use of RequireJS when generating the CDF code of the dashboard. When the box is checked, CDE will generate the code using RequireJS. When rendering a dashboard with this option checked, by default, CDE will require a collection of the base modules. This way, the developer does not need to specifically require them when building custom JavaScript code. By default, the loaded modules are:

  - ° **Logger**: This is represented as `Logger`
  - ° **JQuery**: This is represented as `$`
  - ° **Underscore**: This is represented as `_`
  - ° **Moment**: This is represented as `moment`
  - ° **Cdo**: This is represented as `cdo`
  - ° **Utils**: This is represented as `Utils`

The perspectives toolbar

You should know that there are three perspectives and a preview button, as shown in the following image. The other three buttons or perspectives are as follows:

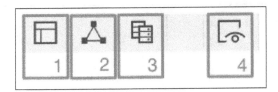

1. **The layout perspective**: This is used to switch to the layout perspective of the editor. You should use this perspective to define the layout of your dashboard. When clicking the layout button, you will get the available and used layout elements. The properties panels will change according to the element selected, displaying all the available properties.

2. **The components perspective**: This is used to switch to the components perspective of the editor. You should use this perspective to define the components to apply to the dashboard. When clicking the components button, the perspective and properties panels will change accordingly and will show you the available components you can use for your dashboard, and also the ones already added to the dashboard.

3. **The data sources perspective**: This is used to switch to the data sources perspective of the editor. You should use this perspective to define the data sources to be saved on the CDA file that will be directly related to the dashboard you are working on. When clicking the data source button, the perspective and properties panels will change accordingly and show the data sources available to be used, and the ones already defined.

4. **Preview the dashboard**: This is the rightmost button, and it allows you to preview the dashboard. When pressed, you will get a new dialog, with the dashboard you are working on inside of it. This way, you are able to test the behavior and see how the dashboard would look.

We will now cover each of the perspectives, except for the last one, as there is nothing else to cover there, so we will give you some more details on the first three.

The layout perspective

When clicking on the layout perspective button, you will switch to the layout perspective and get two panels, as you can see in the following image:

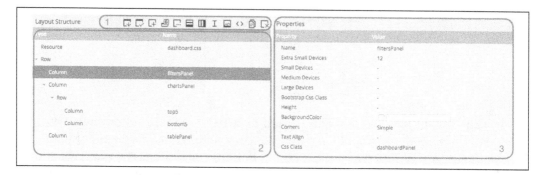

1. **Layout toolbar**: This toolbar is used to create the elements in the layout structure. (See panel 1 in the previous image.) When clicking on the buttons, you will be adding or removing the element, and these changes will be reflected in the layout structure panel.

2. **Layout structure**: In this panel (see panel 2 in the previous image) of the layout perspective, will have represented all the elements that are part of the layout of the dashboard. Whenever you click on an element, the **Properties** panel will be updated and will show you the properties available for the selected element.

3. **Properties**: This panel (see panel 3 in the previous image) shows you the available properties of the selected element in the layout structure, and depending on the type of element, the properties may vary. This is where you can see the value for each of the properties or just set their value.

The Layout toolbar

The toolbar that becomes available when you are in the layout perspective is like the following image. Depending on the elements you have selected in the layout structure, you may find some of the buttons enabled or disabled:

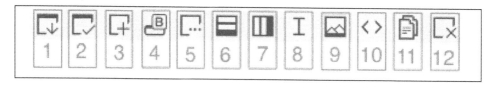

In the image given, we have labelled each button as per their corresponding elements. Now let's look at what each of the buttons is used for:

1. **Save as Template**: You can save the dashboard you are working on as a template. When clicking the button, you will be presented with a dialog like the following image, where you can set the name for the template and the title:

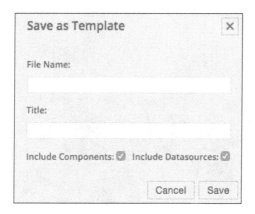

The name and title will be used as previously explained when saving a dashboard. **File Name** is the name of the file inside the repository and **Title** is the text that will be displayed when you are later choosing which template to use.

When saving a template, you should also specify whether you want your template to include components and/or data sources within the template. When these options are checked and when using the template, you are saving all the components and data sources included in the new dashboard. But when those options are unchecked, you will include only the layout of the template in your new dashboard, and nothing else. This will not add new elements to the layout structure.

Templates are saved inside the Pentaho repository

The templates you are saving will become available in the repository inside the `/public/cde/templates` folder.

2. **Apply Template**: Clicking this button will give you a dialog where you can choose from the available templates, as shown in the following image:

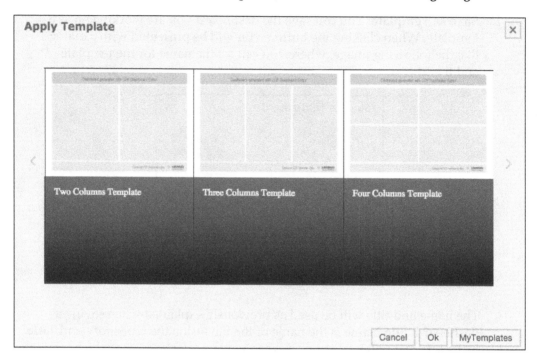

You can choose from the available templates already included in CDE, or you can select from ones you have created and saved. If you want to select one of your own, you should click the **My Templates** button, available at the bottom-right side of the dialog. When selecting this option, you will see the templates you have saved.

To select a template, you only need to click on the template you want to choose and click the **Ok** button.

3. **Add Resource**: You can add resources, JavaScript, and CSS files to your dashboard as a code snippet or as an external file.

   To add a resource, when clicking a button, a dialog box will pop up, similar to the one in the following image. You must select from the dropdowns if you want to include CSS or JavaScript code and if the code will be added as an external resource or code snippet:

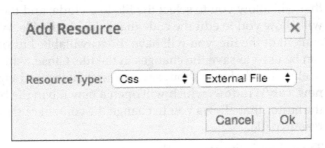

   When adding resources as a code snippet, a line referring to the resource will be added in the layout structure. The properties that become available for this element are as follows:

   ○ **Name**: This is the name you want to use to identify the resource in the layout structure.

   ○ **Resource Code**: When clicking on the button available in the property, a dialog will be presented where you can write, delete, and edit your code. You just need to click **Ok** or **Cancel** to confirm whether you want to add it to the dashboard.

   ○ **Type**: This is the type of the resource, which is automatically set when adding the resource. It will have the value selected in the type dropdown when adding a new resource.

When adding resources as a code snippet, a line referring to the resource will be added in the layout structure. The properties that become available for this element are:

- ○ **Name**: This is the same as the previous.

- ○ **Resource File**: In this property, you can set the URL of the resource, or use the buttons available. The first button will open a new dialog that will allow you to select the file to include, and the second one will allow you to edit the code that is inside the file. When editing the content of the file, you will have three available buttons: **Save**, which can be used to save the changes in the file, **Close**, which can be used to close the dialog without saving the changes, and **Open Tab in new Tab/Window**, which will open a new tab in the browser with the editor that allows you to change the content of the selected resource file.

- ○ **Type**: This is the same as the previous.

When adding a code snippet, the code will be part of the dashboard when it is saved, and this is because it will be saved inside the CDFDE file. When using an external file, the reference to the file will be added to the dashboard.

When generating the code for the dashboard, CDE will also include it as a RequireJS module by using the `require` functions that incorporate its location on the server. Later during the execution of the dashboard, the file will be requested to the server, and the code will become available inside the `require` context of the dashboard.

When adding your code as a code snippet, it will be included inside the dashboard module and will become available inside the dashboard object.

When you are including a resource that uses an external file with your code, you need to define a RequireJS module, because the dashboard will require it. It will then become available in the dashboard module. You can define the code in your file as follows:

```
define(function() {
  var myObj = {
    name: "Joe",
    sayHello: function() {
      return "Hello " + this.name}
  };
  return myObj;
});
```

or

```
define({
    name: "Joe",
    sayHello: function() {
        return "Hello " + this.name }
});
```

This way, you are able to access the code in the dashboard module. Here you can set the name of the resource using the same name as the file, and this will be used to define your module name. Let's suppose you named the resource `myModule` and the name of the file is `myModule.js`. You can later use this code inside your dashboard. For instance, you would set the following code in the `Expression` property for a text component:

```
function f() {
    this.placeholder().text(myModule.sayHello());
}
```

You may also want to include a third-party resource to be used in your dashboard. If they are built as RequireJS modules, you just need to follow the previous instructions. Most of the JavaScript frameworks and libraries have this support, so you should look for it. If the resource is not exposed as an AMD module, you'll need to develop AMD support for it.

You may ask: What option should I use: code snippet or external file? Well, this depends on what you want or are doing, but I always prefer to have all the code in external files. One of the reasons for this is that when you are saving a dashboard, CDE can change the order of the elements inside the saved file, and this will cause problems with version control, especially when you are working as part of a team working on the same files. It will be painful to solve conflicts just because of a small change in the CSS.

Of course, it will be easier to deploy the code to another server if you have the JavaScript and CSS code as snippets, where you just need to worry about deploying the dashboard files, because the code will also be there.

4. **Add Bootstrap panel**: This is used to add a Bootstrap panel to our dashboard, like the examples available at: `http://getbootstrap.com/components/#panels`. If clicked, it will add a parent element containing three child elements. The parent element is a Bootstrap panel, where you can change the properties, and the child elements are panel header, panel body, and panel footer. You can change the properties available for these elements, but you can also add more elements as rows, columns, freeform, and HTML inside each one of these child elements.

For the parent element, identified by the type `Bootstrap Panel`, the properties that become available are:

- **Name**: This will be the unique identifier of the HTML element that is going to be created by CDE and used in the dashboard to render elements. This will correspond to the `id` property of the HTML element being created.

- **Height**: You can specify the height of the panel, but usually we let it be dynamic and let it be larger or smaller depending on its content.

- **Corner**: Let's consider this property deprecated. It was used in older versions of CDE, where it was not possible to use CSS to create a rounded corner. We will not refer to this property again in this book.

- **CSS class**: When creating the element on the page, CDE will add the values of this property as the values of the class property for the HTML element being created. This will allow you to use your own CSS classes and later use them when defining the CSS for the dashboard.

- **Panel Style**: You can select from multiple options available in Bootstrap and depending on the value used, you will have different styles applied to the panel being created. The possible values are: Default, Primary, Success, Info, Warning, and Danger.

  Child elements identified by the type panel header, panel body, and panel footer will have the same properties, except for the panel type, which will not be available.

The Bootstrap panel will include the header and the footer, but if you want to exclude them, you can add some CSS to hide them when needed, or delete them by clicking the **X** button.

Depending on what you are trying to achieve, you may find Bootstrap very useful.

5. **Add freeform element**: Adding rows and columns will just add DIVs to the dashboard, but using the freeform element, you can specify which HTML will be added. When you click the button, the freeform element will be added to the layout structure, and the properties that become available are as follows:

   - **Name**: This corresponds to the value of the `id` property for the HTML element being created. CDE will generate a random and unique ID when the value is not set.

- ° **CSS Class**: These values will be used as the values of the class property of the element being created. This is used to set your own CSS classes for the element. It can have multiple values separated by a space, like the normal CSS property of the HTML elements.

- ° **Element Tag**: Here you should set the HTML type to create. By default, it uses a value of div. This way, you would create a div element, so you should change the default value and write the name of the element to create.

- ° **Other Attributes**: Here you can set the name of the properties and the value to be used for these properties. When creating the element, CDE will also add the property/values that will become available in the dashboard. When clicked, the input field of this property will become available as a dialog, where you should set the property name in the **option** field and the **value** in the value field. To add more properties, you just need to click the **Add** button. At the right side of each row added, you will find a minus button, which, when clicked, will remove that row. Click **Ok** to confirm or **Cancel** to discard:

Property	Value
Name	searchBox
Css Class	inputBox
Element Tag	input
Other Attributes	[["type","input"]]

Let's suppose you added a freeform with properties the same as the previous image. The HMTL code generated by CDE will be as follows:

```
<input id="searchBox" class="inputBox" type="input">
```

You can see that the element is an input type just as specified in the Element Tag property, the id is the value set in the Name property, the class is inputBox as the value of the CSS Class property, and finally, the type property is input as the key value set on the other attributes.

6. **Add row**: Use this button when you want to create a Bootstrap row. A Bootstrap row is just a `div` element with a class value of `row`. This way, the dashboard will use the Bootstrap framework and apply the rules defined for the grid system. Following the best practices of Bootstrap, components should be rendered inside columns and not directly on rows. As referred to previously, you can find more information at `http://getbootstrap.com/css/#grid`. This means that you should always have at least a column inside the row, except for some special cases where you have the need to create a row. The properties that become available are:

    ○ **Name**: This corresponds to the value of the ID property for the HTML element being created. CDE will generate a random and unique ID when the value is not set.

    ○ **Height**: This is used to set the height of the HTML element. It should be left blank whenever possible.

    ○ **CSS Class**: These values will be used as the value of the class property of the element being created. It is used to set your own CSS classes for the element. It can have multiple values separated by a space, like the normal CSS property of the HTML elements.

    ○ Background Color, Corner, and Text Align should be set as the CSS.

7. **Add column**: You should click this button when you want to create a new column to be used by your dashboard. Columns should always be created inside a row element and, not always but usually, used to render the components. If it's a leaf, you always need to set the name, so that we can use the name on the components. When creating a new column, it will become available in the layout structure of the dashboard. The properties are:

    ○ **Name**: This corresponds to the value of the ID property for the HTML element being created. CDE will generate a random and unique ID when the value is not set.

    ○ **Extra small devices, small devices, medium devices, and large devices**: These are used to set the width to be used for the column. This is where you should already have some knowledge about the Bootstrap framework, particularly the grid system.

When creating a row using the CSS Bootstrap framework and the concepts of the grid system, each row can go up to 12 columns, scaling appropriately when the viewport or screen size increases. When creating a column, there is a need to include a class such as `col-<device_size>-<num_columns_to_span>`.

Bootstrap already includes predefined classes that can be used for all the columns spanning from 1 up to 12. So, depending on the device/screen size and the number of columns to span, the CSS rule to be applied can change.

CDE will take care of this for you, you just need to set the number of columns to span, for instance, if you are creating columns that should occupy six columns of the 12 available columns for each row, you just need to set the number 6 for the device size you want to apply to this value. This is why you have these four properties: extra small devices, small devices, medium devices, and large devices, corresponding to `col-xs-*`, `col-sm-*`, `col-md-*`, and `col-lg-*`, where * is the number of columns you wish to span for the specified device/screen size.

Let's analyze this example. We have created a row that contains two columns. The two columns are named `col1` and `col2` and use a value of 8 and 4 respectively for each of the columns of the extra small devices property of each column.

The HTML result would be as follows:

```
<div id="329e160a-625d5a5ds5" class="row clearfix ">
<div class="col-xs-8">
  <div id="col1"> </div>
</div>
  <div class="col-xs-4 last">
    <div id="col2"> </div>
</div>
</div>
```

By analyzing the generated HTML, we can see that we have a row, the first element that has a uniquely random generated ID, because we haven't set the name for it. Inside of it, we have two child elements: the first column uses the `col-xs-8` class and the second one uses `col-xs-4`, because we used a value of 8 and 4 in the extra small devices:

col1	col2

The layout generated would always span the first eight columns available for the row, and use it for `col1` and the span the last four columns also available for the row.

We can also offset the columns by using an additional Bootstrap CSS class `col-<device_size>-offset-<num_columns_to_span>`. More information can be found on this at: `http://getbootstrap.com/css/#grid-offsetting`.

Let's suppose you only wanted to have col1 at the right side of the dashboard using only the last four columns. To achieve this result, you would create just one column with the name col1, a value of 4 in the extra small devices property, but also set the Bootstrap class, the next property to be explained, to have a value of col-xs-offset-8. This would give the following result:

col2

Don't forget that by using CSS, you can extend the position, and the look and feel, by using additional media queries, for instance, to include a max width to limit the CSS for a narrower set of devices.

Similar to the use of offset is the use of the responsive utilities classes, available at http://getbootstrap.com/css/#responsive-utilities-classes.

- ○ **Bootstrap class**: This is a CSS class that will be added to the Bootstrap element. You can refer to the last example of the last property. Here, it is possible to have multiple CSS classes; you just need to separate them with a space, just like when you are defining multiple CSS classes on a HTML element.

- ○ **Height**: This is used to set the height of the HTML element. It should be left blank whenever possible.

- ○ **Background Color, Corners, and Text Align**: This should be set in the CSS.

- ○ **CSS class**: These values will be used as the value of the class property of the element being created. This is used to set your own CSS classes for the element. You can have multiple values separated by a space, like the normal CSS property of the HTML elements.

8. **Add space**: This is used to create a vertical space between elements of the dashboard. If clicked, it will add an element to the layout structure. The following elements become available:

- ○ **Height**: This is used to set the height of the separator. This property is mandatory when using this type of element.

- ○ **Background color, corners, and text align**: This should be set in the CSS.

- ○ **CSS class**: These values will be used as the value of the class property of the element being created. This is used to set your own CSS classes for the element. You can have multiple values separated by a space, like the normal CSS property of the HTML elements.

You should be able to create the same effect when setting the CSS margin at the top or bottom for the elements you want to separate visually.

9. **Add image**: Click this button to add images to the dashboard. The properties that will be available for this element are:

   ° **URL**: This is the URL to the image `${solution:../../images/logo.png}`. It will point to an image of two folders below the current directory of the dashboard, or refer to `http://www.pentaho.com/sites/all/themes/pentaho_resp/_media/logo-pentaho-n.png`, which will point an image on the Internet.

   ° **CSS class**: These values will be used as the value of class property of the element being created. Used to set your own CSS classes for the element. Can have multiple values separated by a space, like the normal CSS property of the HTML elements.

   To be honest, I never use this element and always do it in CSS. To do so, I just add a column where I also set a CSS class that will later be used to load the image using just CSS rules. I do this because it is easier to change in CSS and keep a track of the version control system, but also because, using RequireJS, the HTML will be loaded in the first place and then all the components and CSS. If you set the image directly in the layout, the image will appear on the dashboard first rather than all the other components, so you may see the image being pushed from one side to the other.

   Also, if you later apply some CSS rules to the image, you will see the image changing only sometime after, when the CSS code is loaded by RequireJS. When changing the CSS, I can do it in any text editor or using the referred Community Text Editor plugin.

10. **Add HTML**: This should be used to set HTML on your own. You may find the HTML element very useful when setting some static content, or when you can't do it with all the other elements available in CDE, but I find this very hard to believe. The properties that will become available for this element are:

    ° **Name**: This corresponds to the value of the ID property for the HTML element being created. CDE will generate a random and unique ID when the value is not set.

    ° **HTML**: This is where you can add HTML to include in the dashboard. When clicking the button available on the right side of the property, you will get a dialog you can use the editor to edit the HMTL code and confirm or cancel the changes you have made.

- ○ **CSS class**: Values will be used as the value of class property of the element being created. It is used to set your own CSS classes for the element. Can have multiple values separated by a space, like the normal CSS property of the HTML elements.

- ○ **Font size and color**: As we already saw for some other properties, these two should also be set using CSS.

11. **Duplicate layout element**: Another really useful ability is being able to copy elements, without needing to create all the elements by hand, when you want to replicate structures similar to already existing ones. Selecting one element and clicking the duplicate button on the layout toolbar will create a copy of the selected element and all its children.

12. **Delete**: Selecting one element and clicking the delete buttons will remove the element itself and all its children. Use this button carefully because CDE does not yet have an undo operation.

Nowadays, can also can change the position of the elements inside the layout structure, and to do this, you just need to grade the element to the position you need. You should take a look at the sample provided with the book and available once you upload them to the repository. You can find this under `CTools Book Sample/ Chapter 4`. You should not expect a really a dashboard running queries, but it's good to understand the capabilities of the layout elements and how to use them.

Considerations when creating the layout of your dashboard

You should have noticed that I placed more importance on some properties than others. This is because some of the properties may be deprecated, and they are there just to ensure compatibility with older dashboards that were developed with earlier versions of CTools. Another reason may be because of my preference to have all the styles in CSS files.

Let's use the example of the align property, which allows us to specify the alignment for the content inside the element where element is defined. When defining the alignment in the property of the element, it may not work for all the content you have inside, and you would end up having some CSS to align some of the elements. If you set some properties using CDE and others in CSS, you are not being consistent. We should always avoid inconsistency, and I can point you to some other reasons beside consistency: complexity, maintainability, and also very importantly, reusability.

When developing dashboards, the layout can get a bit complex and you should find a way to build it to make it simple and use a name convention. One way is to find the most correct and simple hierarchical structure, and always set the proper names that can identify not only the element, but also the section and maybe the hierarchy level where it belongs. The name or ID must be unique and never be repeated again. You will see that following one name convention will help you later. A question that you could be asking is: Is the name or ID mandatory for all the elements defined in the layout structure? The answer is no, CDE will make sure you generate randomly unique IDs that will be used for the elements where you are not specifying a name, but never forget that you need to set the names for the leafs, because they probably will be used by a component.

Don't forget that you may be delivering dashboards to a customer or department that may need to make some changes later, so the dashboards should be simple, while always meeting the requirements.

You saw that when defining some of the components using the Bootstrap framework, there are two similar properties: the CSS Class and the Bootstrap Class, so another question you may ask is: What's the difference between the CSS Class and the Bootstrap Class and/or which one should I use? When we add a row/column in the layout panel, CDE will generate two HTML DIV elements. A parent where the value of the Bootstrap class will be applied and a child that will have the value of the CSS Class property. Depending on your goals, you can set both properties. In the Bootstrap Class, you should use the predefined classes available in the Bootstrap Framework, and in the CSS Class you should set your own classes, which you can use later in your CSS files.

When creating rows and columns, CDE always generates DIV elements for your page. The freeform and the HTML elements allow you to create different types of elements in your page. Let's suppose you want to create an input element—you don't have any button in the layout perspective to create these kinds of elements, so the only way to do so is to use freeform elements or create your own code for the HTML structure.

Regarding this matter, one question that I already asked myself was: When should I use freeform or HTML elements? I believe that the answer is use what you prefer, but note that when creating a structure using freeform, you can just keep expanding or collapsing the elements inside the layout panel. You cannot do this when using the HTML element, because you always need to click the edit button on the right side of the element to look at the code. However, it will be faster and more flexible if you define it by hand. To be honest, you will be fine using one or the other, you just need to see what you feel most comfortable using.

The freeform element (layout and component)

We will look at the usage of the freeform component during the next chapter, just to avoid getting confused later by establishing a relationship between the freeform component and the freeform element. They both have the same goal, which is giving more flexibility, but they have different applications. The freeform element is used to provide the flexibility to introduce a different element in the layout, and the freeform component is used to create content that can be rendered inside the other elements of the layout, which could be the freeform element or not.

When editing the content of a resource that was added as an external file, and when we're using the CDE button available in the `Code File` property, CDE will use ACE, a web-based code editor. It has the ability to do syntax highlighting and is a great help when reading or writing code. You also have a bunch of shortcuts that are very useful, and you can learn more about these at the following web page: `https://github.com/ajaxorg/ace/wiki/Default-Keyboard-Shortcuts`. Now you can see some of the shortcuts I often use:

Windows/Linux	Mac	Action
Ctrl + *A*	*command* + *A*	Select all
Ctrl + *Shift* + Right arrow key	*option* + *shift* + Right arrow key	Select word right
Alt + *Shift* + Right arrow key	*command* + *shift* + Right arrow key	Select to line end
Shift + Up arrow key	*shift* + Up arrow key	Select up
Shift + Down arrow key	*shift* + Down arrow key	Select down
Ctrl + *F*	*command* + *F*	Find
Ctrl + *H*	*command* + *option* + *F*	Replace
Ctrl + *Z*	*command* + *Z*	Undo
Ctrl + *Shift* + *Z,Ctrl* + *Y*	*command* + *shift* + *Z, command* + *Y*	Redo

Using Bootstrap to create a responsive dashboard

Creating a responsive dashboard is simple, but don't forget that the components must respond to the changes and not only the layout. It is very important when creating CSS rules that you always use relative widths values and never static values. By default, almost all the components can adapt to changes in screen size, and that's because the CSS which has been included, except for the charts that need some extra code to readapt their size when changes happens to the dashboard. CCC charts, the charts used by default in CDE, are not yet responsive. I will explain this and give you the source code later to make it possible, but for now let's focus on the layout. This can make your dashboard look good and be usable on all device sizes.

We already saw that the Bootstrap grid system appropriately scales up to 12 columns as the device or viewport size increases, and we can make predefined classes for easy layout options, as well as powerful mixins to generate more semantic layouts. But how does Bootstrap do this? Bootstrap uses media queries and some predefined classes we can use to leverage the process, but there are some Bootstrap rules that must be followed, which are as follows:

- Rows must be placed within `.container` (fixed-width) or `.container-fluid` (full-width) to get the correct alignment and padding, and by placing all the elements within a `.container` automatically will take care of alignment and padding.

- Content should be placed within columns, and only columns may be immediate children of rows. We must be careful to say where the components are rendered, so always do this in columns. CDE will take care of applying the correct `row` and `col` classes, but the `col` classes will be set based on the device size and span value.

- For each CDE column element, we need to specify how many of the 12 columns available we will span. When more than 12 columns are placed within a single row, each group of extra columns will, as one unit, wrap on to a new line. We should play with this and the device size to make the layout of the dashboard responsive.

- Grid classes are applied to devices with screen widths greater than or equal to the ones where we had set values. Values set in classes for larger devices will override the values of smaller devices; therefore, applying a value on `Medium Devices` to an element will not only affect the style on medium devices but will also affect large devices, if and only if a value for the `Large Devices` property value is not set.

  For instance, if you set two columns of a row to have the following properties/values:

  ```
  Extra Small Devices: 12
  Medium Devices: 6
  ```

  What you will get is that it will display two columns on different lines for `Extra Small` and `Small` devices and will get the two columns side by side in the same line for `Medium Devices` and `Large Devices`. Setting the right values for these four properties is really an important task when building your responsive dashboard.

Another consideration when building a responsive dashboard would be using utility classes to hide some layout components. It should be used as previously covered in this chapter when talking about offsetting columns. To show or hide layout elements in the dashboard, we can set a class visible-<device_size>-<display_rule> and/or hidden-<device_size>, where <device_size> should be set as xs, sm, md, and lg (for extra small, small, medium, and large devices/screen sizes), and <display_rule> should be set as block, inline, or inline-block, the last one set only for visible. The display rules will make the CSS apply similarly to the CSS display property.

Let's suppose, for instance, that we have created a row that contains three columns. The three columns are named col1, col2, and col3:

- Should be pulled to different lines, each with the full size of the screen, when on extra small and small devices
- Should be seen side by side on medium or larger devices
- The col2 column should only be seen when on medium or larger devices
- The height should be 15px and background colors should be red, green, and blue for col1, col2, and col3 respectively

To accomplish these requirements, you need to set a value of 12 in the Extra Small Devices property for all three columns (col1, col2, and col3), and a value of 3 in the Medium Devices property. In the property of the second column (col2), you should also set a value of hidden-xs hidden-sm to hide the element for those screen sizes. You also need to add the class emptyBox in the CSS class for all the columns and classes red, green, and blue in the CSS class for each one of the corresponding colors. Don't forget that the classes should be separated by a space.

The resulting HTML would be as follows:

```
<div id="responsive" class="row clearfix ">
  <div class="col-xs-12 col-md-4">
    <div id="col1" class="emptyBox red"></div>
  </div>
  <div class="col-xs-12 col-md-4 hidden-xs">
    <div id="col2" class="emptyBox green"></div>
  </div>
  <div class="col-xs-12 col-md-4 last">
    <div id="col3" class="emptyBox blue "></div>
  </div>
</div>
```

If you build a dashboard with the layout set this way, you will get a responsive layout for your dashboard. Please take a look at the sample, which we provide with this book, and edit it. You can find the dashboard files in the `responsiveDashboard` folder within the chapter samples. After opening the dashboard, change the browser size and you will see the magic happening.

Considerations when building responsive dashboards using CDE

For me, it's very important to know the difference between the responsive and adaptive/responsive design concepts. Both concepts attempt to optimize the user experience across different devices, making the necessary adjustments for different viewport sizes, resolutions, and usage contexts, and I really like the Mozilla definition for these two concepts:

> *"Responsive design works on the principle of flexibility. The idea is that a single fluid design based upon media queries, flexible grids, and responsive images can be used to create a user experience that flexes and changes based on a multitude of factors. The primary benefit is that each user experiences a consistent design. One drawback is a slower load time."*

> *"Adaptive design is more like the modern definition of progressive enhancement. Instead of one flexible design, adaptive design detects the device and other features, and then provides the appropriate feature and layout based on a predefined set of viewport sizes and other characteristics. This can result in a lack of consistency across platforms and devices, but the load time tends to be faster."*

It is my opinion that you should not choose between using one or the other; you should use the advantages of both concepts and avoid the disadvantages of both concepts, and this is possible when putting together the Bootstrap framework's capabilities and the dashboards and components lifecycle. I believe this means having a layout that uses responsive concepts and components; the more adaptive concepts would make the perfect dashboard, where you can have only one dashboard for all devices and screen sizes, but just execute or change the behavior of the components depending on the device. This way, we can have the advantage of a unique dashboard for all devices and at the same time control what's being executed so that we can have better response times and avoid the possible lack of consistency across platforms and devices.

Desktops can have better processing capabilities and a lot more memory than mobile phones. When building a dashboard that will be used for various platforms, screen sizes, and even hardware capabilities, we need to be cautious. There are some points that we should consider:

- Mobile dashboards may face some hardware limitations. Processing and memory capabilities are not the same when comparing mobiles and desktops. When using a huge amount of points to represent, CCC Charts may be a bit heavy; anyhow when using a mobile phone the user would not get the best look and feel if you are trying to represent charts that become too tight on the screen. Here you have two options: using the same dashboard, you may use preExecution of the component to control if the chart is rendered on a mobile, or change the parameters and/or the query itself so that you can have an optimized visualization solution.

- You need to adapt the visualizations for the device/screen size. Similar to the last point, you can use the preExecution function of components to prepare the execution of the component. Depending on device/screen size or orientation, you can write some code to change the behavior of the component. For instance, if you have a bar chart, when on a mobile, you could change one property of the chart to have a horizontal bar chart instead of a vertical bar chart. Please refer to the following web page: http://dev. w3.org/csswg/cssom-view/#the-mediaquerylist-interface.

You place the following code in the preExecution of a CCC BarChart, and you will get a chart with vertical bars for screens greater than 840, a chart with horizontal bars if the screen size is between 600 and 839, and not get a chart at all if the screen size is less than or equal to 600:

```
function f() {
    var mq = {};
    mq['<=600'] = window.matchMedia("(max-width: 600px)");
    mq['<=840'] = window.matchMedia("(max-width: 840px)");
    if (mq['<=600'].matches) {
    return false;
    } else {
    if (mq['<=840'].matches) {
      this.chartDefinition.orientation = 'horizontal';
      }
    }
}
```

You should learn about and make use of media queries, using CSS or JavaScript, as they are important when using adaptive and responsive concepts. It may also be important to reduce the number of components being rendered.

- Mobile network communications are usually slower than wired networks, so avoid making lots of requests and requests that need a big portion of data when transferring from the client to the server side or the opposite. This is also the case when building the desktop version of a dashboard; we should be more careful when doing it for mobiles.

- Put your images on a diet, or even avoid using them. Just use icon fonts whenever you can. You have two options available to use in CDE/CDF:

    ○   `http://getbootstrap.com/components/#glyphicons`

    ○   `http://fortawesome.github.io/Font-Awesome/`

- Use relative sizes whenever possible. For instance, when you set a static width for an element, the element will not respond to the screen and orientation changes. The parent elements may change, but the element itself would always have the same size. Try to use relative sizes as percentages when setting the width of elements.

- Similar to the changes in the charts, we should adapt the column content to different device sizes. For instance, when applying an add-in to the columns of a table where we want to have a trend arrow (up or down depending on whether it's a good or bad value), we can change the options so we can also see the value. On a mobile, we would need to hide the arrow or the value. That can be achieved doing something similar to what we saw in the section for the charts, or we could do it using CSS Media Queries.

- Be careful with the number/size of the included libraries. When on a mobile (it is also the case for desktops, but needs more attention on a mobile), we already saw that the communications may be slower, so we need to be careful when loading libraries, and just load the libraries and the parts that are really indispensable.

The data sources perspective

When clicking on the datasources perspective button, you will be switched to the data sources view and get three panels and a toolbar, as you can see on the following image:

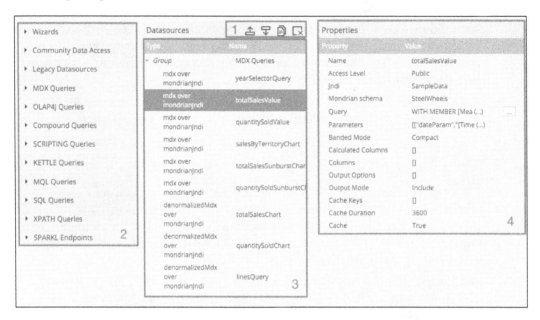

The four panels shown in the previous image are:

1. **The data sources toolbar**: This toolbar is used to change the position of the created data sources, up and down, and duplicate or delete them.

2. **Available groups and types:** This panel shows the available data sources. The data sources types are divided into groups that can be expanded when clicking on the group when selecting one.

3. **Available data sources:** This is where we can select from the data sources that have already been created, and it can be used by the dashboard and components. When selecting a particular data source, the properties will become available inside the properties panel.

4. **Properties:** This is where we can change or just get to know the values that will be or were set for the selected data source. Depending on the data source that is selected, the properties may vary, and the displayed properties may be different from data source to data source. We already saw in the second chapter of this book, the CDA chapter, that for different types, different properties are needed.

The data sources toolbar

The data sources toolbar becomes available when you are in the `datasources` perspective. You will see a toolbar like the following image:

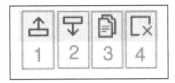

Depending on the position of the selected `datasource`, you may find some of the buttons enabled or disabled:

1. **Move up**: This changes the position of the data source, moving it up.

2. **Move down**: This changes the position of a data source, moving it down.

3. **Duplicate**: This creates a copy of the data source and appends _new to the name.

4. **Delete**: This deletes a data source. It will remove the data source from the dashboard and from the available data sources panel.

Creating new data sources

To define a new data source, we just need to select the group of the data source to create and select the type. You will then see, on the right side of the screen, the palette of properties we need/can set to get the selected data source to work.

You already know which data sources types are available and what the properties are used for, as this was covered in *Chapter 2, Acquiring Data with CDA*. Let's suppose you wanted to create an MDX query. You should expand the **MDX Queries** by clicking on it, and then select **mdx over mondrianJndi**. This will create a new empty data source in the Dashboards data sources panel. The advantage of using CDE is that you don't need to know what the data sources types are or the names of the properties available for each one of the properties. Not that this is a disadvantage, but the difference is that CDE will generate a connection for each data source you set. When you are setting the data sources by hand, you can reuse one of the existing connections. If this is the case, CDE will generate a larger file, but at the end, you will notice the difference.

When you click on a created data source, on the right side, you will get a list of properties for the kind of data source you have created or selected. There are some mandatory properties and some other ones that are not. Some of them are common to all the data sources and other ones will just appear for a particular data source type, because they would not make sense for other types.

Automatically generated CDA files should not be edited and changed by hand

You should not edit and change any of the CDA files by hand that are generated when you save dashboards and have data sources defined. CDE will not read the CDA file, and instead will read the definitions that are inside the CDFDE file and always generate a new CDA file when we save the dashboard. This way, you will lose the changes that you make directly on the CDA file that you have changed by hand. Note that this is the case only for the CDA files that are automatically created with CDE, that is, the ones that have the same name as the dashboard. The CDA file is just read and used by CDA, never by CDE.

When you finish creating your data sources using the CDE editor, and after saving the dashboard, you will get a CDA file with the same name as the dashboard. Double-click on the CDA file and the CDA previewer will open. As we covered in the CDA chapter, you can use previewer to test the queries you just created using CDE.

Data sources properties

When creating data sources, you will see some common properties in all or in almost all the data sources you will create:

- **Name**: This is the name of the data source. This is the name to be used by the components or when selecting the Data Access ID when using CDA directly to run queries, or when using a previewer.

- **Access level**: This should be used for the query to be accessible from the outside or just for internal use. For instance, data sources that are just to be used on compound queries can be set as `Private`.

- **Parameters**: This is used to make queries dynamic. We can add parameters to be used inside the queries, and this parameters will be replaced during the execution. Parameters are very important, so don't forget to also set them in the query. It's also important to set the default values, because these are the values that will be used when previewing the results using the CDA previewer. You can change the parameters values in the previewer when using the CDA previewer or they will be overwritten by the parameters from the dashboard when we also establish the mapping on the components that will use the same data source.

- **Calculated columns**: This is used to set some simple formulas to create new columns based on calculations using other columns.

- **Columns**: Here you can change the header for your columns. You just need to add an element using the add button in the pop-up window and add the index of the column (starting from zero) and the name for the new column.

- **Output options**: This can be used to change the order to repeat a column after getting the results from the source and before sending the results back to the dashboard. You should specify the index of the columns starting from zero.

- **Output mode**: This should be used together with output options. The index of the columns specified will be included or excluded from the dashboard. The possible values are Include or Exclude.

- **Cache keys**: These are the keys that will be used to manage the cache segments where we are writing and getting the results from.

- **Cache duration**: This is the length of time that the cache will store the last results.

- **Cache**: This tells you whether the cache is enabled or disabled. True will enable it and false will disable the cache. Queries will be cached or not using this method.

Some other properties may be found just for some of the data sources types. For instance, the Query property is available for most of the queries, but not for all of them. When using a kettle data source you will not see a query property, but you will see the variables property. This is used to make the matching between the parameters and the variables in the kettle transformation. When the name of the parameters is the same, you don't have to set the matching, but when the name of the parameters is different from the variables defined in the kettle transformation, you need to set it.

JNDI is another example of a property that would appear in multiple data sources types, but not all of them, and allows distributed applications to look up services in an abstract, resource-independent way. At least will become available for SQL and MDX queries. For MDX queries, you will also get the Mondrian Schema to set the name of the schema to use. For both cases, you will see the property query.

Regarding the explanation here, you also can refer to the CDA chapter, the second one.

The components perspective

When you have the layout of the dashboards and the queries ready to get data using parameters, it's time to set the components.

To add components, you need to go to the components perspective. When you click on it, you will be switched to the components perspective and will see three panels, as shown here:

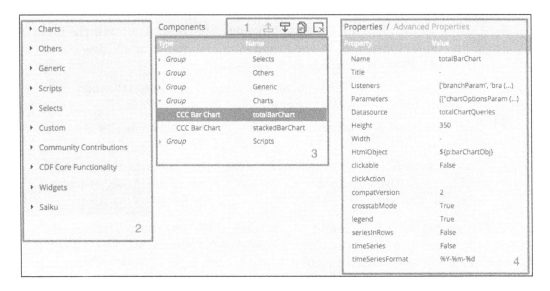

1. **Layout toolbar**: This toolbar is used to manipulate the elements you can see in the dashboard components panel.

2. **Components groups and types**: Here you can select the element type that you want to add to the dashboard. In a wide view, we can classify the components in three different categories:

   ○ **Visual Components**: These are the components that are displayed in your dashboard, including tables, charts (such as lines, pies, bars, stacked, heatgrid, waterfall, and so on), selectors (such as dropdowns, radio buttons, date pickers, or buttons) and a lot more. There is a new component, called template component, where you can build your templates that will be rendered using the model, which is built automatically from the query results or that you can build on your own.

   ○ **Parameters**: These represent values that can be shared by the components. The parameters are crucial for the interaction with the dashboards. They should be set in the input components, and set as listeners in the components that need to be updated when the values are changed.

   ○ **Scripts**: These are pieces of JavaScript code that let you customize the look and feel or behavior of other components, and add code to be executed before or after the execution of the dashboard.

3. **Dashboard components:** This is where all the elements that are part of the dashboard will be represented. Whenever you select an element in the properties panel, some parameters will be updated, and will show the properties available for the selected element. When you add more components, parameter(s), or scripts, you will see them in this perspective panel.

4. **Properties:** This panel shows you the available properties of the selected component, and depending on the type of element, the properties may vary. This is where you can see the value for each of the properties or just set their values.

The components toolbar

This toolbar becomes available when you are in the components perspective and it is shown in the following image. Depending on the elements you have selected in the dashboard panel, you may find some of the buttons enabled or disabled:

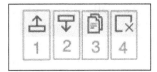

1. **Move up:** This changes the position of a component, moving it up.
2. **Move down:** This changes the position of a component, moving it down.
3. **Duplicate:** This creates a copy of a component and appends _new to the name.
4. **Delete:** This deletes a component. It will remove the component from the dashboard and from the panel.

Dashboard parameters

You saw that we can create parameters using the components perspective. We already covered this, but it's never too much to refer it again. There are two different kinds of parameters, the kind that are set to be used by the queries and the kind that are set to be used by the components in the components. You just need to establish a matching between both the dashboard and query parameters and pass the values stored in the dashboard parameters to the query parameters. To do so, you should use the parameters property available in almost all of the components.

To create a parameter in the dashboard, you need to be in the components perspective and choose the right type from the generic, in the **Components Groups and Types** section. When expanding this group, you will get three different parameters to use. The difference between them is the way you set the default value, because at the end you are just setting a JavaScript variable, so the big difference is the value you are setting for the first time.

- **Date parameter**: You should name the parameter and set a property date value. The available options here are: Today, Yesterday, One week ago, One month ago, First day of month, First day of year, or Pick date.

- **Custom parameter**: Here you should set the name and JavaScript code, and this way you will have all the flexibility you need. You may set a number, a string, a Boolean, a date, a function, or whatever you need, just by setting the JavaScript code to do so.

- **Simple parameter**: For this, you should set the name and a default value that will always be set as a string. Each value you may set will always be interpreted like a string. It's really simple to use, but be careful when using it, because if you're setting it to true or false, it will be set as a string, so it will not be interpreted like a Boolean value. Comparing a Boolean and a string that has a Boolean string inside it is not the same when using JavaScript, so be cautious.

For me, it's always a good idea to set a custom parameter and just ignore the other two types.

You should have noticed that we haven't yet talked about the `bookmarkable` property that is in the parameters. This is a property where you can set a `True` or `False` value. If you want to open a dashboard on a particular state/selection, you can use `bookmarkable` parameters. When you call the dashboard using the URL, you can pass some values into the parameters and make those the values to be used for the parameters, which can make the dashboard work with a particular selection of values.

You will also notice, when using `bookmarkable` parameters, that your URL changes based on the new selections in the dashboard, so you can send the link to another person in the company and when that person opens the dashboard, they will see what you are seeing.

So, the `bookmarkable` parameters are used to accept values that come from the URL when requesting a dashboard. If you are expecting the values of a parameter to come from the URL, you should set the parameter as `bookmarkable`. You can later specify the values for the parameters of the URL, and those values will be automatically used to set the value of the parameter. For instance, if you just created a parameter called country and checked the box for `bookmarkable`, when calling the dashboard, you can just call a line, like in the following example. After the name of the dashboard or other options, you should add the following:

```
&bookmarkState=%7B"impl"%3A"client"%2C"params"%3A%7B"country"%3A"Port
ugal"%7D%7D
```

If it's decoded, you should add the following:

```
&bookmarkState={"impl":"client","params":{"country":"Portugal"}}
```

Appending this example code to the URL of the dashboard with a parameter named `country` will display a dashboard with values for the specified country, in this case, `Portugal`.

Scripts

You can also add some code to your dashboard using scripts. A script is just a JavaScript function or part of code you can add to the dashboard that will be executed at the beginning of the rendering of the dashboard, or called later as a regular function in JavaScript.

To add a script, you should expand the script group in the components groups and types panel that is available in the components perspective. You just need to click on the function component. This will make the script component available in the center panel, and the properties that need to be set are as follows:

- **Name**: This is the name you want to give to this element. The name is just an identifier for your own use.
- **JavaScript code**: This is where you will place the code that you need to include in your dashboard.

Visual components

The last type of components category is the visual components category. There are a lot of groups that belongs to this category — pretty much every group that is not script or generic is a visual component.

When looking at the groups and trying to find some logic, you will most likely be disappointed and you have a good reason to be. To be honest, I think anyone will be able to find the true logic behind the grouping as it is right now, but I also think and truly believe that Pentaho/Webdetails will take care of it and create some real logic there. Well, there is a group where the name is really informative, and that's the selectors group.

To add a visual component to the dashboard, you should act as for the last two categories, you need to expand the groups and types of available components and then click on the component you want to use.

Visual Components should only be set when you have the necessary layout elements and queries ready to be used, because to properly set a component we really need to specify values for some mandatory properties. There are some properties, like `datasource` and `htmlObject`, which are common for most of the components. We already covered these common properties during the CDF chapter, so you should already be familiar with them. Anyhow, let's do a recap:

- **Name**: This is the unique identifier of the component inside the dashboard.

- **Listeners**: This will accept an array of string with the name of the parameters of the dashboard that triggers the component update. This array is crucial in the iteration between components. Here you should check the parameters that will trigger the update of the components when the values of those same parameters are changed by the `fireChange` function. If you remember, this is the function that can be called using your own code, or automatically called by a particular type of component. Suppose that you have a component that needs to be updated when selecting a value from a dropdown, and then you need to check the name checkbox in front of the parameter whose value will be changed by the dropdown, which is also another component. When clicking on the listener's property, you will get a list of names that will correspond to the dashboard's parameters created in the dashboard.

- **Data source**: This is the name of the data source you may have created in the data sources perspective. When typing the name, you will get an autocomplete list of values, that is, the names of the already created data sources. You can also click the bottom cursor arrow to get a complete list, before you start typing. When you type, you may be excluding some of the available values.

- **Parameters**: This accepts an array of arrays, where each array will have the name of the parameters of the query and the parameters of the dashboard with the value to be used. You already saw that we may have parameters defined in the query and in the dashboard. This is where we make the mapping between them in the component. You can have as many rows as you need for each component, and for each row you will specify the name of the parameter of the dashboard on the right side, and the name of the query parameter on the left side. What will happen is that the component will request the execution of the query defined in the data source, and send the values of the parameters that are in the dashboard to replace the parameters that are in the query. This way, the same query can get different results. Just don't forget that the parameters overwritten in the query are the ones where the matching is established, not for any other. Make sure the matching uses correct and created parameter names, otherwise you will not get the expected results, or you will get errors. To avoid this kind of error, you can use the same name for the parameters of the dashboard and for the query, but you will need to define the mapping between them anyhow.

- **Parameter:** For components where user input is required, this is where you set the name of the parameter where a value will be stored for later use. This is different from the last one, because this is where you are saying what the parameter name is where the values are stored, and not to be sent to the query. It is very important to know the difference between a parameter and parameters. You will find a parameter in the components that are under the group Selectors. The parameter should be set with the name of where it will be stored when the value is changed. In the same components, you will be able to get values to use from a query and you may need to pass some parameters to the query, so for that purpose you should use parameters. For this reason, you may need to set both, but definitely, where you have a parameter property, you should always set the name of the dashboard parameter you already created.

- **htmlobject**: This is the name of the layout element that you defined using the layout perspective. It's the ID of the HTML object, which will be the wrapper of the component's contents. The iQuery element can be reached by calling a method from inside the component using `this.placeholder()`. For instance, it can be used inside `preExecution` or `postExecution`.

- **priority**: This is the priority of the components' execution, defaulting to 5. The lowest priorities have the highest priority of execution. Components with the same priority will be executed simultaneously.

- **executeAtStart**: When set to false, the component will not execute at the start of the dashboard, but it can be updated as soon as one of its listeners has changed.

- **preExecution**: This accepts a function that will be executed, which can happen in three different ways: at the beginning of the dashboard, when there is a change in a parameter in the list of listeners of the component, or when directly calling the update function of the component.

- **postFetch**: This accepts a function with an argument that will have the object with the result of the query. As already described in last chapters, that object will be composed of three properties: `metadata`, where the column's name and type are described, `resultset`, where you will find a multidimensional array with the results, and `queryInfo`, with the number of rows in the result.

- **postExecution**: This accepts a function that is called after the rendering/ drawing of the component. The function can be used for you to manipulate the DOM or perform some operations that you can only do after the rendering of the component.

In some cases, there are also two more functions on the components, the ones where user input is required. You can see it like the ones that can act as filters. For instance, when using a select component that would be rendered as a dropdown, when you change or select another option in the dropdown, it will automatically call a `fireChange` (which changes the value and notifies the components that are listening to the parameter that you set in the parameter property) between the executions of the following functions. Those properties, where you can add a function with the code to be executed before and after the parameter value changes, are as follows:

- `preChange`: This accepts a function that is called before doing the `fireChange` to the parameter. You can verify whether it's a valid option and return another value, one that is going to be set in the parameter. If not returning a value, the selected option is used.

- `postChange`: This accepts a function that is called after the `fireChange` to the parameter. You can use this function to execute after confirming the choice. Let's suppose you want to generate another value/parameter based on the choice the user made. Here you are able to do so by adding your own custom code.

For further information or reference, you can always review the CDF chapter.

The remaining properties are more specific to the type of component that you are using. For example, when using a chart, you will see properties that are not available for a table, or when using a table you will not get properties that you would get when using a template component. In the next chapter, I will start teaching you about how to use the most important components, so that's the right place to talk about these specific properties. This is also the reason why, in this chapter, we will not go into detail about using the components. From my experience of building a dashboard with CTools, the most important ones, and the ones that you should know really well are: select, multi select, date range, multi button, button, table, charts, duplicate, freeform, query, text, duplicate, export popup, map, and the new template component.

Not all components are everywhere

Note that some of the components may only be available in CDE and not in CDF. If they exist in CDE, this does not mean that they exist in CDF, and if they exist in CDF, they may not be seen in CDE.

As I just referred to, there are more important visual components than others, and to build an outstanding dashboard you really need to know a few of them, and these will be covered in the next chapter. Anyhow, we can provide an overview and a brief description of all the components here:

- Charts

Type	Description
CCC charts	CCC charts are the charts included by default in CDE. This chart library is built on top of Protovis for older visualizations and D3 for newer visualizations. The advantage of them is that they are extremely customizable and interactive and can accept a result that comes from a CDA query. There will be a chapter dedicated only to CCC charts.
Protovis	This is a kind of component where you can use your own code. You can build your own chart without the need to create a new CDE component. To create the visualization, you should use Protovis.

- Others

Type	Description
Button	This is a component based on a simple button, where you can add some code that is executed when the button is pressed.
Comments	This component can be used to create comments on a dashboard. Another user can then see the comments. It's possible to set a property to control who sees what comments.

Type	Description
PRPT	Using this component, you will be able to render a Pentaho Report Designer report inside a dashboard. For instance, you can create a dashboard to control the execution of reports and the parameters that will be sent.
Freeform	This is a component that allows you to create your own code and embed it inside the dashboard. It's very similar to the Query component; it will not run any query, but it will be inside the lifecycle. It can be very handy.
Navigation	This allows you to create navigation between dashboards.
Query	This is a component that will run a query and will write the results to a variable. It will let you create any kind of elements in the dashboard by making use of the results from a query. It can be used to create custom visualizations that are created to be used once in a dashboard.
Table	This is one of the most important components. It allows you to create amazing dashboards, and you should not think of it as a simple table. You have addins, where you can customize the content of columns or cell or have expandable content inside the row. We will cover this in detail later in the book.
Template	This is a new component that allows you to build content for your dashboard based on Mustache or Underscore templates. These templates will be rendered with the results of a query as the model. You can also use addins and control clicks or some other functionality, which we will also cover later on in this book.
Text	The text component does not run a query, and you just need to define a function that returns the content to be rendered. This can be used to perform the internationalization and localization of your dashboards.
Viz API	It's also possible to render Analyzer Visualizations in CDE dashboards, using the results from a CDA query.
Xaction	This allows you to run an Xaction in a CDE dashboard.
Duplicate	The duplicate component is used to create copies of other components. It will create a copy of the HTML elements, parameters, and component itself. Having also duplicated the parameters, you will have a different result set coming from the query of each of the components.
Export Button	This will create a button on the dashboard that lets the user export the data to a particular component. The formats that you can export to are: XLS, CSV, XML, JSON, and PNG, the last one just for the charts. When using the button, the exported file will use the defined format. If you pretend that the user can choose the format from more than one option, you should use the Export Popup Button.
Popup	This is a way to display some content or components inside a popup. They can be hidden in a hidden part of the dashboard and displayed only when the popup is called.

Type	Description
Export popup button	Similar to export, this will display a popup where the user can select a different format for the data to export.

- Selects

Type	Description
Auto Complete	This is an input box that can have autocomplete, based on a values array or query result.
Check	This is a checkbox element where the options are based on the results of a query or by just defining the values array. As the normal checkboxes, they allow multiple selections.
Radio Button	This is a radio button element, where the options are based on the results of a query or by just defining the values array. As the normal radio buttons, they do not allow single selections.
Date Input	This shows a calendar where you can pick a date.
Date Range	This is used to select a start and end date. It's very flexible and lets you select open periods, so be careful regarding the performance of the queries.
Month Picker	This is similar to Date Input, but it lets you select a month.
Multi Button	This component will generate as many buttons as results from the query, or as many as defined in the values array. You can have single or multiple selections. I always use this in place of radio and check box components. It can also be used to simulate the behavior of tabs.
Select	This is a dropdown selector.
Select Multi	This is similar to Select, but allows multiple selections. There is a new Select component that we will cover, and it's very useful.
Text Area Input	This will use a text area input as a selector. The text entered will fire a change in a parameter. It can handle multiple lines.
Text Input	This is similar to the last one, but it will be a simple text input element with one line only.

- Community and custom

Type	Description
Ajax Request	You can use this component to make Ajax requests and get the results back. Just by setting the properties you would get a result, which you can later use on your dashboard.
New Map	This is a map component you can use in your dashboard. It can use two different engines: Google or OpenLayers. To represent data, you can use shapes or markers. It is very simple to use, but may not have some of the interactions you would expect.
Raphael	If you want to use the Raphael library to build your visualizations, this is the right component. Of course, you need to write your own code for the visualization.
Google Maps Overlay	This is a component that was created by Sinn Technology, a community contribution, and allows you to make use of Google Maps Overlay.
Google Analytics	This is a component that was created by Sinn Technology, a community contribution, and allows you to work with Google Analytics.

Parameter, parameters, and listeners, again

When talking about building an interactive dashboard, you need to remember that parameters are crucial. To have a component using the same query but showing different results, we need to use parameters. When defining the data source, we need to say which parameters will be used and build the query with them inside. Also, we need to have the dashboard parameters where the values we want to use when executing the query are.

When setting the component, we need to specify the data source and the parameters properties, among others, but for now let's focus on these two. In the component, the parameters property is where you specify the mapping of the parameters that you have created in the dashboard, using the components perspective, and the name of the parameters in the data source. This way, the component can get different results, depending on the value of the parameters we have in our dashboard.

Listeners are also crucial. The dashboard parameters will store the value that we want to be used by the queries. When the values inside the parameters are changed, we may need to update some of the components in the dashboard, but for that, the components must be listening to those parameters so that they can be notified about the changes. To have this in place, we need to add the parameters that will trigger the update on the listeners of the component that will be updated on changes.

But how can the parameters be changed and store other values? You can directly call two functions, `fireChange` and `setParameter`, or just let it be done automatically by some components, which are available under the selectors group. The type of components inside this group have another property, called parameter, where we need to set the name of the dashboard parameter that will store the value.

When selecting or writing, depending on the component's type, the component will automatically call the `fireChange` function and set the new value to the dashboard parameter. This way, components listening to those dashboard parameters will be updated, and a query will be executed. Using the matching between dashboard and query parameters, set in the component, the component will know what values should be sent to the query so that the query can use them to get the pretended results.

Putting it all together

Now it's time to build your first dashboard with CTools. These are the steps you should follow:

Create/change the layout: Create the responsive layout for the dashboard using the Bootstrap concepts we covered earlier and add resources (JavaScript and CSS) if necessary:

1. **Define the data sources:** Create the data sources with the queries and if necessary, include these parameters:

     ◦ **Add the parameters and components:** Create the dashboard parameters, add the scripts (JavaScript code, if necessary), add the components to be displayed in the layout elements, and render the data coming from the queries. You will need to set the necessary properties:

       Set the parameter on the components that are in the groups of Selectors

       Set the data source and the parameters to use

       Set the listeners so that the components can be notified about parameter value changes and be updated

       Set all the other properties or, if necessary, some custom code

2. **Overall improvements:** This step is not mandatory, but it can increase the user experience just by adding some improvements to the components and layout, creating some custom behaviors, and adding some CSS to make the dashboard more attractive. These are just some examples of what you could do in this step.

3. **Testing and Quality Assurance:** This is where you, but always someone else that did not work on the backend or frontend, if existing should be done by the QA team, making sure the developments meet all the acceptance criteria, never forgetting the performance. Don't forget that performance is also important.

Once you finish step 3, if it's necessary for any reason, such as bugs, acceptance criteria not being met, or unsatisfactory performance, you will need to go through all the steps again and make the necessary changes to ensure the work delivered is really good. The cycle should be like the following diagram:

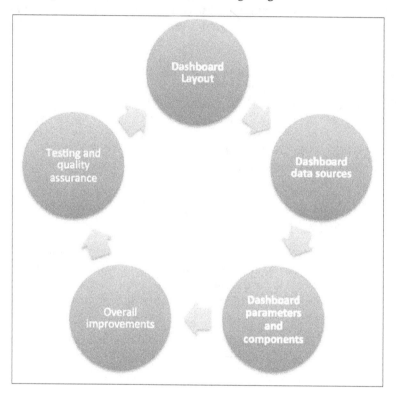

Creating your first CDE dashboard

Now let's create a dashboard using the concepts covered from *Chapter 1*, *Getting Started with CTools* till this chapter. Next you will find some images showing the dashboard design for the desktop and mobile versions:

The dashboard should be responsive, and the layout should adapt to the device/ screen size. It will be created as a sample of the **SteelWheels** sample data. The dashboard has four components: a dropdown selector to select the year for the data to be displayed, and a multi button to select the product lines to display on the table. The table is the three columns with the name, total sales, and percentage. Last, we also have a simple pie chart using the same data used in the table. When changing the selectors, year, and product line, the table and the chart will be updated and fire new queries, so they should be listening to the correct parameters.

Creating the layout

Following are the steps to create the layout:

1. Create a new dashboard using the PUC menu: **File | New | CDE Dashboard**.

    ◦ Start by saving the dashboard in a folder chosen by you.

2. Go to the **Settings** of the dashboard, check **RequireJS Support** and press **Save**.

3. Using the **Layout Perspective,** add the following elements and properties (between curly brackets) respecting the hierarchy:

```
Row (Name="headerBackground", CSS Class="headerBackground")
Row (Name="header", CSS Class="header")
Column (Name="userInfo", Extra Small Devices="12", Medium
Devices="4")
Row (No need to set aby property here)
Column (Name="userImage", Extra Small Devices="2", Medium
Devices="1", CSS Class="fa fa-user userImage")
Column (Name="username", Extra Small Devices="10", Medium
Devices="11", CSS Class="username")
Html (Html="Welcome: <b>CTools Book Reader</b>")
Column (Name="filters", Extra Small Devices="12", Medium
Devices="6", CSS Class="filters")
Row ()
Column (Name="yearFilterTitle", Extra Small Devices="12", CSS
Class="description")
Html (Html="Welcome: <b>CTools Book Reader</b>")
Column (Name="yearFilter", Extra Small Devices="12", CSS
Class="yearFilter")
Row (Name="middlePanel")
Column (Name="dashMiddlePanel", Extra Small Devices="12", CSS
Class="dashPanel")
Row (Name="overview", CSS Class="overview")
Column (Extra Small Devices="12", Medium Devices="3")
Row ()
Column (Name="productLineFilterTitle", Extra Small Devices="12",
CSS Class="description")
Html (Html="Click on the product line to toggle")
Column (Name="productLineFilter", Extra Small Devices="12", CSS
Class="productLineFilter")
Column (Name="overviewTable", Extra Small Devices="12", Medium
Devices="6", CSS Class="overviewTable")
Column (Name="overviewPieChart", Extra Small Devices="12", Medium
Devices="6", CSS Class="overviewPieChart")
Row (Name="footerBackground", CSS Class="footerBackground")
```

Define the data sources

Using `Datasources Perspective`, add the queries for the dashboard. The queries will all be `mdx over mondrianJndi` using a JNDI property with the value `SampleData` and the Mondrian Schema using `SteelWheels`. The data sources types and properties you need to create/define are as follows:

- As data source type: MDX Over JNDI:

  Name: `productLineQuery`,
  Query:
  ```
  WITH
      SET PRODUCTLINES AS { [Product].[Trains], [Product].[Trucks
  and Buses], [Product].[Motorcycles],  [Product].[Vintage Cars],
  [Product].[Classic Cars] }
      MEMBER [Measures].[UniqueName] AS [Product].CURRENTMEMBER.
  UNIQUENAME
      MEMBER [Measures].[Total] AS AGGREGATE(PRODUCTLINES,
  [Measures].[Sales])
      MEMBER [Measures].[Percentage] AS  [Measures].[Sales]/
  [Measures].[Total]

  SELECT
      {[Measures].[UniqueName], [Measures].[Sales], [Measures].
  [Percentage]} ON COLUMNS,
      ORDER(PRODUCTLINES, [Measures].[Percentage], DESC) ON ROWS
  FROM [SteelWheelsSales]
  ```

  Output Options: 1, 0, 2
  Output Mode: include

- As data source type: MDX Over JNDI:

  Name: `yearQuery`,
  Query:
  ```
  WITH
      MEMBER [Measures].[Years UniqueName]  AS  [Time].
  currentmember.UniqueName
      SET  YEAR  AS  UNION( [Time].[All Years] , [Time].[Years].
  Members )
  SELECT
      [Measures].[Years UniqueName]  ON COLUMNS,
      YEAR   ON ROWS
  FROM [SteelWheelsSales]
  ```

  Output Options: 1, 0, 2
  Output Mode: include

- As data source type: MDX Over JNDI:

    ```
    Name: overviewTableQuery,
    Parameters:
    [productLineParam, [Product].[Trains], [Product].[Trucks and
    Buses], [Product].[Motorcycles],  [Product].[Vintage Cars]
    [yearParam, [Product].[Classic Cars]], [productLineParam, [Time].
    [All Years]]
    Query:
    WITH
        SET PRODUCTLINES AS { ${productLineParam} }
        MEMBER [Measures].[UniqueName] AS [Product].CURRENTMEMBER.
    UNIQUENAME
        MEMBER [Measures].[Total] AS AGGREGATE(PRODUCTLINES,
    [Measures].[Sales])
        MEMBER [Measures].[Percentage] AS  ([Measures].[Sales]/
    [Measures].[Total])*100

    SELECT
        {[Measures].[UniqueName], [Measures].[Sales], [Measures].
    [Percentage]} ON COLUMNS,
        ORDER(PRODUCTLINES, [Measures].[Percentage], DESC) ON ROWS
    FROM [SteelWheelsSales]
    WHERE {${yearParam}}

    Output Options: 0, 2, 3
    Output Mode: include
    ```

- As data source type: MDX Over JNDI:

    ```
    Name: totalSalesQuery,
    Parameters:
    [productLineParam, [Product].[Trains], [Product].[Trucks and
    Buses], [Product].[Motorcycles],  [Product].[Vintage Cars]
    [yearParam, [Product].[Classic Cars]], [productLineParam, [Time].
    [All Years]]
    Query:
    WITH
     MEMBER [Measures].[Year] AS [Time].CURRENTMEMBER.PARENT.Name
    SELECT
        NON EMPTY UNION(Crossjoin({[Product].[All Products]},
    {[Measures].[Year]}), Crossjoin({${productLineParam}},
    {[Measures].[Sales]})) ON COLUMNS,
        NON EMPTY {Except(Descendants(${yearParam}, [Time].
    [Quarters]), {[Time].[All Years]})} ON ROWS
    FROM [SteelWheelsSales]
    ```

- As data source type: MDX Over JNDI:

```
Name: quantitySoldQuery,
Parameters:
[productLineParam, [Product].[Trains], [Product].[Trucks and
Buses], [Product].[Motorcycles], [Product].[Vintage Cars]
[yearParam, [Product].[Classic Cars]], [productLineParam, [Time].
[All Years]]
Query:
WITH
 MEMBER [Measures].[Year] AS [Time].CURRENTMEMBER.PARENT.Name
SELECT
    NON EMPTY UNION(Crossjoin({[Product].[All Products]},
{[Measures].[Year]}), Crossjoin({${productLineParam}},
{[Measures].[Quantity]})) ON COLUMNS,
    NON EMPTY {Except(Descendants(${yearParam}, [Time].
[Quarters]), {[Time].[All Years]})} ON ROWS
FROM [SteelWheelsSales]
```

- As data source type: MDX Over JNDI:

```
Name: salesByTerritoryQuery,
Parameters:
productLineParam:[Product].[Classic Cars], [Product].[Trains],
[Product].[Trucks and Buses], [Product].[Motorcycles], [Product].
[Vintage Cars]
yearParam: [Time].[All Years]
Query:
WITH
    MEMBER [Measures].[Sales in Time] AS ( [Measures].[Sales] ,
${yearParam} )
Select
    { [Markets].[APAC] , [Markets].[EMEA] , [Markets].[NA] } on
COLUMNS,
    { ${productLineParam} } on ROWS
FROM [SteelWheelsSales]
Where [Measures].[Sales in Time]
```

Do not forget to test the queries using the CDA Previewer. Correct any mistakes that you may have made.

Add the parameters and components

Now that we have the layout and the queries ready to be used, go to the Components Perspective and add the parameters, components, and scripts to the dashboard. The components and properties you need to create/define are as follows:

- Generic -> Custom Parameter

  Name: productLineParam

  JavaScript: ["[Product].[Trains]", "[Product].[Trucks and Buses]", "[Product].[Motorcycles]", "[Product].[Vintage Cars]", "[Product].[Classic Cars]"]

- Generic -> Custom Parameter

  Name: yearParam

  JavaScript: ["[Product].[Trains]", "[Product].[Trucks and Buses]", "[Product].[Motorcycles]", "[Product].[Vintage Cars]", "[Product].[Classic Cars]"]

- Selects -> Multiple button Component

  Name: productLineFilter

  Parameter: productLineParam

  Multiple Selection: True

  Value as ID: False

  Datasource: productLineQuery

  HTMLObject: productLineFilter

- Selects -> Select Component

  Name: yearFilter

  Parameter: yearParam

  JQuery Plugin: Chosen

  Value as ID: False

  Datasource: yearQuery

  HtmlObject: yearFilter

- Others -> Table Component

  Name: overviewTable

  Listeners: productLineParam, yearParam

Parameters:

- ° productLineParam
- ° yearParam

Column headers: Product Line, Sales Amount ($), %

Column types: string, numeric, numeric

Column formats: %s, $%.0f, $%.1f%

Column widths: 50%, 30%, 20%

Expand on click, Show filter, Info filter, Info filter, Length change, Paginate, Sort data: False

Datasource: overviewTableQuery

HTMLObject: overviewTable

- **Charts -> CCC Pie Chart**

  Name: overviewPieChart

  Listeners: productLineParam, yearParam

  Parameters:

  - ° productLineParam
  - ° yearParam

  Datasource: overviewTableQuery

  HtmlObject: overviewPieChart

  Height: 150

  CrosstabMode: False

  Legend: False

  PreExecution:

```
function() {
    // this code will reset the size of the chart
    if (!_.isNull(this.chart) && !_.isUndefined(this.chart.
options))
        this.chart.options.width = this.placeholder().width();
    // the code bellow will change some of the properties of the
chart. will reset the size of the chart
    var cd =    this.chartDefinition;
    cd.slice_innerRadiusEx = '60%';
    cd.explodedSliceRadius = '0%';
    cd.animate = false;
    cd.colorMap = {"Classic Cars": "#005CA7", "Vintage Cars":
```

```
"#3E83B7", "Motorcycles":          "#5C9FBC", "Trucks and Buses":
"#66C2A5", "Trains": "#22B573"};
}
```

Save the dashboard and execute it, so that you can check the result.

Overall improvements

If you follow the previous steps and render your dashboard, you can see that the elements and components are there and working, but they do not have the look and feel you expect or should be happy with.

Just by applying some CSS, you will definitely have an incredible change in the look of the dashboard. We are providing you with the files you can add to your dashboard. To add the CSS, you can go to the layout perspective and add a resource, CSS as an External File, and point it to the following file: /public/Ctools Book Samples/Chapter 4/SteelWheelsSample-1st/resources/css/steelWheels. css. Don't forget that to be able to use it, you should already have imported the book samples. This file contains CSS that uses the CSS Classes that we defined in the layout perspective, and it will make the dashboard much fancier.

You will not notice a problem when rendering on different devices where you are not resizing the window, but when resizing the window, the layout will adapt to the new size, but not the charts. We will cover this later on in a special chapter dedicated to CCC and will explain the following code; for now just follow the instructions to be able to update the charts when the window is resized. Using the Components Perspective, just add a JavaScript Function to the dashboard under the group Script. You can name it dashboard.postInit and write the following code for the JavaScript Code property:

```
dashboard.postInit = function() {
    var chartsTypeToUpdate = ['CccPieChartComponent',
'CccBarChartComponent'];
    var chartsToUpdate = _.filter(dashboard.components, function(elem,
index) {
        return (chartsTypeToUpdate.indexOf(elem.type) >= 0);
    });

    var resizeChart = function() {
        _.each(chartsToUpdate, function(elem, index){
            elem.chart.options.width = elem.placeholder().width();
            elem.chart.render(true, true, false);
        });
    };

    var throttle = _.throttle(resizeChart, 100, {leading: false});
```

```
    $(document).ready(function() {
        $(window).resize(throttle);
    });
};
```

Now if you save the dashboard and refresh it, you will see that the charts are also updated when the window changes its size. You will find an example of the dashboard after uploading the book samples inside the folder /public/Ctools Book Samples/Chapter 4/SteelWheelsSample-1st. It will also be a good help if you have any trouble creating your own dashboard.

 Please check the samples provided for each one of the chapters. The samples for this chapter are under the Chapter 4 folder. There are two simple but complete dashboards, and also another small sample related to the content covered in this chapter. You are able to render them, but also edit them and check the layout, component, and data sources.

Summary

In earlier chapters, you may have got the idea that working with CTools, you would need to write a lot of code, but as you can see, CDE can save you a lot of work, and you can have a dashboard that works with no or almost no code.

In this chapter, you learned how to use CDE to create a dashboard, so at this time you should already know how to build a CDE dashboard. You are now able to create the layout of a responsive dashboard, define the data sources, and then make use of the parameters and components. At this time, you should already know the importance of parameters, the ones from the dashboard and the ones set on the queries, and how to establish the mapping between them. Also, you learned about how to set the listeners so that the components know when to be updated. We gave you a detailed explanation about the buttons, options, and sections, so that you know where to find them and what they are used for.

We haven't yet covered the visual components in detail, because that's what we will cover in the next chapter.

If I ask you what are the mandatory steps to build a CDE dashboard, what would be your answer? Certainly, it would be: create the layout, define the data sources, and create the dashboard parameters and the components, where we can then set the parameter, the parameters, and the listeners, because this is what creates the interactivity of the dashboard. Of course, we have a lot more to cover, so let's jump to the next chapter.

5
Applying Filters to the Dashboard

Now that you are able to build a dashboard using CDE on your own, you now should see how to take advantage of the most important components. After building some fancy dashboards, you will notice that you are not using all the components, just a subset of them. We will cover these components now.

We've split the chapter into two. The first part covers the filters and the other part covers the data being displayed. Filters, or selectors, can be applied to the dashboard as one way to create an interaction and filter the data you want to be displayed on the dashboard. If you deliver a dashboard with too much information, it will be hard for the final user to understand it at first glance. We already said that a dashboard should be easy to understand and get results from at first look, so by filtering the information, the user will be able to access all the information and it will be simple to understand.

Firstly, you need to know that there is a difference between filters and selectors. A filter component only applies a selection when at least one option is selected, and it will not filter anything if there is no selection, the same as if everything was selected. A selector will always apply a selection on data because it will always have something selected.

In this chapter, you will learn how to work with the select components, at least the ones I consider as the most important and powerful ones. We will also give you some tricks and tips for each of the components and some customizations that will enable you to create even greater dashboards. There is a big focus on the new filter component, which was desired previously and is a long-awaited improvement.

By the end of the chapter, you will be able to apply and customize the filters on a dashboard. You will know what properties are available for each one of the select components covered, and will be able to improve the look and feel of dashboard as well as the user experience. The components that are covered are listed as follows:

- Select and select-multi components
- The filter component
- The multi-button component
- The date range component

The select component

The select component is part of the input components group. Based on the results of a query or based on a values array, it can be set on the properties or on the pre-execution of the component, and the user will be able to select an option from a dropdown. A select component can look like the following image:

To have a select component properly working, the first step is to create a placeholder for the filter, using the layout perspective. The following step is used to set up the query, but it is not needed when you want to set the values on the values array. Another step, and an important one, is to create the dashboard parameter to store the value that is selected by default, and to set the name of the parameter on the corresponding property. The last step is to add the component to the dashboard and set all the properties needed.

By clicking on **Select Component** inside the **Select** group, the component will become available. Once available, you will need to set: the **name**, the **data source** and the **placeholder** (the layout element where the component will be rendered).

Among the properties that are available for the component, some of them are common to all the components, and you already know them from the last two chapters. For these components, there are some properties that you need to be aware of:

- **Value as array**: When we don't want or need to have a query, it's possible to make use of the values array property, setting the ID and value to be used. When using a data source, it will ignore the values array that might be set. The values array accepts a multidimensional array, where each array will be a pair of ID and value.

- **Value as ID**: When you are setting the values array or defining the data source, you may use two columns: one for the ID and another one for the values/description. The first one is used as the ID and the second one is used as the value. If you need to have the value also as the ID, you can set this property to true; otherwise, if you want to display a value but write the ID for the parameter, you should set this property to false. Let's suppose you need to have the following options to be used in the select component:

ID	Value
1	Option One
2	Option Two
3	Option Three

The code to apply such options would be as follows:

```
function(){
  this.valuesArray = [
    ["1","Option One"],
    ["2","Option Two"],
    ["3","Option Three"]
  ];
}
```

When setting false on the **Value as ID** option, you are telling the component that you want to display **Option One**, **Option Two**, and **Option Three** in the dropdown list, but when selecting a choice, you will get the corresponding ID and not the value itself. If you choose **Option Two**, the parameter that stores the value is written with the ID that for this case, would be **2**. This is because you just said that you don't want to have the value as the ID.

When setting the property to true, you will still see in the dropdown the options: **Option One**, **Option Two**, and **Option Three**. If you choose **Option Two**, the parameter will be written with the value and not the ID. If that's the case, the parameter would have **Option Two**. This is because you said in the property that you want to use the value as the ID. When applying a filter and working with an MDX query, you can set the ID as the unique name of the member. When selecting one option, the ID will be written to the parameters that can be used in a query. This can be achieved by setting the values array or using a query that returns the following result:

ID	Value
[Markets].[APAC].[Australia]	Australia
[Territory].[EMEA].[Portugal]	Portugal
[Territory].[EMEA].[Spain]	Spain

- **JQuery plugin**: This is used to set the JQuery plugin, which will be used to generate a fancy selector that will be similar from browser to browser, not like the traditional select HTML, that will have a different look depending on the browser that is being used. Here, you can select from the list of available plugins, or write the available values: Select2, Chosen, and Hynds. No option is selected by default, and a traditional dropdown will be used. You will find more information about the components on the following sites:

  - **Select2**: https://select2.github.io/
  - **Chosen**: https://harvesthq.github.io/chosen/
  - **Hynds**: http://www.erichynds.com/examples/jquery-ui-multiselect-widget/demos

Now let's suppose you want to make use of another JQuery plugin that's not available on the list; are you still able to use it? The answer is yes. You should remember that you are able to manipulate the DOM on postExecution of the component. That's the place to do it. For example, if you are trying to set the bootstrap-select plugin, available at https://silviomoreto.github.io/bootstrap-select/, you just need to download the plugin and add it as a resource using the layout perspective.

Don't forget to also include the CSS files when needed

You should not forget that sometimes, plugins and libraries are not just .js files; they may also need some styling, so do not forget to include these CSS files when you want to customize the styling of your dashboard.

When applying a plugin as shown in this example, we should not specify or set an available plugin, so the JQuery plugin property must be empty.

After including the plugin as a resource, it will become available to be used. On `postExecution`, place the following lines of code:

```
function() {
    var opts = { plugins: ['remove_button'] };
    var selector = this.placeholder('select');
    selector.attr('placeholder','Select your option...');
    selector.selectpicker(opts);
}
```

In the previous code, we are setting an object to pass to the `select-bootstrap` plugin, which contains the options and customizations for the filter, as you can see in the documentation and samples provided on the plugin website. We are setting one option, which won't be used for this example, but that we need for the following component/example.

The second line of the function is grabbing the select HTML that was created by this component, and it returns the JQuery element that we need to add a property. The last line of the function code is just applying the plugin.

Add the minified version of the libraries and plugins when in production

You can add the non-minified version of the plugins or libraries when you are developing the dashboard, which makes debugging easier or even possible. Change to minified files for quality analysis and production. If you are adding the resource as an external file, copy the imported file to the minified and non-minified files to the same resources folder. Later, to change from non-minified to minified, you just need to change the name of the file.

To have a selector working besides the name and layout element where to render it, you need to set the values array or make use of a data source. When a data source is used, the values array will be ignored, even if it was defined. After this, you need also to specify whether the component should make use of one or two columns, to get an id and a value, or just a value that will be used also as the id.

Of course, the visual impact and usability is very important, so you should change the plugin and apply the best setting, depending on your case.

The multi-select component

The multi-select component, identified by the name MultiSelect, is very similar to the select component. The big difference is that we may select multiple options in the selector. When we need to provide the ability to choose multiple values from the selector, this is the component to use.

For you to be able to test it and see how it works, you can create a component with a values array that will display more than the four rows in the preceding example. Render the component and check that you now have multiple selections. The properties that are available are the same as those for the select component.

One important feature that is common to all the components inside the Selectors group is that they can be nested, so the selection of one can depend on the selection of another and so on. The concept behind this is the same as for the remaining components: having to pass parameters to the data sources and listening to the parameters that trigger this update to fetch new data.

Let's build a quick example here. Start by creating two data sources using MDX over JNDI and the Steel Wheels sample data, as follows:

Name	territoryQuery
Jndi	SampleData
Mondrian schema	SteelWheels
Query	WITH
	MEMBER [Measures].[UID] AS [Markets].CURRENTMEMBER. UNIQUENAME
	SELECT
	FILTER(DESCENDANTS([Markets].[All Markets], [Markets].[Territory]), [Markets].CURRENTMEMBER. NAME <> '#null') on ROWS,
	{[Measures].[UID]} on COLUMNS
	FROM [SteelWheelsSales]
Output options	1,0

Name	countryQuery
Jndi	SampleData
Mondrian schema	SteelWheels
Query	WITH MEMBER [Measures].[UID] AS [Markets].CURRENTMEMBER. UNIQUENAME SELECT DESCENDANTS({${territoryParam}}, [Markets]. [Country]) on ROWS, {[Measures].[UID]} on COLUMNS FROM [SteelWheelsSales]
Parameters	[['territoryParam', '[Markets].[APAC]']]
Output options	1,0

Using the layout perspective, add one row, with two columns named territory and country, and using the components perspective, create the parameters and the components.

Two of the parameters should be like the following:

	Terriotoy parameter	Country parameter
Name	territoryParam	countryParam
Property value	territorySelector	

Two of the components should be like the following:

	Territory component	Country component
Name	territoryComp	countryComp
Parameter	territoryParam	countryParam
Listeners		territoryParam
Parameters		[['territoryParam', 'territoryParam']]
Datasource	territoryQuery	countryQuery
Value as ID	False	False
HTML object	territory	country

	Territory component	Country component
`postExecution`	```function() { var opts = {}; var selector = this. placeholder('select'); selector. addClass('selectpicker'); selector. attr({'placeholder':'Select your option...', 'data-width': '100%'}); selector. selectpicker(opts); }```	

After creating all the layout, components, parameters, and queries, save and render the dashboard so that you can see the results, as shown in the next image:

You should see two selectors, one below the other, and on the top you will be able to select the territory; depending on the selected territories, you will be able to select the countries. If you have any trouble, you may import, render, and edit the sample provided in the chapter folder.

The filter component

The filter component is a new and recent component, with more advanced options that will make the interaction of the dashboard even better. It is used as a simple selector or as a more advanced selector with multiple choices. The selection of all or none options is also available and achievable by setting some properties. The component also provides server-side capabilities that can be used when the number of elements to be displayed is too high.

I would dare to say that it's replacing the select and multi-select components. It's more powerful, able to provide single and multiple selections, and has a lot more improvements, besides the fact that it is even more user-friendly when using a select component with a plugin. If you also need to extend its capabilities, you are able to. Do not hesitate—just use it.

As with any other component, you need to at least set the `Name` and the `HTML Object` property where the component should be rendered, and if it's a select component being used, you also need to set the data source/parameters, or the values array. Depending on whether the value and the ID should or should not be different, you should also set the `Values as ID` property.

To have a proper knowledge of how to work with the component, we need to cover some topics such as the expected data format, specific properties, and also how to extend the functionality by making use of add-ins.

Expected data layout

First, we need to bring the data to populate the selector. To populate the selector with values, you need to at least return two columns, the first one for the ID and the second one for the value. The following image is an example of the results of a query that should be used. You can see in the first column that we have the unique name of the members that we use to filter the data using MDX queries, and in the second column, the names that are displayed:

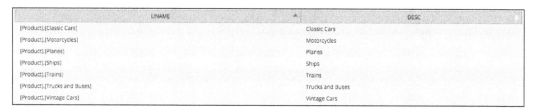

The filter also provides grouping for the options. Let's suppose that you want to be able to select **Product Vendor**, but you want to display them by the product line. If you need to use the grouping, you just need to return four or more columns, and the component will automatically take care of it. The following image is an example of a query that would be needed:

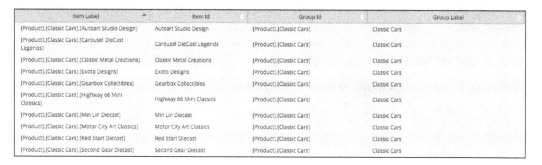

We should respect the order of the columns; there is a way to customize them, but for now, let's focus on the default configuration. First, you should return the columns for the items and next, the columns with the information about the groups. You should have noticed that first, on the left-hand side of the image, there are two columns that represent the id and the value to be used as options on the filter, and only after that are the two columns for the group with the id and value.

Specific properties

After setting the mandatory properties, you will be able to use the selectors. Let's jump now to the specific properties of this component:

- **Title**: This is the label to display on top of the filter.

- **Multiple selection**: This is whether the component should accept multiple selections or not. This property will also change its behavior. If a single selection is selected, when clicking on an option, it immediately closes the filter and writes the selection to a parameter. If a multiple selection is set, the filter only closes if the user clicks outside, cancels, or commits the current selection, and the parameter is only updated when the user presses the **Apply** button. The default value is set to `True`, so a multiple selection is set. The following images are an example of a single selection on the left and a multiple selection on the right:

- **Output format**: This determines how the selection is written to the parameter upon commit. If it is set to `Group and Item Ids`, the filter attempts to write the group's IDs when all of its members are selected. When using groups, we should use `Group and Item Ids` because this will generate a compact array to be written to the parameter. The default value is `Item Ids`, and if this is selected, the group's IDs will not be used.

- **Always expanded**: This accepts `true` or `false`, and it's used to keep the filter expanded. When set to `true`, and an option or the **Apply** button is clicked, the filter will still be opened. The default value is `false`, so the filter will collapse when the options are selected.

- **Selection limit**: This accepts an integer that represents the maximum number of options that can be selected. You should not use a high value, because depending on some other factors, it can affect the performance of the queries that the selection will trigger. This value is valid for all the options selected, independently of the group they belong to. When you have more options than the limit, the **All** selection button will not work.

- **Page length**: This is used to sequentially load pages of items from the server. By default, the filter attempts to load the entire dataset defined by a data source, but sometimes, the list of options might be quite large. For this case, you may want to take advantage of CDA's support for pagination and server-side searching, and you can set the property to `true` so that the component takes care of it for you. This property option accepts an integer value with the number of rows for each load from the server, so when the user reaches the bottom of the scrollbar, a new page is loaded and added to the list of items. We can view this as lazy loading. If no value is set, the component tries to load the entire dataset. When you have a huge number of options, for performance reasons, you might want set a value to activate it.

- **Show icons**: By default, this is set to `true` and an icon, checkbox, or radio button will be displayed next to each item.

- **Show only button**: This is used to specify that for each option, you also want to see a link/button where you can click and unselect all the other options and select only the one that you are clicking on.

- **Show search filter**: This is used to specify whether the search box should or should not be available. This option accepts a Boolean value. When set to `true`, the search will be available. The default value is set to `true`.

Making use of add-ins

Add-ins are an advanced option that you will not need if the standard behavior of the filter is enough for your use case. Either way, you won't lose anything if you learn some more advanced concepts, such as how to do some customizations here.

This component also has some properties that are related to the use of the add-ins. If you check the properties, you will find some where the name ends with **Addin**, and these are the properties we will be covering now. In some ways, they are similar to the add-ins that you will see in the next chapter for the table and template components. Here, they are used to customize the default behavior of the component by associating them to slots.

An add-in is basically a snippet of reusable code capable of modifying a component, so let's start to check the add-ins that are available:

- `notificationSelectionLimit`: This is used to show a notification that the selection limit has been reached
- `sumSelected`: This is used to calculate the sum value for the list of the selected items
- `selectedOnTop`: This is used to keep selected items on top
- `insertionOrder`: This is used to keep the insertion order
- `sortByLabel`: This is used to sort items alphabetically, using their labels
- `sortByValue`: This is used to sort items by their values
- `sumValues`: This is used to sum the values of the items
- `template`: This is used to apply a mustache template, so that the HTML of the item can be customized
- `accordion`: This makes the filters of a particular group behave as an accordion

To get an add-in working, we should apply it to a slot, but what's a slot? A slot is a part of the processing of a filter that can go from data loading to rendering. Slots are being processed between the `postFetch` and `postExecution` functions, at the end of `postFetch` and just before `postExecution`. Let's see what available slots there are:

- **Post update add-ins**: This is used to perform some action when data is added to the model. The identifier of the slot is `postUpdate`.
- **Root header add-ins**: This is used to perform an action on every update of the root header. The identifier of the slot is `renderRootHeader`.
- **Root selection add-ins**: This is used to perform an action when the selection is changed. The identifier of the slot is `renderRootSelection`.
- **Group selection add-ins**: This is used to perform an action when the group selection is changed. The identifier of the slot is `renderGroupSelection`.
- **Item selection add-ins**: This is used to perform an action when the item selection is changed. The identifier of the slot is `renderItemSelection`.
- **Root footer add-ins**: This is used to perform an action when the root footer is changed, and it can be used for notifications. The identifier of the slot is `renderRootFooter`.
- **Group sorting add-ins**: This is used to determine the visual order of the groups where the items will be. The identifier of the slot is `sortGroup`.
- **Item sorting add-ins**: This is used to determine the visual order of the items. The identifier of the slot is `sortItem`.

So, the slots are parts of the code of the component where we can make use of add-ins, but not all add-ins are available for all the slots, so I have compiled the following matrix, where you can see the slots where we can apply each one of the add-ins:

	Post Update	Root Header	Root Selection	Group Selection	Item Selection	Root Footer	Group Sorting	Item Sorting
Notification			X					
Sum selected			X	X				
Select on top							X	X
Insertion order							X	X
Sort by label							X	X
Sort by value							X	X
Sum value			X	X				
Template	X		X	X	X	X		
Accordion	X							

The way to apply an add-in to a slot is to to set the right properties on the component. In the layout perspective, in the component, you can click on the property with the name of the slot ending with **Addin**, and you will get a dialog, where you can start adding the add-ins names. This operation must be done for each row and each add-in. This way, during the execution of the component and for each one of the slots, the add-ins that were added will also be processed.

Add-ins are great, but even greater when we can modify the options of the add-in. The way to do this is by making a call via `setAddInOptions` on the `preExecution` callback of the component itself. The following code is an example of this:

```
this.dashboard.setAddInOptions('postUpdate', 'accordion', {
    group: 'myGroup' //Name of the group who this filter belongs to
});
```

In the preceding code, we are applying options for the add-in `accordion` that will be used in the slot `postUpdate`, which runs when data is imported into a filter's model. The add-in works by hooking a callback to an event emitted by a model whenever the filter is expanded/collapsed. Whenever the user expands a filter, a global event is triggered, so that the remaining filters configured to use this add-in will listen that event. If they share the same group, the same as we set in the earlier options, they will close themselves accordingly. When applying this code, we are setting the group that the filter belongs to, and acts as an accordion, along with the remaining filters that also belong to this group. The group is the only property that we may need to set. The default value here is `group` and if it is not changed, the filter will belong to the group `group`.

For the accordion add-in to work as expected, you will also need to apply the following CSS to the dashboard:

```
.filter-accordion .filter-root-body{
    position: relative;
}
```

For some of the add-ins, you just need to apply them, but when using others, you also are able to change their behavior. For example, for the `sortByLabel` and `sortByValue` add-ins, you can change an option, that is, `ascending`. Setting this option to false would be like the following:

```
this.dashboard.setAddInOptions('sortGroup', 'sortByLabel', {
    ascending: false
});
```

Just don't forget that the add-in should be applied on the `Group Sorting AddIns` property and the name of the add-in, `sortByLabel`, should be added to the list of add-ins to be applied. By default, the list of add-ins is empty.

The add-in `sumValues` can be applied per instance to the render of the root selection slot, and here, the property we have to apply is `formatValue`. This needs to be a function that receives one argument that is the number of selected values and should return the string/value/HTML to be displayed. The name of the option/function is `formatValue`. If you were applying the code, to get it working as the default, you would write the following.

```
this.dashboard.setAddInOptions('renderRootSelection', 'sumValues', {
    formatValue: function(total) {
        return Mustache.render('{{total}}', {
            total: total
        });
    }
});
```

The `template` add-in has two main properties that can be overwritten, which are `template` and `postRender`. For `template`, we should provide a valid string containing the mustache template, but we will get back to the templates later. For `postRender`, it should be defined as a function that will execute/perform some action after the elements appear on the page. The following code is a small example of this:

```
this.setAddInOptions('renderItemSelection', 'template', {
  template:'{{label}}' +
    '<a url="https://www.google.com/#q={{label}}">Google Search</a>',
  postRender: function($tgt, st, opt){
    tgt.find('.filter-item-label a').click(function(event){
      window.open(event.target.attributes.url.value, '_blank');
      event.stopPropagation();
    });
  }
});
```

We are appending a link that, when pressed, will open a new tab in the browser with a Google search about the item clicked on. The `postRender` function will add a click event handler that will open the link in a new tab, and will stop propagation of the event, so that the item does not become selected when only the link is pressed. If the stop propagation was not there, then the item would become selected. The following image is one example of the result:

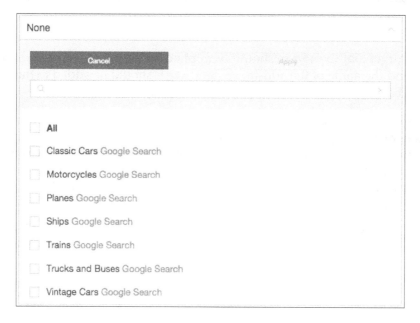

We have already covered the options for the `accordion` add-in.

You can see and check the properties, options, and code in the samples provided for this chapter and component.

Advanced options and configurations

There are more advanced options you can use, and among others, we can customize the strings/messages that are used inside the component. These options are changed in the advanced options property of the component. A function must be defined, and it should return a component object with the options inside.

Changing default messages

To change the default messages, you can use the following function in the advanced options property:

```
function options(){
    return {
        component:{
            Root: {
                strings:{
                    isDisabled: 'No available data'
                }
            }
        }
    };
}
```

The returned JSON structure is changing the string that is applied when there is no data and the component is disabled. Other messages/strings that can be customized are as follows:

- `title`: This overrides the value in the title component property
- `allItems`: This message is displayed when all the items are selected
- `noItems`: This message is displayed when no items are selected
- `btnApply`: This label is displayed for the Apply button
- `btnCancel`: This label is displayed for the Cancel button

This makes it possible and very easy to make the internationalization and localization of the dashboards, but this we will cover in another chapter.

Showing values

It is also possible to show the values related to the available items. The next example will makes it possible:

```
Function options(){
    return {
        component: {
            Item: {
                options: {
                    showValue: true
                }
            }
        }
    };
}
```

You will be able to perform the same operation for the Root and Group elements; you just need to add a similar structure at the same level as for the Item in the previous example.

Now you should be able to make use of the filter component, for single and multiple selections, or even to show the items grouped, using server-side functionality, and apply the add-ins. You should also be able to customize the messages/strings that will be shown. When covering internationalization and localization, you will understand how to apply it here.

Date range input component

With the date range selector, you can select dates within a range of dates. For instance, you can select the last seven days, the last month, or even an interval of dates. Besides the common properties, there are the following ones available:

- **Today**: This option will select today's date as the start and end date.

- **Last 7 days**: This will select the last seven days by setting today's date. The end date will be today's date and the start date will be today's date less seven days.

- **Month to date**: This will select the period starting at the beginning of the current month and ending at the current date.

- **Previous month**: This will select the last day of the last month as the end date and the first day of the last month as the start date.

- **Specific date**: This will let the user select one specific date. The start and end date will be the same.

- **All dates before**: This will select all dates before the selected day. When setting the component, we need to specify the earliest date, starting from today, which can be selected. The start date will always be the start date of the interval specified on the earliest date property. The end date will be the selected day.

- **All dates after**: This will be the opposite of the last one, where we will get all the dates after the selected day until the last date of the interval that is specified as being the latest date. When setting the component, we need to specify the latest date property. The start date will always be the selected day and the end date will be the latest day of the specified interval.

- **Date range**: This lets you select two dates, which will be the start and end date. We need to be cautious when using open dates, as we may get poor performance when making this kind of selection in the MDX queries.

Besides the usual and common properties, we also have available the following:

- **Earliest date**: This can be used to set the date or specific interval to set the earliest date that it is possible to select. The default value is `-1 years`.

- **Latest date**: This can be used to set the date or specific interval to set the latest date that it is possible to select. The default value is `+1 years`.

When setting the earliest and latest date, we can specify a value that can be accepted by the `Date.parse(...)` function. For instance, you can specify a specific date. You can also specify the interval that you want to be calculated, starting from today, such as -1 years or +1 years. You need to specify the operator `-`/`+`, the number, and the time period, such as days, weeks, months, and years.

Default JavaScript date parsing can be different from browser to browser

When parsing dates using different browsers, you will notice that you can and may get different results. On some browsers, you may get a date as expected, but when using another browser, you may not get a date at all. This is because the parsing is done at the browser level and there is not a standard between them.

The available properties to be used besides the common ones are:

- **Single input**: When set to `true`, this will use one input box to show or specify the time interval. When set to `false`, it will use two separated boxes for the start and end dates. The default value is `true`.

- **Input separator**: Used only when a single input is set to `true`. This is used to specify the separator when showing the start and end dates. The default value is >.

- **Can click outside popup**: This is used to specify whether the popup will be closed when clicked outside. The default value is `false`.

- **On open / On close**: This is used to define a function that will be called when the popup opens or closes.

You will notice that on parameters, there is a list of the available parameters, and you must select two of them as being the start and end date. In our example, which you may find in the samples provided, there are two parameters selected, `startDateParam` and `endDateParam`. The first one to be selected will be the start date and the last one will be the end date.

You may have found that there is not a date format property in the date input component. This is not a problem because we can format the dates in `preChange`, after `fireChange` to the parameters. You can specify the format by using the values in the start and end date parameters, and write them to the input box. For instance, you can use the following code:

```
function(start, end) {
    var formatted = Utils.dateFormat(start, 'DD MMM YY') +
                " " + this.inputSeparator + " " +
                Utils.dateFormat(end, 'DD MMM YY');
    this.placeholder('input').val(formatted);
});
```

You can see that I am using the `Utils` module, which is automatically included in the dashboard by CDE, to customize the output of the selected dates.

The multi-button component

From my perspective, the multi-button component can and should be seen as a selector. I have also used it as a tab selector and/or as a radio and checkbox selector, and that's because it's simple to style, and has the same look and feel on all the browsers:

- **Datasource**: When setting a data source, the options available will be the ones from the result of the execution of the query.

- **Values array**: This is used if we want to have to set fixed values without the use of a datasource. It accepts a multidimensional array. Each option should be set using an ID and a value to be displayed.

- **Value as ID**: This was already covered for other selectors. It tells you whether the values and id should be considered as the same.

- **Multiple selection**: This is used to allow or not allow multiple selections. The default value is `false`, so it will not accept multiple options selected at the same time. Set the value to `true` if you want to make it possible.

> **Values array set dynamically inside** `preExecution`
>
> When setting a select component, we should specify one of the properties: `data source` or `values array`. This will set the options that will become available in the dashboard. The values array can be set dynamically in `preExecution`, but for this to be possible, we always need to have a `dummy` value set using CDE. The `preExecution` function will only be executed when one of these properties is defined.

Don't forget that you need to set a parameter so that it's possible to notify another component of the changes. This may also be needed for some other queries.

Please refer to the samples provided with this book, as you will find filters, selectors, and date pickers among the samples. Also, don't forget that you have the samples provided with CDE, where you have a description of the properties that can be used.

Summary

By reading this chapter, you learned about using selectors on a dashboard built with CDE. You should know which components are the most useful and are used to filter data in the dashboard, which does not mean that you can use only components from the selectors group. You will see in the next two chapters that we can also use a table, a chart, or a template component to create interaction on the dashboard.

You should be aware that you can replace the use of the select and multi-select components and make use of the filter component instead. Button and multi-button components can be used to filter data, but can also be used to create interaction on the dashboard, and you can use the multi-button component to replace selections using radio buttons and checkboxes. This is the reason why we didn't cover the radio-button and checkbox components. The multi-button component is much easier to style, and with the knowledge you have gained about the use of other selectors/filters, you should also be able to use them.

6
Tables, Templates, Exports, and Text Components

So, I have told you that we needed to split the last chapter into two. The first one contained components usually used to filter data on the dashboard, and now it's time to present the most important and flexible components to represent data on the dashboard. This is one of the most detailed chapters where you get all the details I could think of.

One important part of building a dashboard is to find the best way to represent data on the dashboard. We should not only focus on showing a table, a chart, or any other component, but also on how to represent the data using that same component. Besides learning how to use some valuable components, you will get a full understanding of the capabilities of those components. I usually see people using few of these capabilities; of components, I believe this is because they don't really know the capabilities and how to apply small changes that can have a huge impact. While reading this chapter, just release your creativity and start thinking about what you could do to with it.

You will learn how to use the table component. It is easy to use, but also very flexible and powerful with some options that allow a lot of customization. The table also allows interaction on the dashboard, by using custom code or expanding the rows to display details. We will also be covering a new component that allows a great level of customization, and all data driven, the template component. The template component leverages the necessary work to repeat some content based on the response of a query. Finally, we will talk about how to export the results to different formats.

There are some more components that can be used, such as queries, freeform, and charts, which will be covered in later chapters, but it's not possible to cover them all. So once again let's focus on the components that are useful for all or most parts of the dashboard.

The components that are covered are listed as follows:

- Table component
- Template component
- Export button component
- Export Popup button component
- Text component

Table component

Besides charts and the template component, the table component is one of the most complete and useful components that we can have on a dashboard. It's very simple to use and we should not think of a table in CDE like traditional tables that we are used to. With the use of add-ins and expanded content we have the ability to create amazing dashboards, which really don't look like a table.

To create tables, CDF uses the `JQuery` plugin `DataTables` (`http://datatables.net/`), which also makes this component exceptional for most parts of the sections on a dashboard. We can extend the capability of `DataTables` itself by using plugins; we just need to know how to use the plugin and the best way to extend the capabilities of the component.

Like any other component, when using it you should set its name, the `htmlObject` where it will be rendered, the data source (in this case it's not an option) and, if needed, parameters and listeners. When setting valid values for the previous properties you can render the dashboard and take a look at the results coming from the query. By default, you will get as many columns on the table as columns on the query results, and the names of the columns will be the names that you have just used on the query or when defining the dashboard data source used for the table.

Besides common properties such as `name`, `parameters`, `listeners`, `htmlObject`, and others that you should already be used to, there are the following properties for the table component. The properties that are available and their usage are explained as follows:

- **Show filter**: It will show a filter at the top right of the table that will allow you to filter the records of the table. The default value is `true`.
- **Searchable cols**: You need to specify the index of the columns that will be searchable when `Show filter` is set to `true`.
- **Info filter**: This is displayed at the bottom right of the table, showing some information about the amount of rows that are being shown.

- **Length change**: This will show a drop-down with some values such as 10, 25, 50, and 100, which when changed will update the number of rows being displayed on the table. The default value is `true`.

- **Page length**: The number of rows to show on. This will be applied once if `Length change` is set to `true`, because later, when changing the size, this value will change. If `Length change` is set to `false` then the table will show exactly the number (integer) of rows that we set in this property.

- **Sort data**: Shows whether the table should allow sorting of data or not. This should to be set to false if you don't want your columns to be sortable. The default value is `true`.

- **Sortable columns**: If you set `Sort data` to `true`, you may also specify the column index and the default sort function, which can be `ASC` or `DESC`. This can also be set in the `preExecution` or `postFetch` of the component by using a multidimensional array such as `[[0, "ASC"], [1, "ASC"]]`.

- **Style**: The style to use on the table, one of the following options: `New`, `Classic`, `Bootstrap`. The default value is `Bootstrap`.

- **Paginate**: Determines whether the table should be paginated. The `page length` will only work when `paginate` is activated. The default value is `true`

- **Paginate on server-side**: We can also activate the pagination on the server-side where you are specifying whether you want the pagination to be handled by CDA. The default value is `true`.

- **Pagination type**: The pagination type that will be used by the final user and that will be displayed below the table. There are some predefined options you can use, or you can set a custom pagination, but of course you need to add the code that needs to be used. The predefined options are:

    ○ Here it shows how it appears:

Showing 1 to 10 of 110 entries	Previous	Next

    ○ Here it shows how it appears as simple numbers:

Showing 1 to 10 of 110 entries	Previous	1	2	3	4	5	...	11	Next

    ○ Here it shows how it appears in full:

Showing 1 to 10 of 110 entries	First	Previous	Next	Last

○   Here it shows how it appears as full numbers:

| Showing 1 to 10 of 110 entries | First | Previous | 1 | 2 | 3 | 4 | 5 | ... | 11 | Next | Last |

○   Here it shows how it appears as two numbers:

| Showing 1 to 10 of 110 entries | | |

Table pagination

You will get the same rows on the table as rows on the `resultset` of the query, but they will all be displayed on the page, or not, depending on some of the property definitions. There are two properties, `Length Change` and `Page Length`, which will change the number of rows to display. If `Length Change` is set to `true` it will be possible for the user to change the number of rows that the dashboard is displaying. `Page Length` is used to define the number of rows to display at the execution of the component. Of course this can also change the number of available pages.

Depending on the number of pages and elements on the table, you can give the user a better experience when navigating through the pages, so choose the pagination type that better adapts to the user experience.

The pagination on the server-side is really useful if you have lots of records that are returned back to the component. Let's suppose you are rendering 100,000 of rows on the dashboard. This will not perform because there are a lot of elements that should be rendered on the page. It will be even worse when using add-ins as they will need some extra code and possibly more elements will need to be displayed. Anyway, it's also not good practice to display rows that the user will not look at and will just make them lose focus on the important aspects.

If you are not trying to display that number of rows but you want to have pagination on the dashboard so as not to display more than 20 rows, per instance, and your query is not very well performed, just use the pagination on the server-side.

Internationalization and localization

The `DataTables` plugin provides a way to implement the internationalization and localization of the table elements, not the content because that's the responsibility of the query. We might or not get the results of the query already translated, but we can specify the translation of the elements that are part of the table it self, such as the pagination and other text that may be in buttons or other elements. The following properties are available for internationalization and localization:

- `oLanguage`: Used to set the language information presented by `DataTables`. Should use a JSON object such as `https://www.datatables.net/plug-ins/i18n/English`.

- `Language`: Used to set the language information presented by `DataTables`. Should specify the file where the JSON object containing the translation is available.

You can download or make use of **Content Delivery Network (CDN)** files that are available as alternatives to the static files on your server. The property `oLanguage` overwrites the `Language` property. So when setting `oLanguage`, CDF will not look to `Language`.

When setting the object without using an external file, we should set `oLanguage` as:

```
{
    "emptyTable":      "No data available in table",
    "info":            "Showing _START_ to _END_ of _TOTAL_ entries",
    ...
    "search":          "Search:",
    "zeroRecords":     "No matching records found"
}
```

An example of the `Language` property is:

```
{ "url":"//cdn.datatables.net/plug-ins/1.10.7/i18n/English.json" }
```

Another, more dynamic, option to use is `preExecution`, which defines the language to use. The code should be similar to the following:

```
function() {
    var cd = this.chartDefinition;
    var languages = {
        'en_US': "//cdn.datatables.net/plug-ins/1.10.7/i18n/English.
json",
        'pt_PT': "//cdn.datatables.net/plug-ins/1.10.7/i18n/
Portuguese.json"
```

```
    };
    delete cd.oLanguage;
    cd.language = {
        "url": languages[this.dashboard.context.locale]
    };
}
```

Draw function

Property	Default Value	Description
Draw Function		Used to place a function that will be executed every time we change the table, when rendering, sorting, filtering, changing the page, and changing the number of visible rows. This can be used to manipulate the DOM of the table each time the table suffers a change. Those kinds of change will not trigger postExecution, so we can't use it for this case.

The use of drawFunction is pretty much the same as postExecution except for the fact that it will be triggered almost every time any change happens to the table. We should therefore avoid using it, and when doing so, we should be very cautious with the code so that performance does not suffer.

Column formats, types, width, and headers

Property	Default Value	Description
Column Format		Here we can set the column format and specify the format for the content of the cells of each column. The format should be specified as the sprintf options already covered in *Chapter 3, Building the Dashboard Using CDF*.
Column Types		Column Types are to specifies the behavior of the cells for each one of the columns or even for the rows.
Column Widths		Column Widths is used to specify the width of each one of the columns. Don't forget that you should avoid absolute values such as px and instead use relative values such as %. This is very important when building a dashboard that needs to be responsive and/or adaptive.

Property	Default Value	Description
Columns Headers		The table component will use the names that are coming from the query or the column names that you just defined on the data source being used.

If you are building a more advanced and dynamic dashboard, you could set the properties in a dynamic way by using `preExecution` or, even better, using `postFetch`, making use of the results of the query to define what the user will get.

On the sample provided for this chapter, you will find that on the desktop we display all the columns, totals, and values for each territory, but when shifting to a mobile dashboard, we will only get the columns for the totals. This is because there is no space to display all the columns when on a mobile dashboard, like when using a mobile phone. This is done during execution time, so we need to be able to make those changes during the size change of the window. We can make the properties on `preExecution` or even on `postFetch` before rendering the table, but first we need to define the handler when the table should be updated. The first part is to create some code on the `preInit` of the dashboard. Let's forget, for now, the part about responsive charts. We already covered this earlier. Let's focus on the table changes, depending on whether you are using a mobile or another device:

```
dashboard.postInit = function(e) {
  var self = this;
  var resizeTable = function() {
    var screenSize = '';
    if (matchMedia('only screen and (max-width: 992px)').matches) {
      screenSize = 'mobile';
    } else {
      screenSize = 'desktop';
    }
    if (screenSize != dashboard.getParameterValue('changeTable')) {
      dashboard.fireChange('changeTable', screenSize);
    }
  };
  var throttle = _.throttle(resizeTable, 100, {leading: false});
  $(document).ready(function() {
    $(window).resize(throttle);
  });
};
```

The previous code is used on the postInit of the dashboard. The trick is to listen to the changes on the resize of the window, but only notify the table to be updated just when we change from or to mobile. The only change we want on the table is to change the columns to be displayed, because the table will already respond to changes on the size, if we are using Bootstrap as the grid layout system for the dashboard. Of course you may consider a better validation than the one I am using to check whether we are using a mobile version. Here we are just checking the max-width of the screen and changing the behavior based on that.

So, the preExecution of the chart should look like this:

```
function() {
    this.lifecycle = {silent: true};
    var screenSize = this.dashboard.getParameterValue('changeTable');
    if (screenSize=='desktop') {
        cd.colFormats = ["%s","%d","%.0f","%.1f","%d","%.0f","%.1f","%
d","%.0f","%.1f","%d","%.0f","%.1f","%d","%.0f","%.1f"];
        cd.colTypes = ["string","numeric","numeric","trendArrow","nume
ric","numeric","trendArrow","numeric","numeric","trendArrow","numeric"
,"numeric","trendArrow","numeric","numeric","trendArrow"];
    } else {
        cd.colFormats = ["%s","%d","%.0f","%.1f","%d","%.0f","%.1f","%
d","%.0f","%.1f","%d","%.0f","%.1f","%d","%.0f","%.1f"];
        cd.colTypes = ["string","numeric","numeric","trendArrow","hidd
en","hidden","hidden","hidden","hidden","hidden","hidden","hidden","hi
dden","hidden","hidden","hidden"];
    }
}
```

On the previous block of code, in the preExecution of the table, we can see that the first line of the table is this.lifecycle={silent:true}, and it's used to silent the lifecycle by setting its value to true, so we won't see spinning when updating the table. The remaining code is used to check whether we are displaying the table on a desktop or on a mobile screen. If not on the desktop, we hide most parts of the columns because they will not fit.

You can avoid the spinning wheel that blocks the UI

When a component is updated, you will get dashboard interactivity blocked, showing a spinning wheel. This means that components are waiting for queries to be executed while rendering the elements on the dashboard. This is useful to notify the user that we are still waiting for results and avoids the user having to change the selector again. If, for some reason, you want to disable it for a particular component, you just need to apply the following code on the preExcution or postExecution of a component: this.lifecycle={silent:true}.

We still have a problem because, the first time the components are rendered, the parameter screenSize is still not filled with a value, because this is only done when the document is finally ready and when the code in the preInit function is executed. The previous code, show how we are able to do this validation on the preExeution of the table component. We should also place some code on the preInit of the dashboard. The following block of code shows exactly what we need. To check the screen size and set the value using a parameter that we can later use in the components, use the following:

```
dashboard.preInit = function(e) {
    this.addParameter('changeTable', '');
    var screenSize = '';
    if (matchMedia('only screen and (max-width: 992px)').matches) {
        screenSize = 'mobile';
    } else {
        screenSize = 'desktop';
    }
    if (screenSize != dashboard.getParameterValue('changeTable')) {
        dashboard.fireChange('changeTable', screenSize);
    }
};
```

You should be conscious that there are multiple ways to achieve this, and it's a good exercise to think of another way to do it. The first thing to do would be to create a function to involve the repeated code on the preInit and postInit functions. Another way would be to place all the code in preInit. It should work because the code that will be executed will only be executed when the document is ready.

When resizing the dashboard, we are requesting it to be updated, so on the postExecution we can check whether we have a windows size capable of displaying the full set of columns. If not, we will just stick with the totals by changing the column types and changing some of the columns to c hidden type.

Expanding content

There is another great functionality on table components: the expanded content, or the ability to show content below the row that was clicked. This way we can display details for a particular row on a table. The content to be displayed inside the tables is defined by the developer, as with any other content to be displayed on the dashboard. The difference is that, at the start of the dashboard, these elements will not be available. The following are the properties that you define when you want to create expandable content:

- Expand On-Click: Expand allows you to have a container inside a table row the table. When clicking on a row of the table, you can get content below the row. This property enables this feature. The default value is false.

- Expand Parameters: Parameters that will target a fireChange. We need to specify the parameter(s) and column(s) index(es) of the table. The index will be used to get the value that will be filling the parameter. Index(es) start from 0, as the first column. It accepts an array of arrays, where each array is a pair of parameter and column indexes. This will only be used when Expand on-click is set to true.

- Expand Container: This is the parent container, with the layout elements that will be displayed below the clicked column. This will only be used when Expand On-Click is set to true.

Let's suppose that we wanted to show some details about a row on the table. The following screenshot is an example. You can see three charts inside the row that was clicked; the example we are going to build just uses one chart. The options that you need to apply for one chart are the same as for the others.

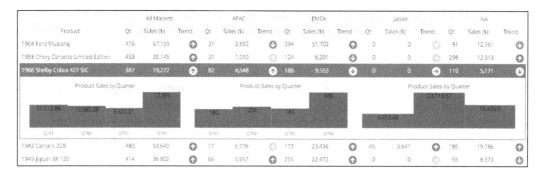

To achieve this result, you need to start by enabling the `Expand On-Click` option on the table, so the very first step is to change the value of this property to true. The second step is to create the layout, queries, and components that we want to be displayed as details. For that we need to specify a parent container that will be hidden, and that table component will make it visible below the row that has been clicked.

On the layout perspective, create a row and a column to be the placeholder for the table. You should also create another row and as many rows inside as components to display. The names could be `salesByProduct` and `prodSalesByTerritory`.

The second row should have a name, as we need to use it to specify to the parent container where all the HTML will be displayed when we click on the row. So, set a second row with the name `tableDetailsContainer`.

On the components perspective you should create a parameter such as `productParam` with the default value of `1968 Ford Mustang`. Using the data source perspective, create two queries using the steel wheels connection and Mondrian schema. The query should be:

```
WITH
MEMBER [Measures].[Trend] as IIF(ISEMPTY(([Time].CURRENTMEMBER.lag(1),
[Measures].[Sales])) OR [Measures].[Sales]=0, 0, ([Measures].[Sales]-
([Time].CURRENTMEMBER.lag(1), [Measures].[Sales]))/[Measures].
[Sales])+0
MEMBER [Measures].[Sales ($)] as [Measures].[Sales]+0
MEMBER [Measures].[Qt] as [Measures].[Quantity]+0
SELECT
NON EMPTY {[Measures].[Qt], [Measures].[Sales ($)], [Measures].
[Trend]} ON COLUMNS,
NON EMPTY {[Product].[Product].Members} ON ROWS
FROM [SteelWheelsSales]
Where [Time].[2004]
```

And another query should be:

```
WITH
    MEMBER [Measures].[Sales in Time] AS [Measures].[Sales]
    SET PRODUCTFILTER AS FILTER([Product].[Product].MEMBERS,
[Product].CURRENTMEMBER.NAME = '${productParam}')
Select
    { [Markets].[APAC] , [Markets].[EMEA] , [Markets].[NA] } on
COLUMNS,
    { PRODUCTFILTER } on ROWS
FROM [SteelWheelsSales]
Where [Measures].[Sales in Time]
```

For this last one you will need to specify a parameter with the name `productParam` that can also have a default value of `1968 Ford Mustang`. The names for the queries are `salesByProductQuery` and `prodSalesByTerritoryQuery`.

The first one will be used in the table, and the second will be used to get details about the selected product when selecting a row on the table. The next step is to create a table with have the following properties.

Property	Value
name	products
datasource	salesByProductQuery
htmlObject	salesByProduct
paginate	True
Expand On-click	True
Expand parameters	[[0, 'productParam']]
Expand Container Object	tableDetailsContainer
Execute at start	True

The table has some common properties such as `Name`, `Datasource`, and `htmlObject` but we also have `Expand On-Click` activated. The `Expand Container Object` is used to specify the parent container where all the HTML to be presented below the row is clicked, and `Expand Parameters` to specify which parameter is needed to be a target for a `fireChange` using the index value of the columns from where we need to extract the value to be set in the parameter. Looking to the second query, you will notice that we are using it to filter the product that the user has selected. On the table component, we are specifying that the first column should be used, so the name of the product will be set to the parameter `productParam`, so that the table can be updated each time we click on a row. This way, the components with the details will be notified that they need to update and be rendered below a row of the table.

There is a need to have a second component to display the details, so let's have a chart. It can be a pie chart or whatever. For now, you can use a bar chart with the following properties:

Property	Value
name	products
datasource	prodSalesByTerritoryQuery
htmlObject	prodSalesByTerritory
listerners	productParam
parameters	[['productParam', 'productParam']]
Execute at start	False

Here we are creating the components where the details for the selected product will be displayed. The properties are already well known, so you just want to make a quick note about Execute at start. This property is set to false because, the first time we render the dashboard, the user hasn't yet selected/clicked a product so we don't want to show the chart with details for a product. Once the user clicks on a row/product, a fireChange will be triggered and the chart component will be notified, because it's listening to the parameter and will be updated with the right values for the selected product. At that time, the component will be rendered inside the htmlObject that is inside the parent container, which has already been placed below the table that was selected.

Making use of add-ins

There are different column types or add-ins, which can change what's displayed as the content of each cell of a column. Inside the community and at Webdetails, the column types are usually referred to as add-ins, and the way to apply them is just by changing the property Column Types and setting the type for each one of the columns that will be available on the table.

By default, the Datatables plugin provides three types:

- string: To display the text in the cell
- numeric: To display a number in the cell
- hidden: When using this type, the column will not be displayed

CDF also extends the column types we can use inside the component. The following image shows the column types or add-ins:

The numbers on the previous image correspond to the column types or add-ins that we are covering using the following numbered list. The ones that are available are:

1. groupHeaders
2. clippedText
3. sparklines
4. dataBar
5. trendArrow
6. circle
7. cccBulletChart
8. formattedText
9. localizedText
10. hyperlink

There is another add-in that is not displayed in the image: the template add-in. We will be covering this in the next chapter.

When you select one add-in just by setting the column type, you will get a result using the default options. If you need to give them a different aspect or behavior, you can customize them by changing the add-in options.

As already explained, we need to change the add-in by setting the type on the column types property. The way to extend the options is to add some code on the preExecution or postFetch functions of the component. Let's see an example using the sparklines add-in.

A Sparkline is a very small line chart that is typically drawn without any axes or coordinates. One use case is to use the variation of a measurement over time, for example for the temperature over the last 12 months.

Just by including the following line inside preExecution, we change the Sparkline type from line to bar:

```
this.setAddInOptions("colType","sparkline", {"type":"bar"});
```

I always like to have the options on a variable as it makes the code more readable. The previous example is not ideal, but we will see in the following example code where the code is so readable at first glance.

Among the properties that are applied to the `Sparkline` add-in, we have the type, which can be, line, bar, pie, and others, but let's cover that later when we go over the properties for this add-in. Using the previous code inside the `preExecution` function will change the representation of the values using bars in place of a line, which is the default value for the type when using this add-in.

This applies to the options for all the columns that use the column type `sparkline`, but what if we want to have a column where the values should be represented by bars and another one by a bar and a line? That's also possible by using a function that, depending on the column that is being processed, returns one object of properties, with the type set to bar, and another one using a line. The following code is one example of this:

```
var options = function(state){
        if(state.colIdx == "3"){
                return {type:'bar'};
        }
    };
this.setAddInOptions("colType","sparkline", options);
```

First, we have a variable that will be a function that receives one argument represented with the name state. This function will be executed for all the cells of the columns that have the column type Sparkline, so inside the function and using the state variable we will get access to one object that represents its context. For each cell, we will have access to `colIdx`, `rowIdx`, `value`, the `target` element on the DOM, and all the table data returned from the query. We can also have access to `colFormat`, if we have defined one using the property column Formats of the table component.

Having all the information mentioned previously, we can change the behavior of the add-in, for each instance, and also have a condition that will return the options for an add-in depending on the row that we are processing, or even the value of a previous row or column.

Now that you know how to change the option to pass to change the defaults and options of an add-in, let's cover add-ins and their options.

The way to apply options to each add-in is always the same; it is just the options that are applied that are different. Let's cover each one of the available add-ins.

groupHeaders

Based on the value of the cell being rendered on a column, the rows can be grouped. In the same columns, if the values of the rows are similar from one row to another, a group can be created. If that's the case, a group header is created and inserted under any of the following circumstances:

- On the first row of all records

- After a higher-level group header, when using group headers for more than one column

- When the value for the current cell differs from the one immediately before it

To be able to create groups, rows must be sorted on the columns where groups should be created. In the CDE samples, there is a great example on how to use the `aoSortingFixed` option of the `Datatables JQuery` plugin, which is provided when you install it and is also available under `/public/plugin-samples/CDE/Require Samples/CDE References/Addins`.

We have already seen that all add-ins have defaults that can be overwritten by passing the options to the add-in. The defaults are:

- `hide`: Its default value is true and will hide the column from the table, because the value is already on the header that identifies the group. If, for some reason, you want to display the column, you just need to set the option to `false`.

- `columnHeadersInGroups`: Repeats the column headers for each one of the groups, meaning that for each group the final user will also see the headers of the columns. The default value is `false`.

- `textFormat`: This is a function that receives three arguments, as follows:
  - **The value**: The value being processed
  - **The status**: A Json object where you can find:
    The row and column being processed or get access to all datasets returned from the query
  - **The option**: The last argument is the option used on the add-in

The function should return a string that will be the name of the group. You can overwrite this function and, based on the value, status, and options passed to the add-in, return a custom string that will be the header for the group. See the following default function:

```
textFormat: function(v, st, opt) {
  return st.colFormat ? sprintf(st.colFormat,v) : v;
}
```

clippedText

The `clippedText` add-in can be used when the text to be displayed inside a cell is bigger than the space that is available. The part of the text that cannot to be displayed on the same line will be hidden and ellipses will be shown.

The options available for this add-in are:

- `showTooltip`: This is for, when hovering over the text, you want to display a tooltip with the full text. The default value is true.

- `useTipsy`: This is if the tooltip shown is not the default HTML tooltip but instead you want to use the Tipsy JQuery plugin to display the tooltip. When set to true it will show a fancier tooltip. The default value is false, so if you want to use it, you will need to set it to true.

- `style`: This is the style to apply to the element inside the cell of the table. The style is an object with CSS.

The following code is one example of how to apply the style to bold text and activate the `Tipsy JQuery` plug-in:

```
var options = {
  showTooltip: true,
  useTipsy: true,
  style: {'font-weight': 'bold'}
};
this.setAddInOptions("colType", "clippedText", options);
```

sparkline

This add-in is based on the JQuery `sparklines`, which generates small inline charts using the data returned by the query. It allows using the properties of the `sparklines` plugin itself and generating different types of inline chart. It can generate inline charts such as line, bar, stacked bar, pie, bullet, composite, discrete, and box plot.

It is a really simple but powerful add-in, which gives the final user a great understanding of the data, and also gives multiple options to the developer. It's a great way to give the final user a distribution of the values over time, or to provide insights if the user needs to get into the details of the values he is looking at.

You can go to the `Try It Out` section at `http://ominipotent.net/jquery.sparkline`. Select the type of chart, change the necessary properties to get the result you expect, and copy the code that is automatically generated, because those are the properties to send to the add-in.

When using this add-in, you need to return from the query, and for the cell you want to have the add-in displayed, a column containing a string with all the values separated by a comma. For each instance, sales by month for a particular year would be:

```
"7498.9,4517.9,0.0,5774.7,0.0,3922.6,9160.4,13063.2,0.0,6934.6,13390.
6,2891.7"
```

There are multiple ways to achieve this result and this will depend on the query type you are using in CDA. If using Kettle, there are also multiple ways to do it. It may be you just need to use one or more steps to join all the values into a string column type; just don't forget to separate them by commas. When using SQL you may need to concatenate all the values but by always combining single values with a comma. When using MDX, it's very simple; you can make use of the Generate function like this:

```
GENERATE(
    DESCENDANTS([Time].[2004], [Time].[Months]),
    CAST(([Measures].[Sales]+0) AS STRING),
    ',')
```

You can also get a complete query example on the samples provided for the table component inside the Chapter 6 folder, available in the samples supplied with this book. You will find a subfolder where you will find three samples for the table component.

The only property that is mandatory is the following:

- **type**: It's the type of the chart and also a property that is passed from the add-in to the Sparkline Plugin. The default value is line, which will generate a line chart with the remaining default values for the line chart of the Sparkline Plugin.

By going to the Try It Out section of the Sparkline Plugin you can check that the properties will differ from chart type to chart type. There are also some advanced options that the Sparkline Plug-in has, which are perfectly usable inside the add-in, and that's because what the add-in does is make a call to the plugin, and passing the options you have set. For each instance, if you want to generate one bar chart and change some of the properties, you would use code such as:

```
var options = { type: 'bar', barWidth: 6};
this.setAddInOptions("colType", "sparkline", options);
```

dataBar

This add-in is used to display a horizontal bar that represents the values returned from the query. The size of the bar is the relation between the value and the minimum and maximum values for all the rows on that same column. The add-in makes use of the Raphael JavaScript library to draw the bar, which is an SVG element, and the available options for the add-in are:

- `width`: Used to define the size of the parent container, the element that will contain the SVG representing the bar. The default value is 98%.

- `widthRatio`: This is the ratio of the bar to the parent element. The size of its parent is set by the width option. The default value is 1.

- `height`: Used to define the height in pixels of the bar.

- `align`: Used to define the alignment of the bar. Can be left or right. By default, it will be aligned at the left.

- `startColor`: The color of the bar can be a gradient. This option is used to define the color to the top part of the bar. The default is #55A4D6.

- `endColor`: Used to define the color to the bottom part of the bar. The default is #448FC8.

- `stroke`: Used to specify the color of the border.

- `max`: The maximum and minimum values are used to calculate the size and left and right position of the bar. This option is used to specify a fixed value or a function that returns a value. When it is not set, the value will be the max value for all the rows for that same column.

- `min`: The same as previous, but for the minimum value.

- `includeValue`: Used to specify whether the value should be visible or not. The default is false. Change it to true to also see the value.

- `absValue`: Used to tell the add-in whether it should apply the absolute value of the number to represent.

- `valueFormat`: This function accepts four arguments: the value, format, status, and options.

One example of the code needed to change the options would be as follows:

```
var myself = this;
require(['cdf/dashboard/Sprintf'], function(sprintf) {
  var options = {
    widthRatio:0.6,
    height: 15,
    align: 'left',
```

```
      startColor: "#3366cc",
      endColor: "#3366cc",
      stroke: null,
      absValue: true,
      includeValue: true,
      valueFormat: function(v, format, st, opt) {
        return "" + sprintf(format || "%.1f", v);
      }
    };
    myself.setAddInOptions("colType", "dataBar", options);
  });
```

The previous code is wrapped by a require function, because we need to use a sprint function that's not available in the scope of the `preExecution` of the component.

trendArrow

The `trendArrow` add-in is very simple, it presents an up or down arrow depending on whether we have a value below the threshold, which by default, is set to zero. This means that values above the value defined as the up threshold will be represented with a green and upper arrow, and values below the value defined as the down threshold will be represented with a red arrow pointing down. Values that are between the ranges defined as the threshold are represented by a yellow equals symbol.

There is also the chance that values below the threshold are good values, so the add-in is also able to handle that. Values above the threshold are shown with a red arrow pointing up, and when below the threshold will be represented by a green arrow pointing down. To achieve this, we only need to set the good option to false, that means that upper values are considered bad, and lower values are considered good. Setting this option will change the color witch upper or lower values are represented. The threshold is also configurable, so it's better to cover now the options that are available:

- good: Used to define whether values above the thresholds are considered good or bad values. By default, it's set to true meaning that the values above the thresholds are good values. When set to false it will set the opposite.

- threshold: It sets the upper and lower thresholds. The threshold accepts an object with two keys, up and down, to set both threshold values. For each instance setting a range would be like {up: 30, down: 60}. You can see in the following sample code, where the valueFormat property is explained.

- includeValue: Used to set whether the value will be shown together with the trend arrows. By default, it is set to false. If you need the value to be displayed, just set it to true.

- `valueFormat`: Is a function used to format the value to be displayed together with trend arrows when the option `includeValue` is set to true. The function accepts four arguments: the value, format, status, and options. The `value` is the value that comes from the query to that same cell of the table. The `format` is the format specified in the columns format of the table component. The `status` is where you can get to know what columns and row is being processed at the time, or where you can get access to the full dataset returned from the query. Finally, the `options` parameter, is where you can find the options that were set to be used by the add-in. The code to apply the options would be as follows:

```
var myself = this;
require(['cdf/dashboard/Sprintf'], function(sprintf) {
  var options = {
      good: true,
      includeValue: false,
      valueFormat: function(v, format, st, opt) {
        return sprintf(format || "%.1f", v);
      },
      thresholds: {up: 0, down: 0}
  };
  myself.setAddInOptions("colType", "trendArrow", options);
});
```

It's possible to change the CSS to change the arrows, showing other symbols and/or colors. To be honest I don't like the default ones, so I always change them.

For each instance, if you have some images that you want to use, you may do so by changing the CSS. You may add the following CSS to your dashboard and the defaults will be overwritten; you just need to change the path and filename of the image. Do not forget that, if the images have a different size, you may also need to change a few more rules:

```
.trend.up.good { background: url("img/up-good.png"); }
.trend.neutral { background: url("img/neutral.png"); }
.trend.down.good { background: url("img/down-good.png"); }
.trend.up.bad { background: url("img/up-bad.png"); }
.trend.down.bad { background: url("img/down-bad.png"); }
```

I always avoid using images on the dashboards as using icon fonts has more advantages. You can change the size (without losing any definition), change the colors, or apply a shadow just by using CSS. Besides that, your page becomes lighter.

To apply an icon font, perform the following:

```css
table .trend {
    position: relative;
}
table .trend:after {
    position: absolute;
    background: none;
    font: normal normal normal 20px/1 FontAwesome;
    top: -5px;
    left: -3px;
}
table .trend.down.good {
    background: none;
}
table .trend.down.good:after {
    content: "\f0ab";
    color: red;
}
table .trend.up.good {
    margin-top: 5px;
    background: none;
}
table .trend.up.good:after {
    content: "\f0aa";
    color: green;
}
table .trend.neutral.good {
    background: none;
}
table .trend.neutral.good:after {
    content: "\f0a9";
    color: #ccc;
}
```

You can find more information about using icon fonts by looking at:
https://fortawesome.github.io/Font-Awesome/icons/.

You will find the code inside the table samples of this book. Notice that this example was only set when values upper of the threshold are good. Otherwise you would need to make similar rules but using bad besides good.

circle

This add-in can be used to represent values as circles. The circles are represented through an SVG, which is the result of the use of the Raphael JavaScript Library. Here we always need to set some options, otherwise you would always get the same size and color that, by default, have default values of four for the size and black for the color. The options are:

- `canvasSize`: Used to set the size, width, and height of the SVG element. By default, its value is set to 10. It accepts a fixed value or a function that can return the value to use as the size. The same value will be used for the width and height.

- `radius`: Used to set the radius of the circle. The default value is set to 4, but you can use a function to return the value to use as the radius. The function will receive one argument that is the value, and the value can be a string. Don't forget that, to see a full circle, the radius should not be higher than half of the `canvasSize`.

- `color`: Used to set the color for the circle. You can return any value that represents a valid color when representing SVGs. By default, its value is set to black. It accepts a fixed value or a function that can return the string, which represents the color.

- `title`: Used to set a function that returns the value to display when hovering the circle. The default value is:

  ```
  title: function(st, opt) { return "Value: " + st.value; }
  ```

Let's suppose that you wanted to show a circle where the radius is calculated based on the percentage relative to the maximum value of the quantities sold, where the lowest value will have the smallest radius and the highest value will have the highest radius. The color is calculated based on the values of sales. To be able to achieve this, we need to get two values from the query, quantity, and sales. For this example, the value is a string that will be a concatenation of both values separated by a comma. You can do it the way you want; we just used a member calculated as:

```
MEMBER [Measures].[circle] AS
  CAST(([Time].[2004], [Measures].[Quantity])+0 AS STRING) ||
  "," ||
  CAST(([Time].[2004], [Measures].[Sales])+0 AS STRING)
```

The code to apply the options would be as follows:

```
var options = {
    canvasSize: 20,
    radius: function(st) {
      var values = st.tableData.map(function(e){
        return Number(_.first(e[st.colIdx].split(',')));
      });
      var tblMax = _.max(values),
          tblMin = _.min(values),
          value = Number(_.first(st.value.split(','))),
          size = (value-tblMin)/(tblMax-tblMin);
      return (20*size)/2;
    },
    color: function(st) {
      var values = st.tableData.map(function(e){
        return Number(_.last(e[st.colIdx].split(',')));
      });
      var tblMax = _.max(values),
          tblMin = _.min(values),
          value = Number(_.last(st.value.split(','))),
          size = (value-tblMin)/(tblMax-tblMin),
          red = Math.min(255, Math.round(510-2*255*size)),
          green = Math.min(255, Math.round(2*255*size));
      return "rgb(" + red + "," + green + ",0)";
    },
    title: function(st, opt) {
      var sales = Number(_.first(st.value.split(','))),
          quant = Number(_.last(st.value.split(',')));
      return "(#): " + Utils.numberFormat(sales, "0") + " " +
             "($): " + Utils.numberFormat(quant, "0.0");
    }
};
this.setAddInOptions("colType", "circle", options);
```

The inside options we are defining are the size for the SVG element, and functions for the `radius`, `color`, and `title`. The `radius` function will return the radius to be used based on the calculations using the value, min, and max values for all the rows being displayed. Color is also a function that will return the RGB string with the colors for red and green, also based on the value passed as an argument.

cccBulletChart

This can represent a bullet chart with the values that come from the query for the same cell. Here you need to return all the values to use on the bullet chart, separated by a comma. The options that you have available are all the options for the CCC charts that we are going to cover later, but the following is the code to apply the default options:

```
var options = {
    height: 40,
    animate: false,
    orientation: "horizontal",
    bulletSize: 16,
    bulletSpacing: 150,
    bulletMargin: 5,
    bulletRanges: [30, 80, 100],
    extensionPoints: {
        "bulletMarker_shape": "triangle",
        "bulletTitle_textStyle": "green",
        "bulletMeasure_fillStyle": "black",
        "bulletRuleLabel_font": "8px sans-serif",
        "bulletRule_height": 5
    }
};
this.setAddInOptions("colType", "cccBulletChart", options);
```

formattedText

This add-in is used to specify a custom format to the value that is supposed to appear on the table. The default option is the following:

- **textFormat**: This is used to return the value to display on the table. The function receives three arguments. The arguments are the `value` being processed, the `status` where you can know the row and column being processed or get access to all datasets returned from the query, and the last argument is the `options` used on the add-in. See the following default function:

```
textFormat: function(v, st, opt) {
    return st.colFormat ? sprintf(st.colFormat,v) : v;
}
```

This is a really simple but useful add-in. We will see later that we can extend and write our own add-ins, but if using this add-in you can almost do whatever you want. Of course, if writing a new add-in, we have the ability to include the JavaScript file. When using this add-in you would need to include some code on the preExecution or postFetch of the component. You can overwrite the textFormat function and, based on the arguments that are passed, the value, status, and options passed to the add-in return a string that will be rendered on the cell of the table being processed. Here you can return a string that is the HTML to be rendered inside the cell, so as you can imagine you have almost no limits here.

Let's see a small example where you need to display the negative value using red. If that's the case, just using the columns format will not be sufficient, so the formatted text add-in is an option, maybe the easiest one. You would need to include the following lines inside the preExecution of the table component:

```
var myself = this;
require(['cdf/dashboard/Sprintf'], function(sprintf) {
  var options = {
    textFormat: function(v, st, opt) {
      var cssClass = ((v < 0) ? 'negative' : 'positive'),
          value = st.colFormat ? sprintf(st.colFormat,v) : v ;
      return '<div class='+cssClass+'">'+value+'</div>';
    }
  };
  myself.setAddInOptions("colType", "formattedText", options);
});
```

We also need to add some CSS similar to the following line:

```
.formattedText .negative {color: red;}
```

You will find on the JavaScript code the textFormat function returning a div element with the formatted value, which will use the mask specified on the columns format of the table. We can get the specified format from the st.colFormat from the st object. This way we could execute the sprint function and format the value with that mask. The div element will have a CSS class that will be negative if the value is less than zero, and positive otherwise, so that we can apply some CSS and turn the negative values to red. All of the code is wrapped by a require function because we need the sprintf library to be included and available when executing the code.

localizedText

The `localizedText` add-in allows the table to display content based on a language that is set for the browser. Using this add-in you may delegate to i18n the translations of the values returned from the query.

If the range of values returned is not too big, and if they are not changing over time, it's fine to use this add-in; otherwise, we have a drawback because you need to have all the translations in one file, and if there is no translation for the current value being displayed, i18n will not be able to do it. When adding new rows in the database, we would also need to add them on the property files that are going to be used by i18n. So, if the range of values is too big and change over time, maybe you should consider doing it on the back end, using a Dynamic Schema Processor, SQL Generator, or any other technique available in Pentaho; but that is not the purpose of this book, so let's skip this option.

So, if you have to meet the requirements to use the add-in, or for any other reason you need to use it, let's see how to do it. We have not yet discussed how to use i18n on the dashboards but we will do it later, but we need to have a brief introduction.

When building a dashboard that needs to handle internationalization and localization, and they all should, you must specify a file with the name `messages_ supported_languages.properties`, which should be in the same folder as the dashboard. That's the way i18n will read the message files and their content will be key/value pairs where:

- key: will be the `<language>` and/or `<language>_<COUNTRY>`, where `<language>` is the lowercase code for the language and `<COUNTRY>` is the uppercase country code
- value: can be any description of the language/country

One example of the `messages_supported_languages.properties` file would be:

```
en=English
en_US=English (United States)
en_UK=English (United Kingdom)
pt=Portuguese
pt_PT=Portuguese (Portugal)
pt_BR=Portugues (Brazil)
```

Here we don't need to specify the fallback file, it will use the one with the name `messages.properties`. We can delegate i18n messages to three specific files, which need to be placed in the same folder as the dashboard. The standard in Pentaho is to have the names using the following rules:

- `messages_<language>_<COUNTRY>.properties`: These files are the ones that contain the translations for a particular country for a language, where `<language>` should be replaced by the lowercase language code and `<COUNTRY>` should be replaced by the uppercase country code (per instance: `messages_en_US.properties`, `messages_en_UK.properties`, `messages_pt_PT.properties`, and `messages_pt_BR.properties`).

- `messages_<language>.properties`: These files are the ones that will contain the translations for a particular language, not specifying the country, where `<language>` should be replaced by the lowercase language code (per instance: `messages_en.properties` and `messages_pt.properties`).

- `messages.properties`: This is the fallback file, where no language or country is specified. Here we will not need to specify a language or country.

Messages, or translations, can and should be shared by the different files and whenever that happens the following rule applies:

- The messages keys placed at `messages_<language>_<COUNTRY>.properties` will override similar ones placed at `messages_<language>.properties`, which in turn will overwrite the `messages.properties`

If we wanted to display a hierarchical structure of the `messages.properties` files, it would look as follows:

```
+ messages.properties
++ messages_en.properties
++++ messages_en_US.properties
++++ messages_en_UK.properties
++ messages_pt.properties
++++ messages_pt_PT.properties
++++ messages_pt_BR.properties
```

We will need to specify the `messages.properties` files, which are also a list of key/value pairs where the key will be translated to the values specified. As an example, let's suppose we have a column that reveals which month had the highest value of sales. If the fallback language is English, the `messages.properties` file should be specified like:

```
Jan=January
...
Nov=November
Dec=December
```

The `messages_EN.properties` files would be similar, but `messages_PT.properties` would be:

```
Jan=Janeiro
...
Nov=Novembro
Dec=Dezembro
```

The previous samples do not specify messages for countries but, as already covered, you would be able to do it, and the content would also be based on key/value pairs. We can avoid repeating key/value pairs that are similar and use the hierarchical priority rules to specify only the key/value pairs that are different from file to file.

Regarding the options available for this add-in, I can't see any advantage to changing the defaults; there is only one option, which is the localize function. The only reason I can see to change this function would be to add a prefix or suffix to the value coming from the query and to match the key of the messages files. In the following code we are applying the same function by default, but it can give you an idea of the code needed to change the function:

```
var options = {
  localize: function(v, st, opt) {
    return dashboard.i18nSupport.prop(v);
  }
};
this.setAddInOptions("colType", "localizedText", options);
```

Please refer to the sample provided for this chapter. You will find the example on the add-in's sample dashboard.

hyperlink

The hyperlink is an add-in that can provide links to any URI that is recognized by the HTML and the browser. You need to return a string with a valid URL from the query. It expects a URI string, for example: `http://www.pentaho.com`. The add-in will create an HTML element that provides a link the user can click in order to interact.

The following are options that we can use to customize the appearance and the behavior:

- `openInNewTab`: Used to open the URI on a new tab of the browser. By default, it is set to `true`. When set to false it will be opened on the same tab.

- `prependHttpIfNeeded`: Used to tell the add-in to prepend the string `http://` to the URL provided when the URI does not include one. We should avoid it when providing an e-mail address as the URI.

- `Regexp`: We can provide a regular expression to check whether the provided URL is valid. The regular expression is just to check whether it's valid or not. If it's valid then the add-in can create the link. By default, it's set to null, avoiding the validation.

- `pattern`: This is the regular expression that will extract the strings to use as the label and as the URI.

- `urlReference`: Used to tell from which group index we get the URI. By default, its value is set to `2`.

- `labelReference`: Used to tell from which group index we get the label. By default, its value is set to `1`.

Let's suppose that the query returns something like `[Link to Pentaho] [http://www.pentaho.com]`, where we first have the label and finally the URI. We would need to overwrite some of the default options, which would look something like:

```
var options = {
  openInNewTab: true,
  prependHttpIfNeeded: true,
  regexp: null,
  pattern: "/\[(.*?)\]/g",
  urlReference: 2,
  labelReference: 1
};
this.setAddInOptions("colType", "hyperlink", options);
```

The previous code defines a `pattern`, used to extract the label and the URI from the string that's returned from the query. By default, `urReference` and `labelReference` have this but, if needed, we could also change it and get those values from other indexes of the resulting application of the regular expression.

We are also able to extend them because CDF provides the capability to create new add-ins, but we need to cover this in a later and more advanced chapter.

Template component

The template component is a component that allows us to create custom visualizations based on templates and models, all based on the data that we have acquired from a data source. The concept of building HTML content is not new, just the fact that we now have a component that allows us to do that. Maybe you don't need them for simple use cases, as using the query or freeform component can be an alternative, but it doesn't take too much complexity before the use of a template component becomes a good decision.

One of the big advantages of using templates is that we can have the same template making use of the same model with different data. So, if the model is the same but just the data has changed, which can be the result of a query, it will leverage the work you need to build a section of a dashboard. It also lets you split the structure of the content to display from the data that needs to be displayed, so your dashboard will have less complexity when building custom visualizations. This is because the alternative would be a custom component, which would take you more time and effort.

You should use this component when you have visualizations that cannot use another component, or if the use of another component becomes hard and you can represent the data coming from a query using HTML. In other words, to be used when you need to loop in data driven HTML representation. We will see later, in this chapter, that it's also possible to use add-ins like we can on tables, handle events for interactions, and create functions for custom formatting, which makes the component even more dynamic.

First of all, you need to understand the concept of templates and how they work. It's not the purpose of this book to get into the details, we will just give you the basic concepts. You should refer to the documentation about template engines (https://github.com/janl/mustache.js and http://underscorejs.org/#template) we can make use of inside a CDF/CDE dashboard. You will find some examples on the CDE samples or on the samples provided with the book. There are also plenty of examples on the use of templates on the Web, which you may find interesting.

Templates are based on a template itself and the model. The template defines the formatting and structure, while the model provides the data that is going to be used on the template. So, when making use of templates, we can separate the formatting and structure from the content, where the JavaScript template engine makes the JavaScript business logic inject content into the template. The template component specifically uses JavaScript-powered templates and was developed to work with two libraries that provide template capabilities, with the advantage of already being included in CDF. The libraries are: Mustache and Underscore.

To have a better understanding of the differences between them, let's use the same example to create the content for the dashboard based on the template. For both engines, the model will be the sales by territory for a particular year, so the final result we want to get is:

```
<div class="title"> Sales by territory: </div>
<ul>
    <li>EMEA: $168479</li>
    <li>APAC: $601606</li>
    <li>Japan: $168479</li>
    <li>NA: $1821247</li>
</ul>
```

The model, where data is?, will be represented by a JSON structure such as:

```
var model = {
  territory: [
     { name: 'EMEA', sales: 168479},
     { name: 'APAC', sales: 601606},
     { name: 'Japan', sales: 168479},
     { name: 'NA', sales: 1821247}
]};
```

Mustache is a logic-less template syntax, because there are no logical conditions, such as if statements, else clauses, or for loops. Mustache makes use of tags that are replaced by either a value, nothing, or a series of values. It can be used for HTML, configuration files, source code, or anything else. Mustache works by expanding tags in a template using values provided in a hash or object, and it's very clean with a small learning curve. It is a very popular template language, which is evident from its many platform implementations.

A Mustache tag begins with two opening braces and ends with two closing braces and, as you might have guessed, the "{{" and "}}" delimiters are where Mustache gets its name from. We can use {{...}} to access a variable and {{#...}}...{{/...}} to display a chunk of markup if a certain condition is true (or false), or to repeat sections, which let you display lists of values. If you have a need to escape HTML, you have the option to use {{{...}}}.

Following the provided example, using Mustache we would need to define a template such as:

```
var template = '<div class="title"> Sales by territory: </div> ' +
               '<ul>' +
               '   {{#territory}}' +
               '      <li>{{name}}:{{sales}}</li>' +
               '   {{/territory}}' +
               '</ul>';
```

And the instruction to get the rendered HTML string is:

```
Mustache.render(template, model);
```

You don't need to run the render when using the component

You won't need to run the render when using a template inside the component; you just need to specify the template engine that you want to use, and the component will take care of it for you.

Underscore is a library that offers functional programming utilities, but it does have an easy template method with a lot of flexibility. By default, it uses more complex delimiters that can easily be modified, and makes use of braces, similar to Mustache. Underscore provides the capability of having logical conditions such as if or for loops, among others. It allows you to make use of JavaScript inside the template, so it's much more flexible than Mustache, but of course its learning curve may be a little harder.

Template functions can both interpolate values, using <%=...%>, and execute arbitrary JavaScript code with <%...%> and this is how all loops will be created. If you wish to interpolate a value, and have it be HTML-escaped, use <%-...%>.

Following the example using Underscore we would need to define a template such as:

```
var template = '<div class="title"> Sales by territory: </div> ' +
               '<ul>' +
               '<% _.each(model.territory, function(elem) { %>' +
               ' <li> <%= elem.name %>: $ <%= elem.sales %> </li>' +
               '<% }); %>' +
               '</ul>';
```

Among other options, the way to render the template to an HTML string is:

```
_.template.render(template, model);
```

I am used to the syntax, but you may find it harder to understand because of the tags that Underscore uses by default. That can be changed just by placing the following code before using the component:

```
_.templateSettings = {
    evaluate:    /\{\{(.+?)\}\}/g,
    interpolate: /\{\{=(.+?)\}\}/g,
    escape:      /\{\{-(.+?)\}\}/g
};
```

Make the same changes on the component

It's also possible to apply these changes to the component. We can place this code just before returning the template to use, which should be done on the template component property.

If that's the case we can build a template such as:

```
var template = '<div class="title"> Sales by territory: </div> ' +
               '<ul>' +
               '{{ _.each(model.territory, function(elem) { }}' +
               ' <li> {{=elem.name}}: $ {{=elem.sales}} </li>' +
               '{{ }); }}' +
               '</ul>';
```

If the project is relatively simple, you can use Mustache, but when the template must be more complex, you will need to use Underscore.

I tend to think of myself as the father of this component, and I have some great ideas and improvements that will make it even greater, so keep an eye on the updates.

Automatically generated model and root element

When we make use of the template component, we also want to get data from a server. We need to define a data source using the data sources perspective, making use of CDA to get the data back to the dashboard, but when doing it the data is returned to the component using the standard CDA format. The component will automatically generate a model you can use when building your template, but you can also do it by yourself when you need to build a more complex model that fits your requirements.

Let's suppose that the query returns sales by territory, so we will have a row for each territory, and on the columns we will have the name and the sales for that same territory.

The resulting dataset would be something like:

APAC	1281705.9
EMEA	5008224.3
Japan	503957.6
NA	3852061.4

The resulting model is based on the result set so the model will be a multidimensional array. I already mentioned that the model should be an object, so a JavaScript object will wrap the multidimensional array with a key that, by default, is items. One example would be:

```
{
    items = [
        ['EMEA', 168479],  ['APAC', 601606],
        ['Japan', 168479], ['NA', sales: 1821247]
    ]
};
```

There is a property that we can cover right away because it will be the key of the root element of the returned model:

- **Model root element**: Used to change the key of the root element of the model. By default, it's set to items. The template needs to refer to the root element so you can use a name that you feel comfortable with. It's not mandatory to change it.

Template and engine

Besides the properties that are available for other components, and that we need to define, such as the name, data source, parameters, listeners, and the HTML object, we also need to have at least the template and the template type well set:

- **Template library**: Used to specify the engine that will be used to render the template. There are two options available: Underscore and Mustache, and the default value is Underscore.

- **Template**: Used to define the template to be used. You need to define a valid template for the selected engine. The property accepts a function that should return a string with the template to be used. An example of the code to create an Underscore template for the automatically generated model sample would be:

```
function() {
  var template = '<div class="row">' +
    '<% _.each(items, function(elem) { %>' +
    ' <div class="col-xs-6 col-md-3 single">'+
    '   <b> <%= elem[0] %>:</b> $<%= elem[1] %> '+
    '   <div> <%= addin("3,5,7,3,4,2", "sparkline", "sparkline") %>
</div>'+
    '   </div>' +
    '<% }); %>' +
    '</div>';
  return template;
}
```

The template creates a parent element that will wrap all other elements. Since each row is the same as one element of items, the root key of the model, the template generates a `<div>` that's going to have the name of the territory and the value. You should have noticed that we are using CSS classes, the bootstrap CSS classes that will make this content responsive to screen size changes.

Model handler

We already covered in earlier chapters and/or sections the fact that we can use **Pentaho Data Integration (Kettle)** transformations to return data to the dashboard. When using MDX, we may return some more complex value parsed in a string and, when this happens, you may also need to manipulate the model so that it will let you build a really advanced visualization. Let's suppose that you are returning the sales for each territory and country, and you want to display a card by territory where you will include all countries' sales, such as in the following image:

What we need to do is to group the result by territory, because if we can have an object for each one of the territories then we can have all countries inside it. It's easy to build a template that can bring those results to the screen:

```
function(data){
    if (data.queryInfo.totalRows > 0) {
        var model = {};
        var territories = _.groupBy(data.resultset, function(elem){
                return elem[1];
            });
        model[this.rootElement] = territories;
        return model;
    } else {
        return null;
    }
}
```

On the previous code, first we are checking whether we get results from the query, otherwise we want to return `null` to notify the component that it will not have data to display. If we have data on the result, then we will use the `groupBy` function to group all rows based on the second column (index one) that contains the territory. What we are getting is an object where the key will be the territory and the value will be the array of countries/values that belong to that same territory. After getting the result object we also need to put it on a root key, which is represented by `this.rootElement`, so we are using the property that has been set on the component (default value is items) so that we can iterate on each territory inside of it. An example of the model that is returned to the component is:

```
{ items: {
  APAC:   [["Australia", "APAC", 630623,  "0,49637,0,…,0,37905"], …,
           ["New Zealand", "APAC", 535584,"0,0,36409,…,0,102523"]],
  EMEA:   [[…],…,[…]],
  Japan:  [[…],…,[…]],
  NA:     [[…],…,[…]]
}
}
```

Based on the model, we can now build the template. We will need to iterate on each element of items, getting each one of the territories, where we will iterate on each one of the arrays inside it. When inside each country we can access the value by using the proper index such as `0` to get the country, `1` to get the territory, or `2` to get the value for sales:

```
function() {
 var template = '<div class="row">' +
  '<% _.each(items, function(tVal, tKey) { %>' +
  ' <div class="col-xs-6 col-md-3 single territoryContainer"> '+
  '  <div class="category"> <b> <%=tKey%> </b> </div>'+
  '  <% _.each(tVal, function(cVal, countryKey) { %>' +
  '   <div class="row countryContainer"> '+
  '    <div class="col-xs-4 country"> <b> <%=cVal[0]%> </b> </div>'+
  '    <div class="col-xs-3"><%=formatter(cVal[2],"sales")%></div>'+
  '    <div class="col-xs-5"><%=addin(cVal[3],"sparkline"%></div>'+
  '   </div>' +
  '  <% }); %>' +
  ' </div>' +
  '<% }); %>' +
  '</div>';
 return template;
}
```

You will see two loops that are coded using the _.each function. First, iterate for each one of the territories and then for each one of the countries. When on the territory, we are using the key to create an element that will have the category or territory. When on the country, we will build three elements to display the name of country, the sale of the year, and a `sparkline` that represents the value for each one of the months for that same year.

You will notice two function formatters and add-ins, but don't worry; we are going to cover them now.

Formatters

Formatters are very useful because, most of the time, we can't get the value formatted from the query, as we want it to be displayed on the dashboard. Let's suppose you have a query that can be used to get data to more than one component, taking advantage of the already cached data. If that's the case and if you want to display the values on a different format, then you need to handle it on the client-side. It's also easier changing the format on the client-side than on the queries, which can also be used by another dashboard or application. The template component has the concept of formatters, which are functions that we can define on the component and later use them inside the template. The values here can be numeric, a date, or a string. This can be done using the following property of the component:

- **Formatters**: Used to define the formats that we may need to apply to the values returned from the dashboard and that will be displayed on the dashboard. When you click on the property you will get a popup where you will have to define the identifier/name for the formatter and the function that receives an argument, the value, and returns the already formatted value. Let's suppose you wanted to display the numbers, not to eight decimal places but just one. For that we would create a formatter with the identifier/name `floatFormatter` and a function such as:

```
function(value, id){
    return Utils.numberFormat(value, '$0.0a')
}
```

Formatters are defined as a property. When you click on the property, you have the ability to add as many as you want.

To make use of the formatter inside the template, we need to use a function that is a formatter and receives two arguments: the value to be formatted, and the identifier/name of the formatter to use. This is because you can define and use multiple formatters on a template. One example of a template that would make use of the formatter would be as follows:

```
function() {
 var template = '<div class="row">' +
  '<% _.each(items, function(elem) { %>' +
  ' <div class="col-xs-6 col-md-3 single">'+
  ' <b><%=elem[0]%></b><%=formatter(elem[1],"floatFormatter","")%>
'+
' </div>' +
  '<% }); %>' +
  '</div>';
 return template;
}
```

You can see in the code that this way we are displaying all the sales by territory, but the values of sales are being formatted to have only one decimal place. The formatter function is being used and called from the template.

Add-ins

We already covered the use of add-ins in the table component. They are really useful and easy to create on the tables, and here on the template component this is also very easy. We can create new add-ins or make use of the ones that are already there by default. The way to apply add-ins that already exist is a bit different from tables.

Here on the template component, since we are defining the layout for our visualization you also need to define it on the template. You can make use of it by using the `addin` function that receives three arguments, the data to be used by the add-in that will create the visualization, the name of the add-in to use, and the name of the column that comes from the query because the add-in may need to access the column. Another reason to specify the ID is because, when using the same add-in on the same template but for a different purpose, you may want to have a different format, as is possible on the table component. Let's suppose you want to display `sparklines` but using lines and bars for different purposes. By including the id, you may do so. Just don't forget that the id must match the column name that is returned from the query.

Let's suppose you want to display `sparklines` like you can do on the table component. For that you should have the string with comma-separated values, and let's suppose that the third column of your query is returning it for you. You would need to apply a template as follows:

```
function() {
    var template = '<div class="row card">' +
      '<% _.each(items, function(elem) { %>' +
      ' <div class="col-xs-6 col-md-3 single territory"> '+
      '   <div class="category"> <b> <%= elem[0] %> </b> </div>'+
      '   <div class="value"> <%=formatter(elem[1], "sales", "sales")%>
</div> '+
      '   <div class="addin"> <%=addin(elem[2], "sparkline",
"sparkline")%> </div>'+
      ' </div>' +
      '<% }); %>' +
      '</div>';
    return template;
}
```

You can see the `addin` function being used, passing as arguments `elem[2]` where the string containing the values separated by commas is, and another argument with the name of the add-in to use.

We may also want to change the default options for add-ins, and here it's the same as on the table component. We need to use the `setAddInOptions` function to override the default values. The function should be placed on the `preExecution` function of the component:

```
function f(){
    var opts = {
        type: 'bar',
        height: 20,
        barWidth: 6
    };
    this.setAddInOptions("templateType","sparkline", opts);
}
```

The result of the add-in would be something similar to that displayed in the following image:

You need to be sure that the add-in that you are using is registered, otherwise it will not work. The add-ins that are available for the template component are not the same; some will be available and others will not. During the writing of this book I also created approximately ten add-ins, some of them almost a copy of add-ins used in the table component. The following image is an example of the add-ins that can already be used inside the template component:

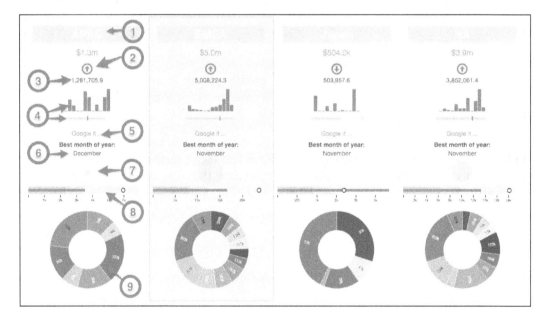

You can see on the image some numbers pointing to the add-ins; let's cover them and use the numbers so that you can easily identify them. The add-ins that we are covering for the template component are very similar to the ones on the table component so you already have most of the information. Don't forget that these options should be set inside the `preExecution` function of the component:

1. `clippedText`: The same as the table add-in plugin used when we have text larger than the space we have to display it. It will show the full text when we hover over it. The options available are:

    ° `showTooltip`: To show a tooltip when hovering over the text. The default value is `true`.

    ° `useTipsy`: Use the Tipsy JQuery plugin to show a fancy and customizable tooltip. The default value is `true`.

    ° `applyFormat`: This is a function that receives an argument that is the value to show on the tooltip and returns the formatted value. One example would be:

    ```
    var options = {
      showTooltip: true,
      useTipsy: true,
      applyFormat: function(value) {
      return value;
    }          }
    this.setAddInOptions("templateType","clippedText", options);
    ```

2. `trendArrow`: This add-in is very similar to the trend arrow of the table component using the exact same behavior and properties. It will display an arrow up/down and red/green depending on whether it's up/below and whether it's a good/bad value. This is the same behavior as the `trendArrow` table add-in, so please refer to the documentation. The properties are the same:

    ° `good`: This property says that a good value is above the threshold upper interval. The opposite applies if we set a value of false. The default value is true.

    ° `thresholds`: Defines the up and down thresholds. The default for up and down thresholds is zero:

    ```
    {up: 0, down: 0}.
    ```

- includeValue: Used to specify that we will also see the value side by side with the arrow. The default value is false. Here the difference to the add-ins available on the table component is that I have used font icons to display the arrow. Color and sizes can be changed just by changing/overriding some CSS. By opening the trendArrow.css file when debugging your dashboard, you will find the CSS classes that you need to override and customize the size, icon, and color. The following image is an example of the template add-in showing the trendArrow pointing down or up depending on a negative or positive trend compared to the sibling period:

3. formatted: I consider this a multiuse add-in because you can use it to easily apply some formatting or even customize, and have complete control over, what you will display. You can use the add-in to send HTML to the dashboard, so it gives you great flexibility. By default, the add-in format will be applied using one of two functions. You can format numbers and/or dates. This is quite different from the one we have discussed for the table component; it's simpler to use but powerful as well. The three main properties are:

- formatFunction: Here you should specify a string with the name of the function that you want to use from Utils. Use numberFormat to format a number or dateFormat to format a date. The default value is numberFormat.

- formatMask: You should remember from the section where you covered the Utils number and date formatting functions that we also need to specify the format mask, so this property is used to specify it. You should set a string with the format to use on the function that you specified as formatFunction. The default value is #,#.#. To get more information, please refer to the date and number formatting of the CDF chapter, *Chapter 3, Building the Dashboard Using CDF*.

- ◦ applyFormat: By default, the functions used are the formatFunction and formatMask properties, so it will do the formatting based on what you have specified for those properties. But if you want to customize the content to display, you can overwrite this function. If so, you need to define your own function, which needs to receive the value as the argument and return the text/HTML to be presented on the dashboard:

```
var options = {
applyFormat: function(value) {
 return '<div class='customContent'">'+value+'</div>';
  }
};
this.setAddInOptions("templateType","formatted", options);
```

The previous code is an example of the code to be placed on the preExecution function of the component to extend the options, if we want to customize the content to return to the dashboard when applying the formatted add-in inside the template component.

4. sparkline: Allows you to use the JQuery Sparkline Plugin just like we covered on the table component. Options should be the ones available on the plugin; just make sure the value returned is a string, represented with comma-separated (,) numbers. This is the only property that you will need to define, but you can use more. You can go to the Try It Out section of the Sparkline Plugin to check that the properties will differ from chart type to chart type:

- ◦ type: It's a chart type and also a property that is passed from the add-in to the Sparkline Plugin. Here the default is bar.

Per instance, if you need to display bars to represent the values chart and change some of the properties you would use code such as:

```
var options = { type: 'bar', barWidth: 6};
this.setAddInOptions("templateType", "sparkline", options);
```

Please refer to the `sparkline` add-in section of the table component. You will find all the information you need, which will also work on the template component. The following images are also examples of what you can achieve when using the add-in:

The previous image uses the bullet chart options, while the following image uses the bar chart options to represent the values that should be represented:

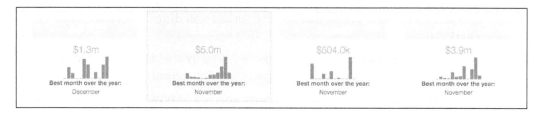

5. `hyperlink`: hyperlink is an add-in that can provide links to any URI that is recognized by the HTML and the browser. You need to return a string with a valid URL from the query. The use is exactly the same as on the table component, so please refer to that section to get more information. The options are:

    ◦   `openInNewTab`: Used to open the URI on a new tab of the browser. By default, it is set to true. When set to false it will be opened on the same tab.

- ○ `prependHttpIfNeeded`: Used to tell the add-in to prepend the string `http://` to the URL provided when the URI does not include one. We should avoid it when providing an e-mail address as the URI.

- ○ `regexp`: We can provide a regular expression to check whether the provided URL is valid. The regular expression is just to check whether it's valid or not. If it's valid then the add-in can create the link. By default, it's set to null, avoiding the validation.

- ○ `pattern`: This is the regular expression that will extract the strings to use as the label and as the URI.

- ○ `labelReference`: Used to tell from which group index we get the label. By default, its value is set to 0.

- ○ `urlReference`: Used to tell from which group index we get the URI. By default, its value is set to 1. To use the add-in, the value returned can be something such as: `[Pentaho Website] [http://www.pentaho.com]`, and if that's the case you will need to apply the following options to the add-in:

  ```
  var options = {
          pattern: /\[(.*?)\]/g
  };
  this.setAddInOptions("templateType","hyperlink", options);
  ```

6. `localized`: This is similar to the `localizedText` add-in on the table component. Please refer to the documentation on the table component section.

7. `bubble`: This add-in will draw a bubble where the size of the bubble is the relation between the value and the minimum and maximum values for all the rows on that same column, where the biggest bubble will be the highest value of all. The available properties are:

  - ○ `containerSize`: Sets the size of the parent container where the bubble will be. The default value is 30. The size of the bubble should be returned as a percentage, which will be the relative size for the bubble inside the parent container.

- ° valuesArray: This is the function used to return the array of values where we should be searching for the max and min values, so that we can calculate the size of the bubble. By default, it will use the id passed when applying the add-in on the template, where the id should match the name of the column that we want to use to get the max and min values. Therefore, it's very important to have the id of the column passed when making the call of the add-in on the template. Based on the `modelHandler` function and the model you are returning to the component, the `valuesArray` function may need to be changed to get the proper array of values from the returned model. The function receives an argument that is the status but, as it's called from the radius and/or color functions that we also may override, you may include more arguments on it:

```
function(st) {
    var colNames = _.map(st.data.metadata, function(elem) {
        return elem.colName;
    });
    var colIdx = _.indexOf(colNames, st.id);
    var values = st.data.resultset.map(function(e) {
        return Number(e[colIdx]);
    });
    return values;
}
```

- ° radius: The default value is a function that will calculate the size based on the value for this same element. It accepts a function that receives the status as an argument. From the status, we can get the value that should be represented by the bubble, the data returned from the query, and the id for the add-in, which should identify the name of the column that should be used to find the min and max values that can be used to calculate the size of the bubble. If there are some add-ins that can work without the id being passed, this is not the case. By default, the following code is applied:

```
function(st) {
    var values = this.valuesArray(st);
    var tblMax = _.max(values),
        tblMin = _.min(values);
    var value = Number(st.value),
        size = (value-tblMin)/(tblMax-tblMin);
    return size*100;
},
```

- ○ `color`: The color to be used for the bubble. This option accepts a function that receives as an argument the status, where we can find the value, all the data returned from the query, and an id that identifies that unique add-in. The default function is:

```
function(st) {
    return "rgba(200, 200, 200 , 0.6)";
}
```

- ○ `showTooltip`: To show a tooltip when hovering over the bubble. The default value is `true`.

- ○ `useTipsy`: Use the `Tipsy` JQuery plugin to show a fancy and customizable tooltip. The default value is `true`.

- ○ `applyFormat`: This is a function that receives an argument that is the value to show on the tooltip, and returns the formatted value. The default value is:

```
function(st, opt) {
    return "Value:" + Utils.numberFormat(st.value, '#,#.#');
}
```

- ○ `tipsyOptions`: The options to be passed to the Tipsy JQuery plugin. This way Tipsy can be customized. The default value is:

```
{ gravity: 's', html: false }
```

The following image is an example of the result of applying the Bubble add-in:

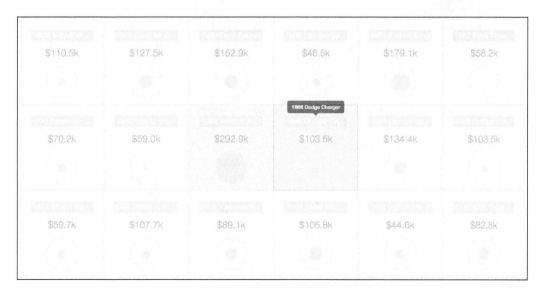

8. `bulletChart`: This is used to represent a bullet chart with the values that come from the query for that same cell. Here you need to return all the values to use on the bullet chart, separated by a comma. The options that you have available are all those available for CCC charts, which we are going to cover later. The options for the chart should be set inside the `chartDefinition` object. The following code is an example of how to set the properties:

```
var options = {
  chartOpts: {
    compatVersion: 2,
    height: 60,
    orientation: "horizontal",
  }
}
this.setAddInOptions("templateType","bulletChart", options);
```

When using the default properties, you get a bullet chart similar to the ones in the following image:

9. `cccChart`: This add-in allows you to display any CCC chart, but it's tricky. We will see later in this book, when we cover CCC charts, that CCC can receive from the query any result set and still display the chart. You may need to change some properties to have data displayed as expected. This is the tricky part here. What is the best way to represent the data so that we can have it represented correctly? Depending on the chart and on the properties that you set for the chart to represent it, you may need to adapt the result set. It would be easier to set the query, choose the chart to represent it, and then just adapt some of the options to adapt the chart to the data format that is returned. You may be a little bit confused with this, but do not worry, you will get the information to understand it. For now, let's focus on the properties that can be used to customize the behavior of the add-in:

- ° `type`: Used to set the kind of chart to represent data. Possible values are: `BarChart`, `LineChart`, `PieChart`, `DotChart`, `StackedLineChart`, `StackedAreaChart`, `HeatGridChart`, `WaterfallChart`, `BoxplotChart`, `MetricLineChart`, `TreemapChart`, `SunburstChart`, and `BulletChart`. You won't need the last one since you have an add-in capable of doing the same thing. The default value is set to `PieChart`.

- ° `chartOptions`: Used to set the options for the chart; you should take a look at the CCC documentation pages and check what properties are available. You can also directly change some of the properties of the chart and check the results. Those are the options/properties that you can set here. One example would be:

```
chartOptions: {
    compatVersion: 2,
    height: 100,
    animate: false,
    crosstabMode: false,
    seriesInRows: false,
    timeSeries: false
}
```

The `crosstabMode`, `seriesInRows`, and `timeSeries` properties are the ones that will make the difference when CCC is interpreting the results. This will definitely change the data you are displaying. The `compatVersion` is used to inform CCC that the chart should be rendered using version 2, which has a lot of improvements and fixes. In this case there is a property that's really mandatory, the `height` for the chart. Without this one the chart will not be rendered.

- ° `transformData`: A function that receives the data as an argument and returns the complete result containing the `metadata` and `resultset`. Please refer to the *Chapter 2, Acquiring Data with CDA* to get more information if you can't remember the format expected. You won't need to include the `queryInfo`:

```
function(data) {
    var result = { metadata: [], resultset: []};
    try {
        data = JSON.parse(data);
        var colMetadata = [];
        _.each(data, function(row, index) {
            if (index == 0) {
                _.each(row, function(col, index) {
                    result.metadata.push({
```

```
                colIndex: index,
                colName: "Col"+index,
                colType: "String"});
            });
        }
        result.resultset.push(row);
    });
} catch(e) {
    return null;
}
return result;
}
```

The following code accepts as an argument an array of arrays. For each row we need to add it to the new result set, and in the case of the first row, we also need to add the metadata to it.

The following image is one example of a pie chart being displayed inside the template component:

Events

It's also possible to handle clicks on the elements created by the template component. You can use events to expand a particular section, to make a fireChange creating interaction between components, or to get details for the clicked section. Since you are creating a function, you can do whatever you need inside.

To create an event, you need to use the Events property of the component. For the right-most value you will need to define the event that you want to handle, followed by the selector of the element from where you want to handle the event separated by a comma (,). On the left you will need to define the function and write the code (it can only be a fireChange) so that other components can be notified and updated.

Let's suppose that you wanted to get details for a particular territory, the one that is clicked; the template would be like:

```
function() {
  var template = '<div class="row card">' +
    '<% _.each(items, function(elem) { %>' +
    ' <div class="single clickable" data-territory="<%=elem[0]%>"> '+
    '   <div class="category"> <b> <%=elem[0]%> </b> </div>'+
    '   <div class="addin"> <%=addin(elem[4],"trendArrow")%> </div>'+
    ' </div>';
    '<% }); %>' +
    '</div>';
  return template;
}
```

You can see that for each of the items/territories, we are creating a parent container that includes `data-territory` attribute with the name of the territory and a CSS class where the value set is the `clickable` value. The `data-territory` attribute will be used to get the territory we are clicking on, and the CSS class will be used to get the HTML element where we will attach the event.

To handle the event, we will need to add an event handler on the events property of the component. To do it you will need to use the left field `click` , `.territory` and the following function on the right field of the dialog that pops up:

```
function(event) {
    var $elem = $(event.currentTarget);
    var selected = $elem.data('territory');
    $elem.toggleClass('selected');
    this.dashboard.fireChange('selectedParam', selected);
}
```

Inside the function this will refer to the add-in, so on the first line we are getting the element that we clicked on. After that, we are using the JQuery data function to get the data from the attribute data category from where we will know which value should be used to set the parameter value. But first, we also need to toggle the CSS class to know which territories are selected. At the end we add a `fireChange` so that the value is written to the parameter, and the components that are listening it can be notified about the change. Don't forget that, for this to work, you will need to create the parameter to store the selected territory name. In our example the name is `selectedParam`.

Besides `fireChange`, you can expand the container you are clicking on and display some more information. This doesn't need to be an element outside, as in the samples provided with the book.

Extendable options

On the template component it's possible to customize the messages that you get in the event of an error, and for that we can use the following property:

Extendable options: Accepts a function that returns the JSON object structure with all the messages to override it. The function to return the messages, which is used by default, is the following:

```
function() {
  var opts = {
    messages: {
      error: {
        noData: "No data available.",
        invalidTemplate: "Invalid template.",
        invalidTemplateType: "Invalid template type.",
        generic: "Invalid options defined…."
      },
      config: {
        style: {
          error: {icon: "remove-sign", type: "danger"}
        },
        template: ""+
        "<div class='alert alert-<%=type%>' role='alert'>" +
        "  <span class='glyphicon glyphicon-<%=icon%>' aria-
hidden='true'></span> " +
        "  <span> <%=msg%> </span>" +
        "</div>"
      }
    },
  };
  return opts;
}
```

The function will return an object with customized error messages but also the Underscore template that is used to build the error message that will be displayed. If you look deeper into the template, you will find that I used a Bootstrap alert component and also made use of the icons to display on the alert. The alert type to use and the icons are defined inside `messages.config.style`. It will work as a template model where the template will act as the template and the style as the model. If needed, you can also overwrite the `processMessage` function that takes care of building the message. The function accepts two arguments, the message and the type, and returns a string with the HTML to be displayed as a message.

If you have no row to display, by default, the following will be shown:

> ○ No data available.

As you can see, the template component needs to be improved, mainly by making it easier to use, but without losing the flexibility to adapt and create new and impacting visualizations. We are in an era where the request to have prescriptive solutions and real-time prescriptive solutions is already a reality. I will be working on a similar component that can have real-time results presented on a dashboard using your custom visualization, so I am expecting to be able to have a real-time template component in the near future.

Export button component

When presenting content on a dashboard, which uses a query to present the content, we can make the export of the data to a specific format. It can be done only for a component, so the results of only a query and not the full dashboard will be exported. When using this component, you can export data to one of two formats, csv or xls; no other format is available on this component.

The properties that you need to set are:

- **Label**: The label that will be displayed on the button.
- **Component name**: The name of the component from where to export the data. This should be the name that you gave to the component. Since you need to export the data from a component, you should already have a component set and ready to be used.
- **Output type**: The format to export data to. Available options are the ones already mentioned, csv or xls.

Export Popup button component

The Export Popup button component is more flexible and will let you have more options. When using this component, the final user will have a link available where he can click to do the exporting. When clicking on the link, the user will get a popup with the options to export to different formats, and one option should be selected to make the export. The formats available are the same that are available in CDA, so you are able to export data to csv, xls, json, and xml. Besides that, if you have a chart, the final user will also be able to export the chart to svg or png format.

The options that you have available are:

- **Title**: This is the text that will be displayed on the dashboard, where the final user can click.

- **Gravity parameter**: This is used to set the position where the popup will jump.

- **Chart component to export**: This is the name of the chart to export. Here you can click on the down arrow key to get the list of values and select the component name.

- **Chart export label**: This is used to set the text that will be displayed and to make possible the export of the chart.

- **Chart export type**: Here we need to specify the format to export the chart to. Available options are `svg` or `png`.

- **Data component to export**: This is the name of the component from where data will be exported. Here you can click on the down arrow key to get the list of values and select the component name.

- **Data export label**: This is used to set the text that will be displayed and to enable exporting the data.

- **Data export type**: Here we need to specify the format to export the data to. Available options are `csv`, `xls`, `json`, or `xml`.

- **Name for data export attachment**: This is name of the file that will be exported. The format will automatically be appended to the name of the file.

- **Content linking**: This an advanced option to present the options and set the links that will enable the export. Per instance, when you want to be able to export to CSV and XLS. Using the previous properties you can only specify one format. The content linking property will allow you to specify the text to be displayed and a function that will be executed when the respective link is clicked. Inside this function you will be able to define the component from where to export, the format, and the filename to export to.

When using this property, you will get a dialog where you will be able to add options. Each new line will be an option, and for each line you need to specify an argument and a value. On the text more to the left, you need to specify the text to display as the link. On the text more to the right, you will need to specify the function. Per instance, on the text to display you would set `Export to CSV` and the function would be as follows:

```
function() {
    var comp = dashboard.getComponentByName('${c:myTable}');
```

```
    var cd = comp.chartDefinition || comp.queryDefinition;
    var query = dashboard.getQuery(cd);
    query.exportData('csv', {}, {filename: "filename.csv"});
}
```

The first line of code will get the instance of the component with the name `myTable`, whereas on the second line we get `chartDefinitions` or `queryDefinitions`. Depending on the component, it will return the correct option, because if one is not available we will use the other. The third line gets the information about the query, and by using this last one we can export the data. For that we need to make use of the `exportData` function that should be available for all the components that run a query. This function accepts three arguments; the first is the export type, the second is the overwrite options, and here you can return an empty object, and finally the third one is an object where we can specify the filename and extension for the file that will be exposed.

The following image is an example of what can be produced, out-of-the-box:

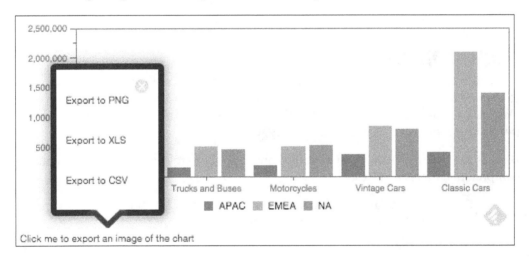

When doing the export, the CDA query will run again, using the same parameters that are selected on the dashboard, and at that time it's already cached. Anyway, you can play around a little with this. It's not unusual to have a request to have quite a different export than we are seeing on the dashboard, so you can imagine a scenario where you will have a component that is hidden and is not executed until an export is requested.

Referring to component, parameters, and to the layout

If you go to the developer tool of your browser and inspect a CDE dashboard code, you can see that, to the names of the components that we set when editing the dashboard, we always prepend with `render_`. So when you want to refer to the name of the component, you should refer to the complete name such as `render_myComponentName`.

When you use code inside the dashboard, which is not valid for code on external files, you can refer to the component as `${c:myComponentName}`. This will be translated when the code is sent to the browser, as it's already referring to the correct name of the component.

This is also valid for parameters `${p:myParameterName}` and for elements on the layout by using `${h:myPlaceholderName}`.

The syntax difference is the letter before the name and inside the `{}`. You can use `c` for components, `p` for parameters, and `h` for elements on the layout.

Text component

The text component is another component that is really simple to use. It allows you to display text on the dashboard. This component will not trigger a query, but is still executed as part of the lifecycle of the dashboard, so it's very useful. It can be used, per instance, to display the user that is logged in.

Besides the properties that you already know and that are common to the remaining components, there can also be:

- **Expression**: A function that should return the text/HTML to be displayed on the element of the layout associated to this component.

  One example would be:

  ```
  function() {
      return this.dashboard.context.user;
  }
  ```

The previous code is returning the username of the user that is using the dashboard, but we could have returned HTML to display.

Summary

By reading this chapter, you should have learned how to use the table component, template component, export buttons, and text component. You should be able to use the table component to display details for each one of the rows, or just trigger some changes to other components when the user clicks on a row. You also should have learned to apply add-ins and customize tables, understand the capabilities provided by functionality on the server-side, or just customize what we see displayed (and the how of it). You have also learned how to use the template component to display data the way you need to. The template component provides many ways to display the results of a query, customize messages, or just apply some functions to customize formatting.

Besides the fact of learning how to use the components, you should be able to make the most of them and be able to find the best way to present data to the user using these two components. Hopefully you also understand what you should use, or should avoid, so as to not decrease the performance of the dashboard, or even queries triggered. Performance is very important.

At the end of the chapter, besides learning how to use the text component, you also learned how to export data and the way to do it. We have covered the way to export an image from a chart. There is a dedicated chapter for charts, as they are one of the best ways to represent data on the dashboard.

The next chapter will cover some advanced concepts that you can use in both CDF and CDE dashboards.

7
Advanced Concepts Using CDF and CDE

Today, when we are requested to build a dashboard, most of the time we find ourselves faced with customers who want you to make the dashboard available in multiple languages, and to be honest, this makes sense. Why would you have a dashboard available only in your language and not in other languages? In this chapter, we will teach you how you can do this.

CDF and CDE provide you with some really cool components that are more flexibility then others, and allow you to build your own visualizations, so we will also cover these components. But for now let's suppose that you are working with a customer who has hired you to build a dashboard but also to train his team to build the remaining dashboards. If there is a visualization that you need to implement/develop, you will certainly be capable of creating a delivery that includes a custom component that they can use/reuse later. This is possible, and we are going to cover how to do it, as well as how to extend template and table components by creating new add-ins.

In one of the sections of the book, we also provided some information about reusing templates and styles, and we already showed you how to create a new template, save it, and reuse it. But we also may want to create a style, and this is the chapter where we are going to do that.

A very interesting possibility is building a dashboard and embedding it in another one. Do you realize how cool this could be? Just imagine creating a dashboard that can be used a section of another dashboard, and reusing it multiple times. You must be having some ideas already, so let's start with the chapter.

The topics covered include:

- Creating new add-ins for table and template components
- Making use of the template add-in for table and template components
- Creating and changing the style of the dashboards
- Using the dashboard component to reuse dashboards
- Creating new add-ins and new components
- Making use of `bookmarkable` parameters

References to components, parameters, and layout elements

First, I want to start by covering one important concept in CDF, and don't forget that concepts in CDF also extend to CDE. If you open the developer tools in your browser and start inspecting some CDE dashboard code, you will see that the names of the components are always prepended with `render_` with the name of the components that we set when editing the dashboard. This way, when you want to refer to a component using its name, you should use the complete name of the component such as:

```
this.dashboard.getComponentByName('${c:myComponentName}');
```

This would be the same as:

```
this.dashboard.getComponentByName('render_myComponentName');
```

When you use this code line inside a dashboard, where it is not valid for code in external files, you can refer to the component as `${c:myComponentName}`. This is possible because, when using this syntax, it will be translated and replaced by the full name of the component, so you don't need to worry about the name that CDE may have given to it.

This is also valid for the parameters or elements created in the layout perspective. When you use a dashboard embedded in a dashboard, like we are going to see later, and you take a look at the code, you will see that the name will not be exactly the same as the one you gave it. You should worry about this, because you can use the syntax previously referred to.

Since this is also valid for components, parameters, and layout elements, we should have a way to distinguish them. This is done by changing the letter before `:`. You should use a p for parameters, a c for components, and an h (from HTML) for the layout elements, like the following:

- Components, which has already been covered:

```
this.dashboard.getComponentByName('${c:myComponentName}');
```

- Parameters:

```
this.dashboard.getParameterValue('${p:myParameterName}');
```

- Layout elements:

```
$('.${h:myLayoutLementName}').text('Hello World');
```

When you select the name of parameters, the elements of the layout, and the component's name using the drop-down, CDE will automatically create a reference to the proper object of the dashboard, using the correct syntax. It won't work, if you type the name yourself nor when writing your own code. For this reason, I always advise you to select the values using the drop-down, and select the value from the list, otherwise you might be creating issues.

The query and freeform components

The components we have covered will give you the freedom to do almost everything you need to do to build an amazing dashboard. However, sometimes we need to go further, and we might be able to do this just by using the available components. To build custom visualizations, you can also make use of the query and freeform components, but what's the difference between them? A very frequently asked question is where to use one or the other. So now let's answer this question and learn how to use these components.

The query component will trigger a query, but you want to display some custom content inside your dashboard. Here you can't avoid setting a valid query, so the freeform component is useful here. The freeform component will not trigger any query so you can use it as you want/need. You may be thinking, If it does not do anything, why would I use it? Well, it's because sometimes you have the need to execute some code that respects the lifecycle (a good example can be internationalization/localization, or just adding static HTML to the page/dashboard) of the dashboard; as with any other component, these two components have their own lifecycle. When using `require`, if you add HTML elements with text directly to the layout of the dashboard, you will see that text displayed in the first place, will give you a bad look and feel. You can use a text component to add the HTML, which will just be added to the page when the dashboard is being rendered.

For both, query and freeform components, you will be able to specify the priority of `execution` and the `preExecution` and `postExecution` functions, as well as the component that should be executed at the start of the dashboard, by setting true or false in `executeAtStart`. For the query component, we are also able to specify the properties `datasource`, `parameters`, and the `postFetch` function, which will be executed as soon as the component gets the results, just after the `preExecution` function and before the `postExecution` function.

So the difference between the query and the freeform components, is that, for the query component, a data source will be used and, for the freeform, it will not. Just use them when you need to present content that you are not able to present with any other component provided by CDF and CDE.

The query component

As already said, we can use the query component to present custom content to the dashboard. The properties that are available along with the common ones are:

- `Result var`: This is the name of the dashboard parameter that is going to be used to store the result set from the query. This will not include the metadata, but just the `resultset` itself. It will store a multidimensional array with all the rows and columns returned. There is no default value—you should specify the name of a parameter. When you leave it blank, no parameter will be set. To access the parameter that could be named `myResultset`, you should use the same methods as for any other parameter in the dashboard, as in the following code:

  ```
  var data = this.dashboard.getParameterValue('${p:myResultset}');
  ```

- Asynchronous mode: This tells us that the component should work in an asynchronous way. The default value is `true` and, when set to `false`, only after the component's rendering is complete, the components with a low priority (higher values) will be executed. My advice is to always use the default value. Pretty much, the property is there to retain compatibility with older versions of dashboards/components, so keep this property set to true.

You can also get more details on Pedro Alves' blog at the following links:

- `http://pedroalves-bi.blogspot.co.uk/2012/11/making-cdf-calls-asynchronous.html`
- `http://pedroalves-bi.blogspot.co.uk/2013/01/cdf-async-support.html`

Let's suppose that you wanted to display the product line to be displayed as an accordion, where for each product line item we display the products and sales for that same line. There is no component, out of the box, that would build what was described in last sentence. Anyhow, you can build a custom component if you want to use it multiple times in multiple dashboards; otherwise you can just use the query component. The reason for using the query component is because the results that are going to be displayed come from a query, and we still don't have them in the dashboard.

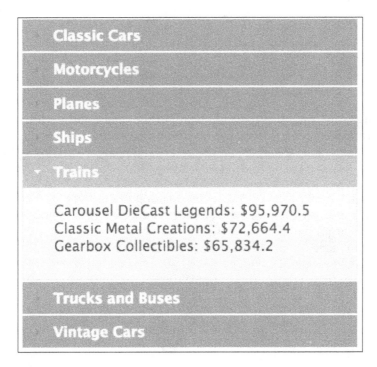

We could use the query component in one of two ways. The first way is to use the variable to create and write the elements to the page on the postExecution function, only after postFetch. The following code is an example of creating the accordion with the accordion from JQuery UI (more information is available at: https://jqueryui.com/accordion/):

```
function() {
    var data = this.dashboard.getParameterValue('${p:myResultset}');
    var $placeholder = this.placeholder(),
        $accordion = $('<div id="accordion"></div>'),
        productLines = _.groupBy(data, function(elem) {
            return elem[0];
        });
    _.each(productLines, function(products, line) {
        $accordion.append('<h3>'+line +'</h3>');
        var $content = $('<div class="container"><p></p></div>');
        _.each(products, function(product) {
            var values = product[1] + ': ' +
                            Utils.numberFormat(product[2], '$#,###.0');
            $content.find('p').append('<div>'+ values + '</div>');
        });
        $accordion.append($content);
    });
    $accordion.accordion({
        heightStyle: "content"
    });
    $placeholder.empty().append($accordion);
}
```

In the previous code, we are getting the result of the query and iterating on each product line, and for each line we are also iterating on the products. This way, we can write the elements to the page. At the end of the code, we are using the accordion plugin and rendering it in the dashboard.

The other way is to use postFetch directly, making use of the argument that is passed. If that was the case, then you will not need to define the variable data, just specify it as argument of the function; where you have data, it will be data.resultset. Don't forget that, when in postFetch, we should return data to the component.

The freeform component

If you have a component that already has the result of a query that fits your need or you just want to render some content in the dashboard that does not depend on the result of a query, you can use the freeform component. The advantage is that the component has its own lifecycle and will be perfectly synced with the lifecycle of the dashboard. You can change the priority of execution, and add code for pre- or post execution.

A property that is different from the other components is:

- **Custom script**: This will accept a function with the code to be executed, just after `preExecution` and before `postExecution`. For this case, and supposing that you had a query component execution before this one, you could use the same code here in the custom script. This would grab the result from the parameters and the same code would be used to build the content for the dashboard.

Even simpler would be a case where you needed to have the freeform component performing `fireChange` to a parameter based on some actions that can be controlled by the lifecycle of the dashboard.

As the component will not make use of a query, you should already have figured out that it will not make a call to `postFetch`.

Creating add-ins

We have seen that both the table and template component can make use of add-ins. We can also extend CDF and create new add-ins that can be added to the dashboard. You should always be aware that when using it on a table component the add-in will be used for the cell of the table, so be cautious about what you are showing for each cell, so that the table does not become hard to read due to excessive information. Just because dashboard users get information from a dashboard does not mean you should present excessive information.

To add a new add-in you just need to write a few lines of code and some properties, create a new instance of an add-in, and register it to the dashboard. The definition of the add-ins will be set using a JSON structure with the following elements:

- `name`: This is the name/identifier given to the add-in, which will be used to reference it. This field is mandatory and accepts a string.
- `label`: This will be the description of the add-in. It accepts a string.

- **defaults**: Here we need to set another JSON structure with the default properties of the add-in. These properties are the ones that may be overwritten later when setting the properties of the add-in. For example, for the `sparkline` add-in, it may have the type set as `line` but later we may want to use a `bar`.

- **init**: This is used to execute some code once the add-in is requested. Some preparation code can be executed here. When defining an add-in that will be applied to a table, we also need to specify the sort functions, and the right place to do it. It accepts a function and accepts no arguments.

- **implementation**: This is a function where the code of the implementation will be added. The function receives three arguments:

- **target** or **tgt**: As you will see in the following example, it's a reference to the HTML element where we will be rendering the content to be displayed.

- **status** or **st**: As you will see in the following example, it's an object where we can find the value to be used. The information that will be available inside this argument will depend on the component that is using the add-in. For instance, when used in a table, we may have access to the index of the column (`colIdx`) and the index of the row index (`rowIdx`) being processed. Since in some cases we may be using a hierarchical structure, we will have access to the add-in identifier (`id`) that is being passed when the add-in is used in the template. For both cases, independently of the component, we will have access to the complete dataset or model (`data` when in the table component and `model` when in the template component).

- **options** or **opt**: Like you will see in the following example, these are the options set by the developer to customize the appearance and/or behavior of the add-in. We should use them if we want to extend the default options.

Let's see what the code would be for an add-in created to be used in a table and another for the template component. Let's suppose you want to create an add-in to format the values that are going to be displayed in the dashboard. For this, you need to use the `numberFormat` function under the CDF utilities, which was already referred to in this book as `Utils`. We should not forget to include the module.

To create and include a new add-in in your dashboard, you will need to add a new resource, using the layout perspective, and give it a name. After setting the name, you should place the code inside it, something like:

```
define(['../../../AddIn','../../../Dashboard',
        '../../../dashboard/Utils','../../../Logger',
        '../../../lib/jquery','amd!../../../lib/underscore',
        'amd!../../../lib/datatables'],
```

```
function(AddIn, Dashboard, Utils, Logger, $, _) {
  var formatted = {
    name: "numberFormat",
    label: " numberFormat",
    defaults: {
      formatMask: '#,#.#'
    },
    init: function() {
      $.fn.dataTableExt.oSort[this.name+'-asc']=
        $.fn.dataTableExt.oSort['string-asc'];
      $.fn.dataTableExt.oSort[this.name+'-desc']=
        $.fn.dataTableExt.oSort['string-desc'];
    },
    implementation: function(tgt, st, opt) {
      var opts = $.extend(true, this.defaults, opt),
          Value = Utils.numberFormat(st.value, opts.formatMask);
      $(tgt).empty().text(Value);
    }
  };
  var addin = new AddIn(numberFormat);
  Dashboard.registerGlobalAddIn("Table", "colType", addin);
  return formatted;
});
```

In the previous code, first we are using require to create the add-in, including all the modules (JavaScript and CSS). When all modules are there, we need to start creating the code for the add-in. We start by creating a JSON structure, the name, label, and defaults as well as the init and implementation functions. The name will be the identifier of the add-in, in this case the formatter. For the defaults, we are defining the format mask, which will be applied when no other format is passed to the add-in.

The init function is being used to define the sort functions of the jQuery Datatables plugin. This will only be used by the add-ins that we create and apply for the tables. It will not break if applied to the template; it will just not be used.

The implementation function has the code that will be executed every time it's called by the table or by the template components. On the first line of the implementation function, we are extending the default options with the options that may be passed to the add-in on the pre-execution of the component. On the second line, we are setting a variable with the format, which is defined in the options and applied to the value that we can grab from the status. Here, using jQuery, we are cleaning the actual content that might be there and writing the already formatted value.

After this is complete, and now that we have the formatted JSON with the definition of the add-in, it's time to create a new instance of the add-in. And last, we are registering the add-in in the dashboard and as available as a column type of the table.

When developing the add-in for the template component, there are two main differences between the add-in for the table component. One difference is that we would not need to define the `sort` function inside the `init` function, because that may not make sense when applying a template. That way, we would also not need the `datatables` module.

The other difference is when registering the add-in for the dashboard. As you can see in the following code line, we are registering it to be used for the template component. Just look at the first two arguments of the function. We are using `Template` and not `Table`, as we are also using `templateType` and not `colType`:

```
Dashboard.registerGlobalAddIn("Template", "templateType", addin);
```

The template add-in

There is one other add-in that was not covered, and it's available for the template component but also in the table component. The way it works is pretty much the same as the template component.

There are three ways for the add-in to use the data being processed. The first one is by working on the query to return a string with the JSON structure that will be parsed by the default `modelHandler` function. There is another way: overwriting the `modelHandler` function by writing your own code and returning a custom and valid JSON structure as the model. If none of the earlier options return valid JSON, then the value will be treated as a string. Please refer to: http://www.json.org for more information.

Just use the method that you are most comfortable with, prepare everything in the query/backend, or use the available function to return a valid model that can be applied to the template being defined.

The way to apply options to the add-in is the same as already covered for the other add-ins, and the ones available are:

- `templateType`: You must select the template engine to use. Those currently available are *underscore* and *mustache*. The last one is the default value.

- `template`: This is the template to be used.

- `rootElement`: This is the name/key that will wrap the model/value being processed.

- `formatters`: This accepts a multidimensional array. Each formatter will be represented by an array that will have two elements. The first element will be a string with the name of the formatter and the second will be the function that accepts two arguments: the value to be formatted and the identifier of the add-in being executed. It should return the formatted value.

- `events`: This is similar to the last option, and here it accepts a multidimensional array. Each event will be an array with two elements. The first element is a string that has the event being handled and the selector of the element, separated by a comma (`,`). The second element is a function with the code to execute when the event is triggered in the selected element. The function accepts one argument that is a reference to the event itself, just like writing a function such as a regular JavaScript event.

- `modelHandler`: This is a function that accepts data being processed by the component. The function is used to return a valid model to be rendered in the template of the add-in.

- `postProcess`: This is a function where you can write some code after the elements are rendered on the page.

For any of these functions, please refer to the template component documentation to get more information:

```
var templateOpts = {
    templateType: 'underscore',
    template:
        '<% _.each(items, function(value, idx) { %>' +
        '   <div class="row clickable productLine" data-
id="<%=value[1]%>"> '+
        '       <div class="category"> <b> <%= value[1] %> : </b> </
div>'+
        '       <div class="value"> <%= formatter(value[2],
"abbreviation") %> </div>'+
        '   </div>' +
        '<% }); %>',
    formatters: [["abbreviation",function(value, id) {
        return Utils.numberFormat(value, '$0.0A');
    }]],
    events: [["click, clickable.productLine", function(event){
        alert('You clicked: '+$(this).data('id'));
    }]],
    modelHandler: function(data, opt) {
      var model = {};
      model.items = data;
      return model;
```

```
    },
};
this.setAddInOptions("templateType","template", templateOpts);
```

You may also apply the options and use this add-in in the template component so you just need to apply the options in the template and make a call to the add-in of the template using the following instruction:

```
this.setAddInOptions("templateType", "template", options);
```

In this code, you will see that we are setting the options to be used by the template add-in. First we are setting the template type, which for our case is *underscore*.

You will also see the template and, inside it, you will find a call to the formatter. We are passing two arguments to the formatter: the value to be formatted and the name of the function to be used. We could and should also specify another argument (a third one) that is the identifier and is useful when we want some conditional formatting.

We can have multiple formatters, so we need to define them as a multidimensional array. Each element of the parent array will have two elements: the first one is the name of the function and the second one is the function that is executed when the formatter is used inside the defined template. The second element, the function, accepts two arguments: the value to be formatted and one identifier. The identifier is really useful if we need to define a formatter that can be used multiple times with different options for the same template.

We can also see that we are specifying an event, and to do so we are specifying one array with one event and one **Document Object Model (DOM)** element. The events will also accept a multidimensional array and, once again, each element of the main/parent array will have another two elements. The first element is the event and the selector, which identify the target in the HTML, while the second one is the handler function triggered when the event is fired. The first and second elements of the array should be separated by a comma (,).

In the previous sample code, we are just showing an alert message with the product line where we are clicking. The last option is `modelHandler`, where we are returning the array wrapped in a JSON structure where the root element is *items*, used in the template. The last instruction registers the options for the add-in.

Take a look at the examples of dashboards provided with the book, and you can get a clear idea of how it works. Anyhow, it's the concept that we covered earlier for the template component, but applied to a table add-in.

Extending CDF and CDE with new components

When we covered the query component, you must have been asking: If I want to use this for multiple dashboards, do I need to apply my own code over and over again for every dashboard? The answer is, no. With the custom components, you are perfectly able to create components that can be reusable in CDF or in CDE.

What changes between CDE and CDF, is that, for CDE, you also need to include a XML file with the information about what should we see in the dashboard editor. Let's see how can you create your custom components.

Extending CDF

I would like you to consider two different kinds of components: those that allow filtering and those that allow you to display data in the dashboard. Of course, the ones that display information can also be used as selectors, but just add functionality to those that are really to allow visualizations of data on the dashboard.

You should remember from *Chapter 3, Building the Dashboard Using CDF*, that components can run asynchronously among those with the same priority of execution. If they have different priorities of execution, then they will run synchronously.

It's important to realize that, when I am talking about asynchronous execution, what I am really saying is that simultaneous AJAX requests will be executed, but the browser only allows a limited amount of concurrent calls, so they may be divided into multiple batches. That will depend on the number of components and the limit of simultaneous calls for the browser being used.

To be able to take advantage of some concepts of the **Object-Oriented Programming (OOP)** languages, CDF makes use of libraries that ease the pain of OOP in JavaScript. One of them is Base, which can be found at `http://dean.edwards.name/weblog/2006/03/base/`. This is a simple class and extends the object `Object` by adding two instance methods and one class method.

When creating a new component, you should be sure to create it in a way that it can run synchronously or asynchronously. This can be achieved by extending from existing *classes*. The UnmanagedComponent class is one of those cases. It already inherits from BaseComponent, which also inherits from Base class, so a lot of properties and methods/behaviors can be inherited. To take advantage of the existing base classes, we need to use UnmanagedComponent. This means that UnmanagedComponent is an advanced and more complete version of BaseComponent. It allows you to have control over the lifecycle when implementing components.

When using UnmanagedComponent, the class will make the calls to preExecution, postExecution, and even to postFetch when triggering a query. This will also make sure the listeners are handled and that the parameters are sent to the queries when the component is executed. This way, the calls to these functions are entirely the responsibility of CDF, and the component doesn't need to worry about them.

There are three functions that we can use when creating a component, and one of them needs be used. They are:

- synchronous: This implements a synchronous lifecycle identical to the core CDF lifecycle

- triggerQuery: This implements a simple interface to a lifecycle built around query objects

- triggerAjax: This implements a simple interface to a lifecycle built around AJAX calls

Creating a Hello World! component would be something like:

```
define(['cdf/components/UnmanagedComponent','amd!cdf/lib/underscore'],
function(UnmanagedComponent, _) {
  HelloWorldComponent = UnmanagedComponent.extend({
    update: function() {
      var render = _.bind(this.render,this);
      this.synchronous(render);
    },
    render: function(data) {
      var message = this.message || 'Hello World!';
      this.placeholder().empty().text(message);
    }
  });
  return HelloWorldComponent;
});
```

This example code doesn't make use of a query, so `this.synchronous(render)` should be used. Managed automatically by the CDF lifecycle, the `render` function will be called just after `preExecution` and before `postExecution`. In the example, the render function is being called using the synchronous function. The render function will show the `Hello World` text if a property `message` is not defined in the component.

In the following example, we are making use of a query to show the result of the query. Here `this.triggerQuery(this.queryDefinition, render)` will be used, so `postFetch` will be also called, just before the `render` function, where we are making use of the data that we fetched. Inside the call of the query function, you can see that we are making use of the definitions of the data source/query for this component, so the definitions will be used to trigger the correct data source/query.

```
define(['cdf/components/UnmanagedComponent','amd!cdf/lib/underscore'],
  function(UnmanagedComponent, _) {
    ShowResultComponent = UnmanagedComponent.extend({
      update: function() {
        var render = _.bind(this.render,this);
        this.triggerQuery(this.queryDefinition, render);
      },
      render: function(data) {
        this.placeholder().empty().text(JSON.stringify(data));
      }
    });
    return ShowResultComponent;
  });
```

The `queryDefiniton` object should look like the following, where `dataAccessId` is the identifier of the CDA datasource defined, and `file` will by default point to the same name and folder as the dashboard:

```
{
  dataAccessId: 'myQuery',
  file: '/path/to/my/datasourceDefinition.cda'
}
```

Since the methods (`synchronous`, `triggerQuery`, and `triggerAjax`) expect a callback that handles the actual component rendering, the conventional style is to have that pointing to a `redraw/render` function. Also, to follow the standards we should use the `bind` function, as you can see in the two previous examples. This function will ensure that, inside the `redraw/render` callback, these point to the component itself.

Now let's suppose you want to create some kind of a select component and you may want developers to be able to make use of a values array and not a query. If that's the case, you can switch between static values and the result of a query:

```
define(['./UnmanagedComponent', 'amd!../lib/underscore'],
function(UnmanagedComponent, _) {
  ShowResultComponent = UnmanagedComponent.extend({
    update: function() {
      var render = _.bind(this.render, this);
      if(this.valuesArray && this.valuesArray.length > 0) {
        this.synchronous(render, this.valuesArray);
      } else {
        this.triggerQuery(this.queryDefinition, render);
      }
    }
    render: function(data) {
      this.placeholder().text(JSON.stringify(data));
    }
  });
  return ShowResultComponent;
});
```

In reality, we have been acting on modules where the components are defined. We can include the component in the dashboard, or we can make it available for CDF in such a way that all dashboards will have access to it. You can have your custom components inside the Pentaho Repository—just create a folder such as /Public/ cdf/components, and place your components there. For instance, you should save the code of the first example provided for this section, Hello World, in a file called HelloWorldComponent.js, so you can use it later in dashboards.

Now let's take a look at how you can make use of that same component, the custom Hello World. You will need to build a CDF dashboard like the one you can see here:

```
<div id="showTextHere"></div>
<script language="javascript" type="text/javascript">
  require([
    'cdf/Dashboard.Bootstrap',
    CONTEXT_PATH + 'api/repo/files/public/cdf/components/HelloWorld/
HelloWorldComponent.js'],
  function(Dashboard, HelloWorldComponent) {
    dashboard = new Dashboard();
    dashboard.addComponent(new HelloWorldComponent({
      name: "HelloWorld",
      type: "HelloWorldComponent",
```

```
        htmlObject: "showTextHere",
        message: "Hello World",
        executeAtStart: true
      }));
      dashboard.init();
    });
  </script>
```

You will see that we are requiring a resource using the Pentaho Repository API, and from there we just use any other component. Don't forget that , as it's a CDF component, you could also define and make use of the preExecution and postExecution functions, like you can for any other component.

When creating a component that acts like a filter, when an action is triggered (such as a click on the **Apply** button), it will change the parameter to store the selected values. We should make use of the following code:

```
this._value = selectedValues;
this.dashboard.processChange(this.name);
```

In this code, we can see the first line where we are setting the selected values of an internal variable _value, which will be used later to get the values that were selected.

The processChange function accepts an argument that is the name of the component making the call, and it's responsible for grabbing the selected values. This is done by calling the getValue function, so this function should also be defined in the component code.

Here is one example of the getValues function:

```
getValue: function() {
  return this._value;
},
```

You can see that the getValue function is just returning the values that were selected, so that the processChange function can proceed with its work. The processChange function now knows the values that have been selected, so it will make a call to preChange from the component if it exists, do the fireChange function using the parameter defined for the component, and call the postChange function.

We don't need to worry about calling preChange, fireChange, and postChange; we just need to define the getValue function and call the processChange function. The dashboard lifecycle will take care of the rest for you.

Extending CDE

Now that we have a component working as a CDF component, we can also extend CDE to use that same component. We already saw that CDE is provided by a friendly interface that allows you to build the dashboard. But CDE needs to know what components are available, what properties may be used, and which types of values are accepted for each one of the properties.

The big difference between a CDF and a CDE component is that a CDE component is also provided with some kind of a metadata file that should be specified using XML. Reading this XML file is the way that the server knows how to build the editor HTML page that will be rendered by the browser.

You should give the same name to the file as for the component; that way, if you have multiple components inside the same folder, you will know which component belongs to which file. Another reason is because you can use different folders for the XML and JavaScript/CSS files. You have names that can identify them and will make your life easier, not only for you, but also for someone in your team who needs to understand them. For our example, we will show you the folder structure that we can have. But you should find out what the best approach is for you.

The XML file with the definition of the component should also be placed inside the folder `/Public/cde/components`. The main structure of the file will be similar to:

```xml
<?xml version="1.0"?>
<DesignerComponent>
  <Header>
    <Name>Hello World</Name>
    <IName>HelloWorld</IName>
    <Description>Hello </Description>
    <Category>OTHERCOMPONENTS</Category>
    <CatDescription>Others</CatDescription>
    <Type>PalleteEntry</Type>
    <Version>1.0</Version>
  </Header>
  <Contents>
    <Model>
      <Property>title</Property>
      <Property>executeAtStart</Property>
      <Property>htmlObject</Property>
      <Property name="parameters">xActionArrayParameter</Property>
      <Definition name="chartDefinition">
        <Property type="query">dataSource</Property>
      </Definition>
      <Property>preExecution</Property>
```

```
          <Property>postExecution</Property>
          <Property>postFetch</Property>
          <Property>parameter</Property>
          <Property>tooltip</Property>
          <Property>listeners</Property>
          <!-- START: Template Component Properties -->
          <Property>message</Property>
          <!-- END: Template Component Properties -->
        </Model>
        <Implementation>
          <Code src="HelloWorldComponent.js"/>
          <Styles>
            <Style src="style.css" version="1.0">Style</Style>
          </Styles>
          <Dependencies>
            <Dependency src=" lib.js" version="1.0">Library</Dependency>
          </Dependencies>
          <CustomProperties>
            <DesignerProperty>
              <Header>
                <Name>mesage</Name>
                <Parent>BaseProperty</Parent>
                <DefaultValue>Hello World</DefaultValue>
                <Description>Model Handler</Description>
                <Tooltip>Message to display.</Tooltip>
                <InputType>String</InputType>
                <OutputType>String</OutputType>
                <Order>0</Order>
                <Advanced>false</Advanced>
                <Version>1.0</Version>
              </Header>
            </DesignerProperty>
          </CustomProperties>
        </Implementation>
      </Contents>
    </DesignerComponent>
```

You will get a lot of examples in your `Pentaho solutions` folder, under the CDE plugin folder, and inside the following folder: `<your pentaho folder>/pentaho-solutions/system/pentaho-cdf-dd/resources/custom/components`. This is where CDE components are placed, so you can have access to all the sources of all the CDE components.

Based on the knowledge that you have about using the lifecycle and the CDE components, the example code we just gave is almost self-explanatory. An important part is that we have a main tag `<DesignerComponent>` where we set all the other definitions. Inside it we will have headers and content.

In the `<Headers>` tag we are setting the name, description, and category/group for the component, where the following properties are being used:

- `Name`: The name of the component.

- `Iname`: The `interface` name of the component, which is very useful for a legacy dashboard. It should not have any special characters or blank spaces. It would be a good practice to set it with the same name as the RequireJS module.

- `Description`: This is just a description of the component.

- `Category`: This is the ID of the group where the component will become available. Another way to say this is to set the group of the layout perspective where we can select this component from.

- `CatDescription`: This is the description of the category where the component will be available.

- `Version`: This is just a number that you can use to specify the version of the component.

In the `<Contents>` tag, we are setting:

- **Model**: This is where we have defined the properties that will become visible when using the layout perspective and when the component has been selected. In the previous example, you will find the following properties that you already know: `title`, `executeAtStart`, `htmlObject`, `parameters`, `preExecution`, `postExecution`, `postFetch`, `tooltip`, `listeners`, and `chartDefiniton`, where you can find the `dataSource` to be used. If defining a select component, it would also make sense to have `preChange` and `postChange`.

A property that you don't really know is the message property, which we need to specify in the tag `<CustomProperties>`, which we will cover as follows:

- **Implementation**: Here you will find the definition of the component. The previous example code shows two properties in the `<Implementation>` tag; the first one `supportsLegacy` is used to make the component available for a legacy dashboard. Since it's not the purpose of this book to cover legacy but only a RequireJS dashboard, we have set this property to `false`. As the component should work in RequireJS dashboards, we have set `supportsAMD` to `true`. The renaming tags are:

    - **Code**: This property is where we specify the path and filename of the JavaScript file where the code for the component will be placed.

    - **Styles**: This is a tag where you will have all the styles (CSS files) that should be loaded with the dashboard. The `<Style>` tag will have two properties: the `src` attribute where you should specify the path and filename of the CSS file to load, and `version` where you can set the version number (not mandatory). You can add as many `<style>` tags as you want pointing to CSS files.

    - **Dependencies**: This is where you can specify the JavaScript files that should be loaded with the dashboard. If you need to use some third-party libraries/plugins, you need to specify them here. Like the `styles` tag, there are two properties: one to point to the file to be loaded and another to set the version. You can use multiple dependencies when setting multiple `<Dependency>` tags, as you can see in the previous example.

    - **Order**: This is a number that will set the order that should be used when displaying the list of properties.

    - **Advanced**: This property only becomes available when we click on **Advanced Properties** when setting the values of the properties of the component while using it in the layout perspective. It needs to be true or false. Setting it to true will make it available as an advanced property.

    - **Version**: This property is a number inside double quotes where you can set the version.

    - **Custom properties**: The definitions of properties in the model tag are already defined, but not the custom properties we are creating for this specific component.

These custom properties are enclosed inside the header tag, and the ones that you need to define are:

- `name`: This is used to set the name of the component.

- `parent`: This is the `parent` property. It should be set to `BaseProperty`, as it's part of the component.

- `DefaultValue`: This is the value that will be used and is visible by default. It may be changed.

- `Description`: This is the description to display in the property, like a label.

- `Tooltip`: This is a tooltip that a CDE Editor user will get when hovering over the name of a property.

- `InputType` and `OutputType`: These two properties are related to the property type:

  - `InputType` is used by CDE to know what kinds of visual input element will be provided to the user. For instance, when you click to set a value on a `postExecution` property, you get a dialog where you can write your JavaScript code. When setting `parameters`, you get multiple pairs of input boxes where you can select a value or write one. This input type is also used for validation of the values that are being set for the property. You can see the Input type as the behavior that CDE should exhibit in order to allow the input of a value(s). Here, the number of options is big, but we can restrict them to just the most important.

  - `OutputType` is the JavaScript data type that will be used to store the value(s) specified for the property. Here, the options to set are pretty much: `String`, `Number`, `Boolean`, `Array`, `Function`, and `Object`.

    Now let's see what options for the input and output property types are available, and how they combine with each other:

Input Type	Output Type	Description
String	String	Basic input types and mapping. The input will be validated depending on `InputType`. The Boolean input type will also allow you to select between true and false.
Integer	Number	
Float	Number	
Integer	Number	
Boolean	Boolean	

Input Type	Output Type	Description
JavaScript	Function	This will open a dialog where you can write the JavaScript code.
ValuesArray	Array	Displays a dialog like the one used in `parameters`. It allows you to combine a pair of values:
EditorValuesArray	Array	This is like the last one but, in the column to the right, it is possible to write JavaScript code, not just a string or number. Extension points, which we will cover later, are an example.
Array	Array	This displays a dialog where you can add multiple values. Vertical input boxes will be displayed.
ColSortableArray	Array	This is similar to the last one, but the values will be sortable. So you can change their order.
HTML	String	This allows you to write HTML code. This will be translated to a string, so the advantage is that you will get a friendly interface to do it.

You can find a lot of examples in the XML files under `resourses/base/properties` and `resources/custom/properties`. Just look under the `system/pentaho-cdf-dd plugin` folder.

Another way to load styles and dependencies is by setting them in the RequireJS dependencies. The `HelloWorldComponent.js` file; if you compare it with the code used in CDF, you will see the same, so a CDE component is pretty much a file that can be as follows:

```
define(['cdf/components/UnmanagedComponent','amd!cdf/lib/underscore'],
  function(UnmanagedComponent, _) {
    ShowResultComponent = UnmanagedComponent.extend({
      update: function() {
        var render = _.bind(this.render,this);
        this.triggerQuery(this.queryDefinition, render);
      },
      render: function(data) {
        this.placeholder().empty().text(JSON.stringify(data));
      }
    });
    return ShowResultComponent;
});
```

Extending or creating new dashboard types

CDF also provides three types of dashboard that you can use when creating a CDF dashboard. It's also possible to extend the functionality of CDF and create new dashboard styles. The three dashboards types that are available out of the box are:

- **Clean**: When using this, the dashboard does not load any CSS—it's just an empty container. It might create some more work, but it also gives you more flexibility and enables a high level of customization. The way to use this dashboard is by setting the module in the modules dependency of RequireJS. The instruction should resemble: `require(['cdf/Dashboard.Clean'],...)`

- **Blueprint**: When using this, the dashboard loads the blueprint CSS framework, which you can find at `http://www.blueprintcss.org/`. You can use its classes easily without including any more resources. The way to use this is with an instruction, such as: `require(['cdf/Dashboard.Blueprint'],...)`

- **Bootstrap**: Last but not least. When you use this one, the dashboard loads the Bootstrap framework, which is my preferred framework as it provides more flexibility when applying styles to the layout of your dashboards. This is a very well-known and popular framework that you can find at `http://getbootstrap.com/`. The way to use it is by setting it as a dependency/module using RequireJS: `require(['cdf/Dashboard.Bootstrap'],...)`

The great advantage of having a dashboard type is that you or other developers can include some CSS and/or JavaScript frameworks and libraries that you might want to use in all the dashboards. Don't forget that you should be careful when doing this because, if you are loading resources that will not be used, you are just decreasing the load time and other resources.

But how do you create a new type? To create a new type, you should define a new require module. Just create a new JavaScript file and give it the name `myCustomDashboardType.js`. You just need also to include all the dependencies that you will need for your dashboards. There is one module that is mandatory and that you can't avoid: the `Dashboard` module/dependency. You can include that dependency and all the others you need, as follows:

```
define(['./Dashboard'], function(Dashboard) {
  return Dashboard;
});
```

The example just provided will produce the same result as the `Clean` dashboard type, because it does not include any other modules/frameworks/dependencies.

Let's suppose you also want to extend the `Dashboard` module with some methods, options, and so on. You can just do something like:

```
define(['./Dashboard'], function(Dashboard) {
  return Dashboard.extend({
    someCustomCode: function() {
      //...
    }
  });
});
```

The dashboard will now have access to the function and can be used as: `dashboard.someCustomCode()`.

You can require the dashboard type by providing the relative path to it. Let's suppose the dashboard type is in the same folder as the dashboard HTML file, and you can just use the name `myCustomDashboardType` when requiring. See the following example:

```
require([' myCustomDashboardType'], function(Dashboard) {
  var dashboard = new Dashboard();
  dashboard.init();
  dashboard.someCustomCode ();
});
```

It is not possible to apply or extend these types to a CDE dashboard

At this time, creating a new dashboard type, it's only available to CDF dashboards, and cant' be applied to CDE dashboards. Inside CDE, you can choose the dashboard type from three options, but you cannot add more types there.

Creating a new dashboard style/template

Besides the dashboard type, we can also specify a dashboard style that will somehow work as a template wrapper for the dashboards. Here you can include some scripts or just HTML; you can define what is valid for an HTML file.

Extending styles for CDF dashboards

We saw earlier that when creating a CDF dashboard, we should specify the style in the XCDF file similar to `<style>clean</style>`. This will instruct CDF to make use of a particular template/style for our dashboard.

By default, the templates are inside a folder in the filesystem, in the plugin itself. The folder is `<baserver>/pentaho-solutions/system/pentaho-cdf`. When we create styles/templates, we need to have them in one place that is accessible for multiple projects, if needed; however, if we place them in the same folder as the default ones, they will be overwritten on the next update of the plugin. To avoid this, it's possible to place our own templates in a folder, inside the Pentaho Repository, that will not be lost when updating the plugins. It should be created in a folder as: `/public/cdf/templates`, and all the styles/templates will become available for the dashboards.

The name of the file should be: `dashboard-template-myTemplate.html`; when setting it in the XCDF file dashboard, we should exclude the prefix `dashboard-template`. The tag inside the XCDF will be `<style>myTemplate</style>`.

But how should we define the template? To answer that, let's look at the following example, which is exactly the same as the `clean` template:

```
<!DOCTYPE html PUBLIC
"-//W3C//DTD XHTML 1.0 Strict//EN"
"http://www.w3.org/TR/xhtml1/DTD/xhtml1-strict.dtd">
<html xmlns="http://www.w3.org/1999/xhtml">
  <head>
    <meta http-equiv="content-type" content="text/html; charset=utf-8"
/>
    <title>Ctools Book Samples</title>
    <meta name="keywords" content="" />
    <meta name="description" content="" />
  </head>
  <body>
    {content}
  </body>
</html>
```

You can see that this is pretty much an HTML page where you can also add CSS and JavaScript files, and CSS code — well, everything you can have on an HTML page you can also have here. The magic is the expression {content}, which represents the area where the specific code for each one of the dashboards will be placed. This expression will be replaced by the HTML, again including JavaScript and CSS code, from the file that is defined in the template element, such as `<template>myFirstDashboard.html</template>`. So the code inside `myFirstDashboard.html` will be replacing the referred expression, generating a complete HTML page for your dashboard, the file that will be used by the browser to render the web page with the dashboard.

So, when creating our first dashboard with the example code we saw previously, the browser would render similar to the following code:

```
<html xmlns="http://www.w3.org/1999/xhtml">
  <head>
    <meta http-equiv="content-type"
      content="text/html; charset=utf-8" />
    <title>Ctools Book Samples</title>
    <meta name="keywords" content="" />
    <meta name="description" content="" />
  </head>
  <body>
    <style>
    </style>
```

```
    <div class="container-fluid">
      <h1>My first dashboard!</h1>
    </div>
    <script language="javascript" type="text/javascript">
      var dashboard;
      require(['cdf/Dashboard.Clean'],
        function(Dashboard) {
          dashboard = new Dashboard();
          dashboard.init();
        }
      );
    </script>
  </body>
</html>
```

Extending styles for CDE dashboards

It's also possible to extend CDE with new styles/templates. The way to create them is pretty much the same, except for the name and the folder where they should be saved. CDE templates should be saved inside /public/cdf/templates and the names are simple. As we can have legacy and require dashboards, we may need to specify two different files, one for the legacy and the other one to be used when building a require dashboard. The name should be appended by Require before the extension, for instance, myCustomStyleRequire.html. Otherwise on a legacy dashboard, which we are not covering in this book, it would just be myCustomStyle.html.

The tags that will be replaced also change a bit, so here we need to make use of:

- @header@: This is used to include some initialization scripts, such as the dashboard context. It should be part of the header.

- @content@: This is use to be replaced by the content of the dashboard. This is where the dashboard will be rendered. All the layout and code for the execution of the dashboard are placed here.

- @footer@: This is used to include some scripts. It can be part of the footer template.

The way to apply a style/template to a CDE dashboard is to just choose it from the setting dialog of the dashboard. You will see a dropdown where the available styles/templates will be selectable. You just need to select the one for your dashboard and save it. Next time the dashboard is rendered, it will make use of that style/template.

The `CleanRequire.html` style looks like the following code. You can see a clean file where the header, content, and footer will be placed:

```
<!DOCTYPE HTML>
<html>
  <head>
    <meta http-equiv="Content-Type" content="text/html;
charset=utf-8">
    <meta name="viewport" content="width=device-width, initial-
scale=1">
    @HEADER@
  </head>
  <body>
    @CONTENT@

    @FOOTER@
  </body>
</html>
```

Bookmarkable parameters

You have already seen that we are able to create a dashboard that uses filters to be interactive. But let's suppose you want a dashboard to jump to a particular state using some values that could be specified using the URL. That's also possible out of the box using the `bookmarkable` parameters.

A great usage of this is for you to share the status of a dashboard with someone else. When you are exploring data through the dashboard, you may find some insights or just some warnings that you want to send to someone else. You can even send an e-mail with that information to someone else in the company. So now let's see how you can get them working.

When you create parameters, by using the components perspective, you may create a parameter by expanding the *Generic* group, choosing the type of parameter (also covered in this book). Three properties will become available: one for the name, a second one for the default value, and a checkbox to make the parameter a `bookmarkable` one.

If you make a parameter available, and when you start using the dashboard in such a way the parameter value is changed, you will notice that the URL changes and some more information has been added. The changes that you will find in the decoded URL will look like the following, depending on the parameters and the values being sent to them:

```
bookmarkState={"params":{"filterParam":"[Product].[Trains]"}}
```

This line shows that the value that is selected is `Trains`. What this means is that, if you use the entire URL like we are getting in the browser, opening another tab or window for your browser and pasting the complete URL will filter your dashboards and show only trains. If you use the dashboard URL without `bookmarkState` in the URL, then you will get the dashboard filtered with the default value, which in the sample provided is `Classic Cars`.

You will find a short and simple example in the chapter samples of a dashboard that presents a button that will send an e-mail with the URL containing the selection applied. In that case, you could send a message to a particular department or person, providing some insights. The code in the button would resemble:

```
function() {
    var dashboardPath = window.location.href;
    // send email with path to dashboard
}
```

This just gets the current URL with the bookmark state and sends it by e-mail.

Bookmarkable parameters in CDF

The `Bookmarkable` parameters are a CDE functionality, so you can also use them in CDF dashboards as well, if you include the module, `cdf/Dashboard.Bootstrap`.

Internationalization and localization

We can have internationalized and localized dashboards, and these are based on the `i18n` jQuery plugin. When we need to translate a dashboard, we need to create multiple files in the same folder as the dashboard, all of the `.properties` files.

The first one is `messages_supported_languages.properties`, where we need to specify the languages that will be supported. This will dictate the files and languages that should be read. If we want to be able to provide transactions in Portuguese (`pt`) and English (`en`), we use:

```
pt
en
```

Here we should have `<language>` and/or `<language>_<COUNTRY>`, where `<language>` is the lowercase code for the language and `<COUNTRY>` is the uppercase country code.

The `i18n` properties files will be key/value pairs where the names will dictate the language that will be used. We can also make use of a fallback file, but the fallback file doesn't need to be defined in the supported languages file.

We can delegate `i18n` messages to three specific files, which need to be placed in the same folder as the dashboard. The standard in Pentaho is to have the names using the following rules:

```
messages_<language>_<COUNTRY>.properties
```

These files are the ones that will contain the translations for a particular country for a language, where `<language>` should be replaced by the lowercase language code and `<COUNTRY>` should be replaced by the uppercase country code (for instance: `messages_en_US.properties`, `messages_en_UK.properties`, `messages_pt_PT.properties` and `messages_pt_BR.properties`):

```
messages_<language>.properties
```

These files contain the translations for a particular language, not specifying the country, where `<language>` should be replaced by the lowercase language code (for instance: `messages_en.properties` and `messages_pt.properties`):

```
messages.properties
```

That's the fallback file, where no language or country is specified. Here we will not need to specify a language or country.

Messages or translations can and should be shared by the different files; whenever that happens, the following rule applies:

The message keys placed in `messages_<language>_<COUNTRY>.properties` will override similar ones placed in `messages_<language>.properties`, which will overwrite `messages.properties`.

A hierarchical structure of the messages properties files would be:

```
+ messages.properties
++ messages_en.properties
++++ messages_en_US.properties
++++ messages_en_UK.properties
++ messages_pt.properties
++++ messages_pt_PT.properties
++++ messages_pt_BR.properties
```

Each one of these files is a pair of key/value, where the key and value are separated by an equals sign (=). The key will represent the identifier for the transactions while the value will be the translation itself, the text that will be displayed on the dashboard.

Let's suppose that we are creating a dashboard that can translate English and Portuguese. The first step is to create the fallback properties file. From there, we need to create new files for language and country, and just include the keys that need translation.

The `messages.properties` file would look like:

```
DASH.TITLE: Internationalization and localization
DASH.DESC: Internationalization and localization, sample dashboard
```

The `messages_en.properties` file could be empty, because the translation will be the same. When there is no key/value for the requested key, the priority (as explained before) is taken into consideration, so the text from the fallback file would be shown.

The `messages_pt.properties` file would look like this:

```
DASH.TITLE: Internacionalização e localização
DASH.DESC: Exemplo de internacionalização e localização
```

To make use of the translations inside a dashboard, we need to make use of the CDF API, calling the `prop` function from `i18nSupport`. The following line of code grabs the translation from the correct language file and returning it. This is done through a line of code:

```
this.dashboard.i18nSupport.prop('DASH.TITLE');
```

The previous examples do not specify the messages for the countries but, as already covered, you should be able to do it; the content will also be based on key/value pairs. We can avoid repeating the key/value pairs that are similar and use the hierarchical priority rules to specify only the key/value pairs that are different from file to file.

To apply this to the DOM using `postExecution` of the components, you can use jQuery or a text component.

There are some places such as charts or tables where you can also use the function, but make sure you also have a way to return the transactions for the result of a query. This can be achieved using a metadata schema, a dynamic schema processor on Mondrian, or with Kettle (PDI), but it may be harder with a simple SQL query where we can't use parameters to change the column returned.

The dashboard component

Using RequireJS allows great flexibility for the integration of CDE and CDF dashboards in third-party applications. That said, you could start asking: Is there a way to have dashboards inside another dashboard? This way, we could develop *mini-dashboards* that we can reuse inside the same dashboard and/or for multiple dashboards.

Later, we will cover, in *Chapter 10, Embed, Deploy, and Debug,* how we can integrate/embed dashboards into third-party applications, because now reusing a CDE dashboard inside another CDE dashboard is really easy. We can use the dashboard component that you can find inside the *Custom* group of the **Components** panel. The component will only be available when building RequireJS and not a legacy dashboard and, as we said before, the CDF and CDE chapters of this book are really focused on building dashboards using RequireJS.

The dashboard component is really easy to understand and use, and in my opinion it's one of the most desired components for developers and teams who want to reuse code and build more complete and complex solutions with less effort.

One of its advantage is that you can make use of a mini-dashboard in multiple dashboards. If you find a problem or just want to make a change, you just need to apply it to the mini-dashboard, and instantly you will see those changes applied to all the dashboards making using of that mini-dashboard.

The available properties when using this component are:

- **Dashboard path**: This is the path to the dashboard you want to embed inside your main dashboard. Here you can point to a mini-dashboard that in reality is a dashboard. That mini-dashboard will be called and rendered inside the main dashboard.

- **Parameter mapping**: If you want to synchronize some of the parameters between both dashboards, you can do this using this property. You can choose the parameters from the list of available parameters; when entering the name, you just need to click on the down arrow. On the left, you will find the parameters of the main dashboard, and on the right are the parameters that are public on the dashboard that is being instantiated. The following screenshot shows the mapping between the parameters from the main instantiated dashboard:

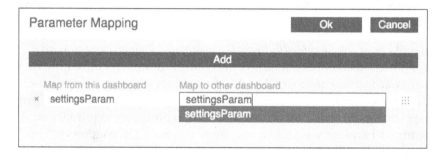

But you should now be asking, why am I referring to a public parameters? Well, it is possible to define the parameter mapping using the parameters of the dashboard being instantiated, and it's necessary that you make them public. When you are creating/editing a parameter, you need to change the **Public** property to **True**. This will make the parameter available to the outside world. The following screenshot is an example of this:

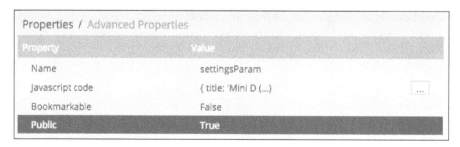

You will see that the **Public** property is set to true, so the parameter will become available when instantiated in the dashboard component.

- **Datasource mapping**: Interesting? Yes, definitely interesting. This can be used to overwrite a data source being used on the instantiated dashboard. This means that we can *replace* the data source and use one defined in the main dashboard. When you create a mapping between dashboards, that data source will be replaced everywhere. So if you have multiple components using the same data source on the instantiated dashboard, this means that those components will use the data source from the main dashboard being mapped.

In the examples from this chapter that you can import to your repository, you will find inside the `chapter 7` folder an example on the use of the dashboard component. There you will find two dashboards. On one main dashboard we use the mini-dashboard four times, displaying different titles, data, and even different chart types.

You can use the dashboard component to create navigation between dashboards, reuse dashboards, and create what in a more limited way CDE made available as widgets (with the use of RequireJS, this does not make sense anymore). I find the dashboard component much more flexible and easy to use, with the advantage that it is possible to define a dummy data source for the mini-dashboards and really use the data sources defined in the main-dashboard.

Summary

In this chapter, you learned some advanced features, tricks, and tips that you can use to build fancier dashboards, just save time developing dashboards, or extend the CDF and CDE capabilities by creating new components. We also covered some important features such as internationalization and localization.

You should also now know how to use the `bookmarkable` parameters to initiate a dashboard from a particular state or just call new dashboards, passing some values to replace the default values for the parameters.

If you create a new dashboard template that will be used to standardize the look and feel of all your dashboards, this topic is also covered in this chapter.

This may be one of the most complex chapters and hard to understand, but it is important when you start to get more complex and advanced requirements for the dashboards. This is really useful when you want to deliver advanced and custom features to your customers or developers. There is no need for everyone to know every single feature and possibility in CDF and CDE so, if you have a team that does not have that knowledge but you want them to be able to reuse some of your code and/or dashboards, you now have the knowledge to make it possible.

Don't forget that is fine to use the query component, but if you are using the same code twice, you may need to consider the development of a custom component and make it easier to reuse.

In the next chapter, you will come to understand the CCC properties and how they can be used for visualization.

Visualizations Using CCC

The **Charts Component Library** is not really a Pentaho plugin, but instead is a Chart library that Webdetails created some years ago and that Pentaho started to use on Analyzer visualizations. It allows a great level of customization by changing the properties that are applied to the charts and perfectly integrates with CDF, CDE, and CDA.

The dashboards that Webdetails creates make use of CCC charts, usually with a great level of customization. Customizing them is a way to make them fancy and really good-looking and, even more importantly, it is a way to create a visualization that best fits the customer/end user's needs. We really should be focused on having the best visualizations for the end user, and CCC is one of the best ways to achieve this, but to do this you need to have a very deep knowledge of the library, and know how to get amazing results.

I think I could write an entire book just about CCC, and in this chapter I will only be able to cover a small part of what I like, but I will try to focus on the basics and give you some tips and tricks that could make a difference. I'll be happy if I can give you some directions for you to follow, and then you can keep searching and learning about CCC. An important part of CCC is understanding properties such as series in rows or crosstab mode, because that is where people usually struggle at the start.

When you can't find a property to change chart styling/functionality/behavior, you might find a way to extend the options by using something called extension points, so we will also cover them. I also find interaction within the dashboard to be an important feature. So we will look at how to use it, and you will see that it's very simple.

In this chapter, you will learn how to:

- Understand the properties needed to adapt the chart to your data source results
- Use the properties of a CCC chart
- Create a CCC chat by using the JavaScript library
- Make use of the internationalization of CCC charts
- See how to handle clicks on charts
- Scale the base axis
- Customize tooltips

Some background on CCC

CCC is built on top of Protovis, a JavaScript library that allows you to produce visualizations just based on simple marks, such as bars, dots, and lines, among others, which are created through dynamic properties based on the data to be represented. You can get more information on this at: `http://mbostock.github.io/protovis/`.

If you want to extend charts with some elements that are not available you can, but it would be useful to have an idea about how Protovis works. CCC has a great website, `http://www.webdetails.pt/ctools/ccc/`, where you can see some samples including the source code. On the page, you can edit the code, change some properties, and click the **Apply** button. If the code is valid, you will see your chart update. As well as that, it provides documentation for almost all of the properties and options that CCC makes available.

Making use of the CCC library in a CDF dashboard

As CCC is a chart library, you can use it as you would on any other web page. But CDF also provides components that you can implement to use a CCC chart on a dashboard and fully integrate with the life cycle of the dashboard. To use a CCC chart on the CDF dashboard, the HTML that is invoked from the XCDF file would look like the following (as we have already covered how to build a CDF dashboard, I will not focus on that, and will mainly focus on the JavaScript code):

```
<div class="row">
    <div class="col-xs-12">
        <div id="chart"/>
```

```
      </div>
  </div>
  <script language="javascript" type="text/javascript">
    require(['cdf/Dashboard.Bootstrap',
             'cdf/components/CccBarChartComponent'],
    function(Dashboard, CccBarChartComponent) {
      var dashboard = new Dashboard();
      var chart = new CccBarChartComponent({
          type: "cccBarChart",
          name: "cccChart",
          executeAtStart: true,
          htmlObject: "chart",
          chartDefinition: {
              height: 200,
              path: "/public/…/queries.cda",
              dataAccessId: "totalSalesQuery",
              crosstabMode: true,
              seriesInRows: false,
              timeSeries: false
              plotFrameVisible: false,
              compatVersion: 2
          }
      });
      dashboard.addComponent(chart);
      dashboard.init();
    });
  </script>
```

The most important thing here is the use of the CCC chart component that we have covered in an example as a bar chart. We can see by the object that we are instantiating, CccBarChartComponent, and also by the type, cccBarChart.

The previous dashboard will execute the query specified as dataAccessId for the CDA file set on the property path, and render the chart on the dashboard. The dashboard code also refers to the crosstab mode for the result set, but the base axis should not be a timeSeries. There are series in the columns, but don't worry about this as we'll be covering this topic later.

The existing CCC components that you are able to use out of the box inside CDF dashboards are as follows. Don't forget that CCC has plenty of charts, so the sample images that you will see in the following table are just one example of the type of charts you can achieve.

CCC Component	Chart Type	Sample Chart
CccAreaChartComponent	cccAreaChart	Not available
CccBarChartComponent	cccBarChart	http://www.webdetails. pt/ctools/ccc/#type=bar
CccBoxplotChartComponent	cccBoxplotChart	http://www. webdetails.pt/ctools/ ccc/#type=boxplot
CccBulletChartComponent	cccBulletChart	http://www. webdetails.pt/ctools/ ccc/#type=bullet
CccDotChartComponent	cccDotChart	http://www.webdetails. pt/ctools/ccc/#type=dot
CccHeatGridChartComponent	cccHeatGridChart	http://www. webdetails.pt/ctools/ ccc/#type=heatgrid
CccLineChartComponent	cccLineChart	http://www. webdetails.pt/ctools/ ccc/#type=line
CccMetricDotChartComponent	cccMetricDotChart	http://www. webdetails.pt/ctools/ ccc/#type=metricdot
CccMetricLineChartComponent	cccMetricLineChart	Not available
CccNormalizedBarChartComponent	cccNormalizedBarChart	Not available
CccParCoordChartComponent	cccParCoordChart	Not available
CccPieChartComponent	cccPieChart	http://www.webdetails. pt/ctools/ccc/#type=pie
CccStackedAreaChartComponent	cccStackedAreaChart	http://www. webdetails.pt/ctools/ ccc/#type=stackedarea
CccStackedDotChartComponent	cccStackedDotChart	Not available
CccStackedLineChartComponent	cccStackedLineChart	http://www. webdetails.pt/ctools/ ccc/#type=stackedline
CccSunburstChartComponent	cccSunburstChart	http://www. webdetails.pt/ctools/ ccc/#type=sunburst
CccTreemapAreaChartComponent	cccTreemapAreaChart	http://www. webdetails.pt/ctools/ ccc/#type=treemap

CCC Component	Chart Type	Sample Chart

`CccWaterfallAreaChartComponent`	`cccWaterfallAreaChart`	`http://www.`
		`webdetails.pt/ctools/`
		`ccc/#type=waterfall`

In the sample code, you will find a property called `compatMode` that has a value of 2 set. This will make CCC work as a revamped version that delivers more options and a lot of improvements, and makes it easier to use.

Mandatory and desirable properties

Among other properties such as `name`, `datasource`, and `htmlObject`, other chart properties are mandatory. The height is really important, because if you don't set the height of the chart, you will not fit the chart in the dashboard. The height should also be specified in pixels.

If you don't set the width of the component, or to be more precise, then the chart will grab the width of the element where it's being rendered it will grab the width of the HTML element with the name specified in the `htmlObject` property.

The `seriesInRows`, `crosstabMode`, and `timeseries` properties are optional but, depending on the kind of chart you are generating, you might want to specify them. The use of these properties becomes clear if we can also see the output of the queries we are executing. We need to go deeper into the properties that are related to the data mapping to visual elements.

Mapping data

We need to be aware of the way that data mapping is done in the chart. You can understand how it works if you can imagine data input as a table. CCC can receive the data as two different structures: relational and crosstab. If CCC receives data as a crosstab query, it will translate it to a relational structure. You can see this in the following examples.

Crosstab

The following table is an example of the crosstab data structure:

	Column Data 1	Column Data 2
Row Data 1	Measure Data 1.1	Measure Data 1.2
Row Data 2	Measure Data 2.1	Measure Data 2.2

Creating crosstab queries

To create a crosstab query, usually you can do this with the group when using SQL; or just use MDX, which allows us to easily specify a set for the columns and for the rows.

Just by looking at the previous and following examples, you should be able to understand that, in the crosstab structure (the previous example), columns and rows are part of the result set, while in the relational format (the following example), column headers or headers are not part of the result set, but are part of the metadata returned from the query.

The relational format is as follows:

Column	Row	Value
Column Data 1	Row Data 1	Measure Data 1.1
Column Data 2	Row Data 1	Measure Data 2.1
Column Data 1	Row Data 2	Measure Data 1.2
Column Data 2	Row Data 2	Measure Data 2.1

The preceding two data structures represent the options when setting the `crosstabMode` and `seriesInRows` properties.

The crosstabMode property

To better understand these concepts, we will make use of a real example. This property, `crosstabMode`, is easy to understand when comparing the results of two queries.

Non-crosstab (Relational):		Crosstab:			
Markets	**Sales**	**Markets**	**2003**	**2004**	**2005**
APAC	1281705	APAC	3529	5938	3411
EMEA	50028224	EMEA	16711	23630	9237
Japan	503957	Japan	2851	1692	380
NA	3852061	NA	13348	18157	6447

In the previous tables, you can see that on the left-hand side you can find the values of sales from each of the territories. The only relevant information is relative to the values presented are the territories. We can say that we are able to get all the information just by looking at the rows, where we can see a direct connection between markets and the sales value.

In the table presented on the right, you will find a value for each territory/year, meaning that the values presented, and in the sample provided in the matrix, are dependent on two *variables*, which are the territory in the rows and the years in the columns. Here we need both the rows and the columns to know what each one of the values represents. Relevant information can be found in the rows and the columns, so this is a crosstab. Crosstabs display the joint distribution of two or more variables, and are usually represented in the form of a contingency table in a matrix.

When the result of a query is dependent only on one variable, then you should set the `crosstabMode` property to `false`. When it is dependent on two or more variables, you should set the `crosstabMode` property to false, otherwise CCC will just use the first two columns like in the non-crosstab example.

The seriesInRows property

Now let's use the same two where we have a crosstab:

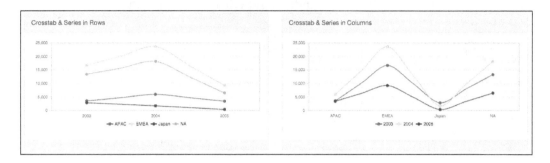

The previous figure shows two charts: the one on the left is a crosstab with the series in the rows, and the one on the right is also crosstab but the series are not in the rows (the series are in the columns). When the crosstab is set to `true`, it means that the measure column title can be translated as a series or a category, and that's determined by the property `seriesInRows`. If this property is set to true, then it will read the series from the rows, otherwise it will read the series from the columns.

If the crosstab is set to false, the community chart component is expecting a row to correspond exactly to one data point, and two or three columns can be returned. When three columns are returned, they can be a **category**, **series and data,** or **series, category and data** and that's determined by the `seriesInRows` property. When set to true, CCC will expect the structure to have three columns such as category, series, and data. When it is set to false, it will expect them to be series, category, and data.

A simple table should give you a quicker reference:

crosstabMode	seriesInRows	Description
true	true	The column titles will act as category values while the series values are represented as data points of the first column.
true	false	The column titles will act as series value while the category/category values are represented as data points of the first column.
false	true	The column titles will act as category values while the series values are represented as data points of the first column.
false	false	The column titles will act as category values while the series values are represented as data points of the first column.

The timeSeries and timeSeriesFormat properties

The `timeSeries` property defines whether the data to be represented by the chart is discrete or continuous. If we want to present some values over time, then the `timeSeries` property should be set to true. When we set the chart to be `timeSeries`, we also need to set another property to tell CCC how it should interpret the dates that come from the query. Check out the following image for `timeSeries` and `timeSeriesFormat`:

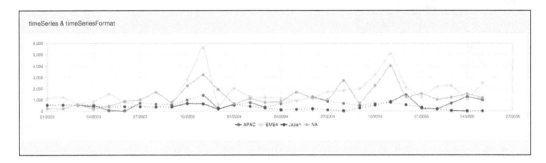

In the example provided with the book, you will find a dashboard that presents data as a `timeSeries` property. The result of one of the queries has the year and the abbreviated month name separate by -, such as 2015-Nov. For the chart to understand it as a date, we need to specify the format by setting the property `timeSeriesFomart`, which in our example would be `%Y-%b`, where `%Y` is the year is represented by four digits, and `%b` is the abbreviated month name.

The format should be specified using the Protovis format, which follows the same format as `strftime` in the C programming language, aside from some unsupported options. To find out what options are available, you should take a look at the documentation, which you will find at: `https://mbostock.github.io/protovis/jsdoc/symbols/pv.Format.date.html`.

Making use of CCC in CDE

There are a lot of properties that will use a default value, and you can find out about them by looking at the documentation or inspecting the code that is generated by CDE when you use chart components. By looking at the console log of your browser, you should also able to understand and get some information about the properties being used by default and/or see whether you are using a property that does not fit your needs.

The use of CCC charts in CDE is simpler, just because you may not need to code. I am only saying *may* because, to achieve quicker results, you may apply some code and make it easier to share properties among different charts or type of chart. To use a CCC chart, you just need to select the property that you need to change and set its value by using the drop-down or by just setting the value:

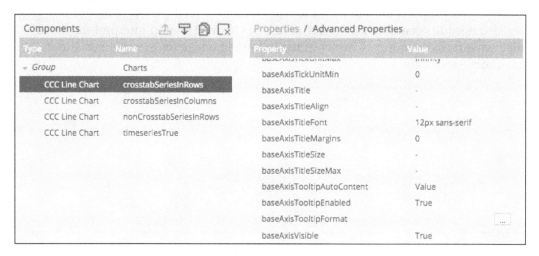

The previous screenshot shows a group of properties with the respective values on the right.

One of the best ways to start to get used to CCC properties is to use the CCC page available as part of the Webdetails page: `http://www.webdetails.pt/ctools/ ccc`. There you will find samples and the properties that are being used for each of the chart. You can use the dropdown to select different kinds of charts from all those that are available inside CCC. You also have the ability to change the properties and update the chart to check the result immediately.

What I usually do, as it's easier and faster, is to change the properties here, check the results, and then apply the necessary values for each of the properties in the CCC charts inside the dashboards. In the following samples, you will also find documentation about the properties, see where the properties are separated by sections of the chart, and after that you will find the extension points.

On the site, when you click on a property/option you will be redirected to another page where you will find the documentation and how to use it.

Changing properties in preExecution or postFetch

We are able to change the properties for the charts, as with any other component. Inside preExecution, the keyword this, refers to the component itself, so we will have access to the chart's main object, which we can also manipulate and add, remove, and change options.

For instance, you can apply the following code:

```
function() {
    var cdProps = {
        dotsVisible: true,
        plotFrame_strokeStyle: '#bbbbbb',
        colors: ['#005CA7', '#FFC20F', '#333333', '#68AC2D']
    };
    $.extend(true, this.chartDefinition, cdProps);
}
```

What we are doing is creating an object with all the properties that we want to add or change for the chart, and then extending the chartDefinitions (where the properties or options are). This is what we are doing with the JQuery function.

> **Use the CCC website and make your life easier**
>
> This way to apply options makes it easier to set the properties. Just change or add the properties that you need, test it, and, when you're happy with the result, you just need to copy them into the object that will extend/overwrite the chart options. Just keep in mind that the properties you change directly in the editor will be overwritten by the ones defined in the preExecution function, if they match each other of course.

Why is this important? It's because not all the properties that you can apply to CCC are exposed in CDE, so you can use preExecution to use or set those properties.

Handling the click event

One important thing about charts is that they allow interaction. CCC provides a way to handle some events in the chart and click is one of those events. To have it working, we need to change two properties: `clickable`, which needs to be set to true, and `clickAction` where we need to write a function with the code to be executed when a click happens. The function receives one argument that usually is referred to as a scene. The scene is an object that has a lot of information about the context where the event happened. From the object you will have access to `vars`, another object where we can find the `series` and the `categories` where the click happened.

We can use the function to get the series/categories being clicked and perform a `fireChange` that can trigger updates on other components:

```
function(scene) {
    var series =  "Series:"+scene.atoms.series.label;
    var category =  "Category:"+scene.vars.category.label;
    var value = "Value:"+scene.vars.value.label;
    Logger.log(category+" & "+value);
    Logger.log(series);
}
```

In the previous code example, you can find the function to handle the click action for a CCC chart. When the click happens, the code is executed, and a variable with the click series is taken from `scene.atoms.series.label`. As well as this, the clicked category `scene.vars.category.label` and the value that crosses the same series/category in `scene.vars.value.value`. This is valid for a crosstab, but you will not find the series when it is a non-crosstab.

You can think of a scene as describing one instance of visual representation. It is generally local to each panel or section of the chart and it's represented by a group of variables that are organized hierarchically. Depending on the scene, it may contain one or many datums. And you must be asking what a a datum is. A datum represents a row, so it contains values for multiple columns.

We also can see from the example that we are referring to atoms, which hold at least a value, a label, and the key of a column. To get a better understanding of what I am talking about, you should perform a breakpoint anywhere in the code of the previous function and explore the object scene.

In the previous example, you would be able to access the category, series labels, and value, as you can see in the following table:

	Corosstab	Non-crosstab

Value	`scene.vars.value.label`
	or
	`scene.getValue();`
		`scene.vars.value.label`
		or
		`scene.getValue();`

Category	`scene.vars.category.label`
	or
	`scene.getCategoryLabel();`
		`scene.vars.category.label`
		or
		`scene.getCategoryLabel();`

Series	`scene.atoms.series.label`
	or
	`scene.getSeriesLabel()`	

For instance, if you add the previous function code to a chart that is a crosstab where the categories are the years and the series are the territories, if you click on the chart, the output would be something like:

```
[info]  WD: Category:2004 & Value:23630
[info]  WD: Series:EMEA
```

This means that you clicked on the year 2004 for the EMEA. EMEA sales for the year 2004 were 23,630.

If you replace the Logger functions with `fireChange` as follows, you will be able to make use of the label/value of the clicked category to render other components and some details about them:

```
this.dashboard.fireChange("parameter", scene.vars.category.label);
```

Internationalization of CCC Charts

We already saw that all the values coming from the database should not need to be translated. There are some ways in Pentaho to do this, but we may still need to set the title of a chart, where the title should be also internationalized. Another case is when you have dates where the month is represented by numbers in the base axis, but you want to display the month's abbreviated name. This name could be also translated to different languages, which is not hard.

For the title, sub-title, and legend, the way to do it is to use the instructions on how to set properties on `preExecution` and the instructions that we already covered in an earlier *Chapter 6, Tables, Templates, Exports, and Text Components* about i18n. First, you will need to define the properties files for the internationalization and set the properties/translations:

```
var cd = this.chartDefinition;
cd.title =  this.dashboard.i18nSupport.prop('BOTTOMCHART.TITLE');
```

To change the title of the chart based on the language defined, we will need to define a function, but we can't use the property on the chart because that will only allow you to define a string, so you will not be able to use a JavaScript instruction to get the text. If you set the previous example code on the `preExecution` of the chart, you will be able to do so.

It may not only make sense to change not only the titles, but for instance it may also be advisable to internationalize the month names. If you are getting data such as `2004-02`, this may correspond to a time series format as `%Y-%m`. If that's the case and you want to display the abbreviated month name, then you may use the `baseAxisTickFormatter` and the `dateFormat` function from the dashboard utilities, also known as `Utils`. The code to write inside the `preExecution` would be:

```
var cd = this.chartDefinition;
cd.baseAxisTickFormatter = function(label) {
   return Utils.dateFormat(moment(label, 'YYYY-mmm'), 'MMM/YYYY');
};
```

The preceding code uses `baseAxisTickFormatter`, which allows you to write a function that receives an argument, identified on the code as a label, because it will store the label for each one of the base axis tick marks. We are using the `dateFormat` method and `moment` library function to format and return the year followed by the abbreviated month name.

You can get information about the language defined and being used by running the following instruction

```
moment.locale();
```

If you need to, you can change the language. If so, please refer to the CDF chapter, as we already covered it there.

What are extension points and how do you use them?

One great thing about the options that you can use is that they are are already implemented. If not, and if they are available as part of Protovis but just not in CCC, you are able can make use of the extension points. So, with extension points you are able to use properties/options that are not implemented directly in CCC. They are one of the great features of CCC charts, because they provide almost direct access to the underlying Protovis marks.

When setting an extension point, we should specify its name and value. The name is a combination of a CCC identification and the Protovis property name separated by an underscore (_). For instance, to define the fill style for the legend, you would need to define legendArea_fillStyle and set a color. First you need to set the visual element, followed by (_) and by the extension point property.

There are no ways to handle the right-click action in CCC, nor is there the possibility to directly listen to the context menu in a Protovis mark, so we can make use of extension points. A good example is:

```
bar_event: [
    ['contextmenu', function(s) { … }],
    ['mouseover',   function(s) { … }],
    ['mouseover', function(s) { … }]
]
```

For each chart type, you will find at the bottom of each chart type the extension points that are available. For instance, the extension points that are available for line charts can be found at: http://www.webdetails.pt/ctools/ccc/#type=dot&anchor=extension-points. The image on the left is an example of it.

When you click on a visual element name such as `baseAxisGrid_`, you will be redirected to another page where you can select the mark, which is the image at the center. Let's suppose that you choose to change the label, you need to add the mark to the visual element like `baseAxisGrid_label`. Finally, after clicking on the marker, you get a list of extension points, which is the image on the right, where you can select the extension point. Let's suppose you have chosen to change the font. It will also need to be added to the property and will end up as `baseAxisGrid_labelFont`.

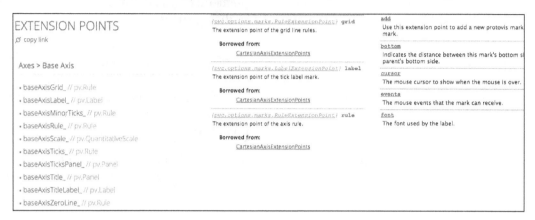

For the provided extension point, we would need to specify the font and size, as specified at: `http://www.w3.org/TR/CSS2/fonts.html#font-shorthand`.

Formatting a basis axis label based on the scale

When you are working with a time series chart, you may want to set a different format for the base axis labels. Let's suppose you want to have a chart that is listening to a time selector. If you select one-year old data to be displayed on the chart, certainly you are not interested in seeing the minutes on the date label. However, if you want to display the last hour, the ticks of the base axis need to be presented in minutes.

There is an extension point we can use to get a conditional format based on the scale of the base axis. The extension point is `baseAxisScale_tickFormatter`, and it can be used like in the code as follows:

```
baseAxisScale_tickFormatter: function(value, dateTickPrecision) {
    switch(dateTickPrecision) {
        case pvc.time.intervals.y:
```

```
            return format_date_year_tick(value);
            break;
        case pvc.time.intervals.m:
            return format_date_month_tick(value);
            break;

        case pvc.time.intervals.H:
            return format_date_hour_tick(value);
            break;
        default:
            return format_date_default_tick(value);

    }
}
```

It accepts a function with two arguments: the value to be formatted and the tick precision, and should return the formatted label to be presented on each label of the base axis.

The previous code shows how the function is used. You can see that a `switch` based on the base axis scale will perform a different format, calling a function. The functions in the code are not pre-defined—we need to write the functions or code to create the formatting. One example of a function to format the date is using the utils `dateFormat` function to return the formatted value to the chart.

The following table shows the intervals that can be used when verifying which time intervals are being displayed on the chart:

Interval	Description	Number representing the interval
y	Year	31536e6
m	Month	2592e6
d30	30 days	2592e6
d7	7 days	6048e5
d	Day	864e5
H	Hour	36e5
m	Minute	6e4
s	Second	1e3
ms	Milliseconds	1

Customizing tooltips

CCC provides the ability to change the default tooltip format, and can be changed using the `tooltipFormat` property. We can change it, making it look like the following image, on the right. You can also compare it to the one on the left, which is the default one:

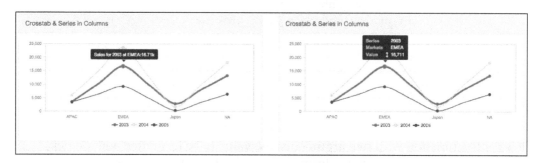

The tooltip default format might change depending on the chart type, but also on some options that you apply to the chart, mainly `crosstabMode` and `seriesInRows`. The property accepts a function that receives one argument, the scene, which will be a similar structure as already covered for the click event. You should return the HTML to be shown on the dashboard when we hover the chart.

In the previous image, you will see on the chart on the left side the defiant tooltip, and on the right a different tooltip. That's because the following code was applied:

```
tooltipFormat: function(scene){
    var year = scene.atoms.series.label;
    var territory = scene.atoms.category.value;
    var sales = Utils.numberFormat(scene.vars.value.value, "#.00A");
    var html = '<html>' +
        <div>Sales for '+year+' at '+territory+':'+sales+'</div>' +
        '</html>';
    return html;
}
```

The code is pretty self-explanatory. First we are setting some variables such as year, territory, and the sales values, which we need to present inside the tooltip. Like in the click event, we are getting the labels/value from the scene, which might depend on the properties we set for the chart. For the sales, we are also abbreviating it, using two decimal places. And last, we build the HTML to be displayed when we hover over the chart.

> **You can also change the base axis tooltip**
>
> Like we are doing to the tooltip when hovering over the values represented in the chart, we can also use `baseAxisTooltip`; just don't forget that use the `baseAxisTooltipVisible` property must be set to true (the value by default). Getting the values to show will be pretty similar.

It can get more complex, though not much more, when we also want, for instance, to display the total value of sales for one year or for the territory. Based on that, we could also present the percentage relative to the total. We should use the property as explained earlier.

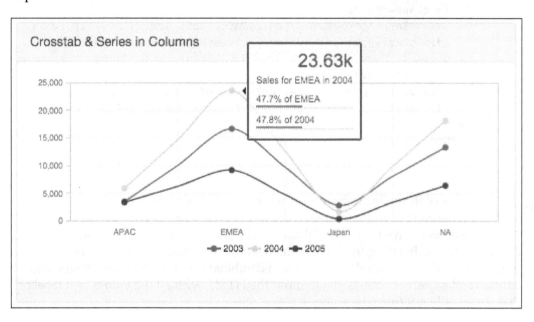

The previous image is one example of how we can customize a tooltip. In this case, we are showing the value but also the percentage that represents the hovered over territory (as the percentage/all the years) and also for the hovered over year (where we show the percentage/all the territories):

```
tooltipFormat: function(scene){
    var year = scene.getSeriesLabel();
    var territory = scene.getCategoryLabel();
    var value = scene.getValue();
    var sales = Utils.numberFormat(value, "#.00A");
    var totals = {};
    _.each(scene.chart().data._datums, function(element) {
```

```
        var value = element.atoms.value.value;
        totals[element.atoms.category.label] =
            (totals[element.atoms.category.label]||0)+value;
        totals[element.atoms.series.label] =
            (totals[element.atoms.series.label]||0)+value;
    });
    var categoryPerc = Utils.numberFormat(value/totals[territory],
"0.0%");
    var seriesPerc = Utils.numberFormat(value/totals[year], "0.0%");
    var html =   '<html>' +
        '<div class="value">'+sales+'</div>' +
        '<div class="dValue">Sales for '+territory+' in '+year+'</div>' +
        '<div class="bar">'+
        '   <div class="pPerc">'+categoryPerc+' of '+territory+'</div>'+
        '   <div class="partialBar" style="width:'+cPerc+'"></div>'+
        '</div>' +
        '<div class="bar">'+
        '   <div class="pPerc">'+seriesPerc+' of '+year+'</div>'+
        '   <div class="partialBar" style="width:'+seriesPerc+'"></div>'+
        '</div>' +
        '</html>';
    return html;
}
```

The first lines of the code are pretty similar except that we are using `scene.getSeriesLabel()` in place of `scene.atoms.series.label`. They do the same, so it's only different ways to get the values/labels, and then the total calculations that are calculated by iterating in all the elements of `scene.chart().data._datums`, which return the logical/relational table, a combination of the territory, years, and value. The last part of code is just to build the HTML with all the values and labels that we already got from the scene.

There are multiple ways to get the values you need; for instance to customize the tooltip, you just need to explore the hierarchical structure of the scene and get used to it.

The image that you are seeing also presents a different style, and that should be done using CSS. You can add CSS for your dashboard and change the style of the tooltip, not just the format.

Styling tooltips

When we want to style a tooltip, we may want to use the developer tools to check the classes or names and CSS properties already applied, but it's hard because the popup does not stay still. We can change the `tooltipDelayOut` property and increase its default value from 80 to 1000 or more, depending on the time you need.

When you want to apply some styles to the tooltips for a particular chart you can do by setting a CSS class on the tooltip. For that you should use the property `tooltipClassName` and set the class name to be added and later used on the CSS.

Pie chart showing the value in the center

There are features that CCC presents and that we don't yet know about, so you should keep an eye on the CCC forum (`http://forums.pentaho.com/showthread.php?161089-CCC-FAQ-Frequently-Asked-Questions-About-CCC`) and Duarte Cunha fiddles (`http://jsfiddle.net/user/duarteleao/fiddles`). The following example has been generated with some simple options that can make a difference. Of course, you also could achieve this with CSS, but it would make your life harder.

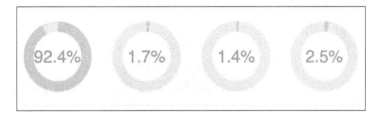

To get the result just shown, for each one of the charts we could apply the following options:

```
function() {
    var cd = this.chartDefinition;
    var options = {
        valuesVisible: true,
        valuesLabelStyle: 'inside',
        valuesFont: '35px sans-serif',
        valuesMask: '{value.percent}',
        label_visible: function() { return !this.index; },
        label_left: null,
        label_top: null,
        label_textAngle: 0,
        label_textAlign: 'center',
```

```
        label_textBaseline: 'middle',
        slice_innerRadiusEx: '70%',
        legend: false
    }
    $.extend(true, cd, options);
}
```

Dimensions

It's important to know that a dimension in CCC is not an MDX dimension. Here it is represented by a subset of atoms. When you want to achieve more advanced results, you can change the behavior of CCC. Well maybe I shouldn't say change the behavior, but help CCC behave in a different way than the default behavior. What we can do is change one dimension, but not change the rest of them; CCC will apply the default options to just those dimensions. Don't forget that these changes are optional and you only want to apply them to change the default behavior of CCC.

When dimensions are not defined, the default dimensions, with the default options, are generated to satisfy the needs of the chart. Anyhow, the data dimensions can be explicitly defined. When defining dimensions, you can define them partially. You will be able to define just one and let the others be automatically generated.

The list of dimension options is defined at: `http://www.webdetails.pt/ctools/ccc/charts/jsdoc/symbols/pvc.options.DimensionType.html`, where you can also get more details.

We have made a table with a complete list and default values and a brief description of them:

Name	Type	Short description (from the CCC website)
label	string	The name of the dimension type as it is shown to the user.
format	string function object	The dimension type's format provider.
isHidden	Boolean	This indicates whether the values of this dimension type should be hidden from the user.
isDiscrete	Boolean	This indicates whether a dimension type should be considered discrete or continuous.
valueType	function	This is the type of value that dimensions of this type will hold.

Name	Type	Short description (from the CCC website)
rawFormat	string	This is a Protovis format string that is to parse the raw value.
comparer	function	This is a function that compares two different and non-null values of the dimension's valueType.
converter	any	This converts a non-null raw value, as read from the data source, into a value of the dimension's valueType.
key	string	This is a function that converts a non-null value of the valueType into a string that (uniquely) identifies the value in the dimension.
formatter	function	This is a function that formats a value, possibly null, of the dimension's valueType.

For instance, if we want to have the dimension, category to be a date, but represented on a discrete and not continuous axis, we would need to specify the following options:

```
dimensions: {
category: {valueType: Date, isDiscrete: true}
}.
```

Readers

One of the options that we have to apply to the dimension is readers. Readers allow you to declare the mapping of columns to dimensions. As it was not always possible to use colName, there was a need to *invent* readers. This will only happen after parsing the data structure and when CCC is already making use of a relational data structure (this could be the result of a data structure parsing from a crosstab).

We can set readers using two different approaches:

- Using visual role names or visual row prefix names: category, series, measure, value, and multiChart. Depending on the chart type, there might be other dimension types available such as median, lowerQuartil, upperQuartil, minimum, and maximum. They are applied on the box plot chart.

    ○ For instance: readers: ['category', 'series', 'value']: this would make CCC interpret the columns as specified, the measure, series, category and at least the value, slightly changing the way it interprets the columns by default

- By using business names instead of defining measures, series, categories, and value.

  ○ For instance: `readers: ['Markets', 'Years', 'Sales']`

  ○ When doing this, we also need to define the mapping for the visual roles:

```
visualRoles: {
value:    'Sales', // <-- mapping defined here
series:   'Years',  // <-- mapping defined here
category: 'Markets' // <-- mapping defined here
}
```

When defining readers, we might use the same visual role names or visual row prefix names that are not defined. These column values will not be mapped to visual roles automatically, but we are still able to use them on, for instance, tooltip customization or event handling. It can be very.

Another way to define readers is using the indexes of the columns being mapped:

```
readers: [
  {names: 'Sales', indexes: 2},
{names: 'Years', indexes: 1},
{names: 'Markets', indexes: 0}
]
visualRoles: {
value:    'Sales',
series:   'Years',
category: 'Markets'
}
```

In the previous example, the first column (`index 0`) of the data source feeds the `Markets` dimension, while the second column (`index 1`) feeds the `Years` dimension and so on.

Visual roles

You might use visual roles even if you are not using the business names as readers. For instance, they might be used to represent a second plot in the chart. Anyhow, the `visualRoles` option allows you to declare the mapping from CCC dimensions to visual roles.

If you want to represent a second plot that should be a boxplot, then you will the code as follows:

```
plots: [
        // Main plot - bars
        {
            name: 'main',
            dotsVisible: true
    },
        // Second plot - boxes
        {
            type: 'box',
            visualRoles: {
                // Comment the ones you don't want represented
                median:         'value',
                lowerQuartil: 'value2',
                upperQuartil: 'value3',
                minimum:        'value4',
                maximum:        'value5'
            }
        }
    ]
```

You can see that we are mapping the visual roles `median`, `lowerQuartil`, `upperQuartil`, `minimum`, and `maximum`, using the row prefix names `value`, `value2`, `value3`, `value4`, and `value5`. This will make it possible to have a second chart using box plot representations for each of the categories.

You are able to check the example provided on the CCC web page at the following link: `http://www.webdetails.pt/ctools/ccc/#type=line&anchor=line-with-5-number-statistics`.

The available visual roles are: `category`, `series`, `multiChart`, `value`, `dataPart`, and `measures`.

Debugging the CCC charts

When you want to customize your options a bit more, you may be entering some advanced features, where it's hard to understand what's being done or what changes we should apply. CCC provides some debugging modes that allow you to have a better understanding and knowledge of what these advanced features are doing.

We will cover how to use developer tools to perform debugging later, but for now just be aware that you have specific debugging levels for CCC. You will see later that you can perform debugging on a dashboard if you add a parameter of your URL (debug=true).

If you have a URL that is http://localhost:8080/pentaho/api/ repos/%3Apublic%3Asample.wcdf/generatedContent, you need change it to: http://localhost:8080/pentaho/api/repos/%3Apublic%3Asample.wcdf/ generatedContent?debug=true. Or if you have http://localhost:8080/ pentaho/api/repos/%3Apublic%3Asample.wcdf/generatedContent?paramcou ntry=Portugal, you need to change it to:http://localhost:8080/pentaho/api/ repos/%3Apublic%3Asample.wcdf/generatedContent?paramcountry=Portugal& debug=true.

To debug a CCC chart and get extra information you can add &debugLevel=5. You need to use it like: http://localhost:8080/pentaho/api/ repos/%3Apublic%3Asample.wcdf/generatedContent?paramcountry=Portugal& debug=true&debugLevel=5.

When you do this, you will get a lot more information that is really important. This information will be available on the console in the developer tools of the browser you are using. The following examples are screenshots taken from Chrome for Mac OS X, version 46.0.2490.80 (64-bit). The image to the left shows the output on the console regarding the options being used to render the chart. The one to the right shows one example of the data source summary that CCC provides. Some examples are as follows:

The following image is also part of the output that we get from debugging CCC. The image on the left gives you information about the `Logical Table` and how CCC parses the result set of the query `seriesInRows` and `crosstabMode`, or for readers:

[pvc.LineChart					]: LOGICAL TABLE
Index	Kind	Type	Name	Label	Dimension
0	C	string	Markets		series
1	R	string			category
2	M	number			value

[pvc.LineChart		]: VISUAL ROLES MAP SUMMARY
Visual Role	Source/From	Bound to Dimension(s)
multiChart	–	–
dataPart	–	–
point.color	point.series	series ("Markets")
point.series	–	series ("Markets")
point.category	–	category ("Category")
point.value	–	value ("Value")

Looking at the table on the right, you will find the `Visual Roles Mapping` that is being used as the default for the options used or as set by you, as explained earlier in this chapter.

If, instead of using a value of 5 for the CCC debugging level, you use a value of 16 (`&debugLevel=16`), when displaying the chart you will be able to see some borders that identify all the panels of the chart. The following screenshot is an example of this. Among other things, it's useful to check whether it's being used as padding or margins for the panels. You can see those margins in the following image:

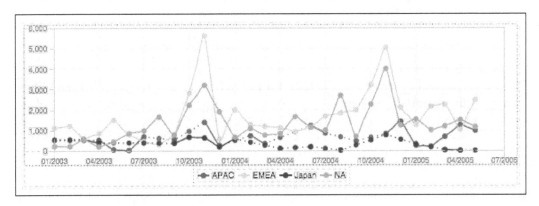

CGG – Community Graphics Generator

CGG is a plugin that allows you to export CCC charts in CDE dashboards as images. CGG will generate the image on the server side, and that's the reason why you will see some JavaScript files related to the charts to be exported. Every time you set a chart to be exportable, it will be provided with a URL that you can use to export the image. This means you can see the generated images of the charts you can embed inside any other dashboard/report/page.

When editing a CDE dashboard, you can press *Shift + G*, which is a shortcut to get to a dialog with a list of charts in the dashboard. By selecting a chart, you will be enabling the option to export the chart using CGG. You can see this in the following image:

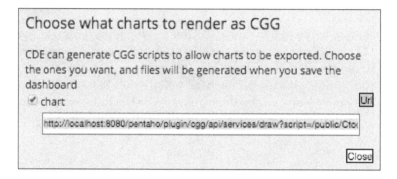

The previous image also shows the URL button, which you can click to get the link to use for the export. For example, for one of the examples provided with the book, the link to the chart will be: `http://<server>:<port>/pentaho/plugin/cgg/api/services/draw?script=/public/Ctools+Book+Samples/Chapter+8/CGGSample/CGGSample_chart.js&outputType=png`.

This URI uses two parameters, the script and the output type. The first one is used to point to where the script to generate the chart is located. This script is only generated when you enable the checkbox in the CGG dialog box and just after saving the dashboard. When you save the dashboard, the script is generated and you can make use of it.

Using CGG, charts can be exposed as a PNG or SVG image. Let's see how we can make this happen. We can change the `outputType` parameter and set the string `png` to get a PNG image or set `svg` to get an SVG image. I always prefer to use SVG but, if you have some incompatibilities, you can use the other option. By default, CGG uses PNG.

References

Other good sources of additional information and examples are the following links:

- http://jsfiddle.net/user/duarteleao/fiddles/
- http://forums.pentaho.com/showthread.php?161089-CCC-FAQ-Frequently-Asked-Questions-About-CCC

Summary

In this chapter, we provided a quick overview of how to use CCC in CDF and CDE dashboards and showed you what kinds of chart are available. We covered some of the base options as well as some advanced options that you might use to get almost a fully custom visualization. Might be that some of the properties are not available in the CDE GUI, but the properties and respective values might be used in the preExecution or postFetch function of the CCC component being used.

You should now know about internationalization and how to customize tooltips, and even how to deal with the click event, creating interaction with new components. When starting out using CCC, you might not be interested in debugging, but if you are or are intending to be an advanced user, you should start looking into it. We also covered what an extension point is and how to use it.

In the next chapter, we are going to cover the Pentaho App Builder and you'll see how to build a Pentaho plugin with it.

Pentaho App Builder

9

Pentaho App Builder is one plugin you can use to build your Pentaho plugins. The most interesting part of it is that you don't need to create any code to get it working. Yes, you heard right, no code.

In this chapter, you will learn about:

- Pentaho App Builder
- Community Plugin Kick-starter
- Creating a dashboard
- Making a plugin available on the marketplace

By the end of this chapter, you will understand Pentaho App Builder and how to work with it. There was a time when you would have needed to know how to write Java code for the back end of the plugin, but now it's much more simple and more accessible to many more people.

You will also know what the **Community Plugin Kick-starter (CPK)** is and its relationship with Pentaho App Builder. You really need to understand the concepts behind CPK, because that's where most of the magic happens. Pentaho App Builder is just a graphical interface that leverages the work. You will also see that with CPK, you are able to make use of jobs directly, and not just transformations like in CDA. We'll give you some tips and tricks that you will find very useful.

Understanding Pentaho App Builder

"Sparkl, or Pentaho App Builder, is a plugin creator instrument that sits on 2 major cornerstones of Pentaho: CTools and PDI, aiming to leverage as much as possible of our existing stack."

– Pedro Alves

The main idea is to use both of the two most amazing tools in Pentaho: the CTools and Kettle (also known as Pentaho Data Integration). If you know how to build Kettle jobs and transformations and also know how to build a dashboard, you should be able to build a Pentaho plugin. If not, it's about time to learn. I can recommend you two books: `https://www.packtpub.com/big-data-and-business-intelligence/pentaho-data-integration-beginners-guide-second-edition` and `https://www.packtpub.com/big-data-and-business-intelligence/pentaho-data-integration-4-cookbook`.

If you didn't know Java code, it would be hard for you to create a plugin, but that's not the case anymore as you are able to do it without the need to write Java code. You can also create a CTools dashboard without writing a line of code; however, as I already told you earlier in the book, you will need to write some JavaScript to build remarkable dashboards. Not that you need to know a lot of JavaScript; you just need to understand it and adjust some code in the book or in the included samples. We are making the absolute most of the existing skills of data developers. When we talk about building a web application, usually we will talk about having a back end and a front end.

Pentaho App Builder works on top of CPK. CPK provides a way to simplify the structure of a Pentaho package application, where the UI can be built as a CDE dashboard and the back end as a Kettle transformation/job. There are other options, such as making the back end using JavaScript or Java code. However, there is no need to do this if you can use Kettle.

Installing Pentaho App Builder

You can install Pentaho App Builder using Marketplace, and you just need to refer to the instructions in the first chapter. Pentaho App Builder has some dependencies, so make sure you have them installed:

- **CPF**: Community Plugin Framework
- **CDE**: Community Dashboard Editor
- **CDF**: Community Dashboard Framework
- **CDA**: Community Data Access

Create a new plugin

Open Pentaho App Builder using the PUC menu, or directly from `http://localhost:8080/pentaho/plugin/sparkl/api/main`. When you start Pentaho App Builder, you will be in the following *dashboard*. I referred to the dashboard, because Pentaho App Builder is itself dashboard:

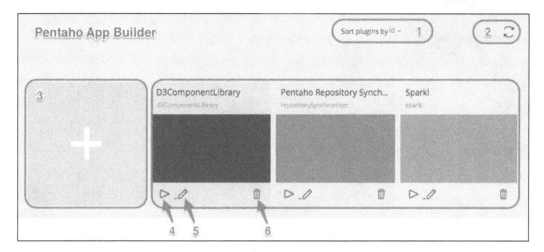

In the preceding image, you will find the following buttons/options:

1. **Sort plugins by**: This is to sort the plugins that are available in your Pentaho instance. Here, you only see the plugins that were built using Pentaho App Builder or CPK.

2. **Refresh**: This refreshes the list of available plugins.

3. **Create a new Plugin**: Click this plus sign to be able to create new plugins. You will learn more about this later in the chapter.

4. **Play**: This will open/execute the main dashboard of the plugin.

5. **Edit**: You will be redirected to another window where you can edit the metadata of the plugin, or create/edit/remove end points.

6. **Remove**: This deletes the plugin from the system folder. The files will be removed from the `system` folder of the server.

When you create a new plugin using option 3, you need to enter the name of the plugin and click on the **Create plugin** button. You will get a message to restart the server. So please proceed. In future versions of Pentaho 6.X and new releases of Pentaho App Builder for Pentaho 6.X, it will be possible to generate a new plugin that becomes immediately available.

After the restart, you need to go into Pentaho App Builder and edit your plugin. If you didn't set the metadata of the plugin, it's a good time to do it. Just fill out the form data and click on **Apply Changes**. The following image is an example of what you will get:

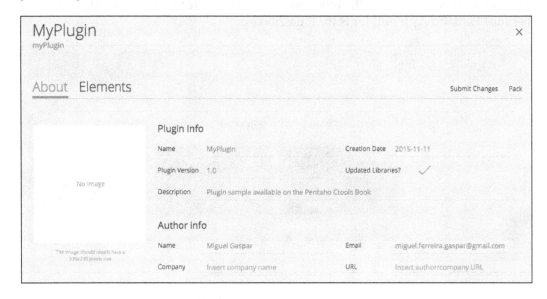

You will see two tabs: **About** and **Elements**. **About** is the information/metadata of the plugin. **Elements** is about the endpoints of the plugin:

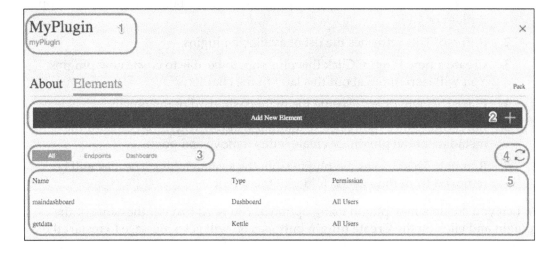

In the preceding image, we can identify the following sections:

1. **Plugin name**: The plugin's ID/name.

2. **Add new element**: You can click on this plus button to add a new endpoint. It can be a dashboard or a Kettle job/transformation. We will cover these separately in this chapter.

3. **Display options**: You can select the type of add-in you want to be displayed. It can be a dashboard or a Kettle transformation/job, or both at the same time. In the image, you can see a dashboard that can be used as the front end and a Kettle transformation/job as part of the back end.

4. **Refresh button**: This will let you refresh the endpoints available. You can add a dashboard or transformation/job to the endpoints folder in the plugin system folder, and you can then refresh the plugin to see the endpoints listed, so there is no need for a restart.

5. **Available endpoints**: Here you will get a list of the available endpoints. The list will include the name, type, and permissions. The type will give you information about whether it's a dashboard or Kettle endpoint.

Creating a new endpoint

An endpoint can be considered as a URI and HTTP method that directly gets a response from the server. For instance, when invoking the URI, we might get a dashboard or the result from a Kettle job/transformation. It does not need to be invoked from the plugin itself, as you can run a Kettle endpoint from another application, but of course one of the use cases it to use the end points inside the plugin itself.

We saw in *Chapter 2*, *Acquiring Data with CDA*, that we can use CDA to get data from a Kettle transformation, but using Pentaho App Builder to do so, you can also use jobs to execute some actions and return success or error messages, download a file/multiple files, or have a custom format. Note that you should use Pentaho App Builder only if you're building one application/plugin, otherwise you might build a normal dashboard or use CDA endpoints to get data. If you can't do this with a regular dashboard and CDA data sources, then use Pentaho App Builder.

Like we have already covered, there are two kinds of endpoints that you can use in Pentaho App Builder/CPK. When creating a new element, you need to specify its name and type:

- A Pentaho Data Integration (Kettle) job/transformation
- A CDE dashboard

Creating a job/transformation

To create a new Kettle endpoint, you will need to specify the name and the type **Kettle Endpoint**. You will also need to choose from **Clean Job** or **Clean Transformation**. You can also create a Kettle transformation that can be executed only by an administrator:

After the endpoint has been created, you will see it as shown in the following image:

There are two buttons here you can use for each Kettle endpoint:

1. **Execute the endpoint**: This will trigger the execution of the endpoint.

2. **Remove/delete the endpoint**: This removes the endpoint, and will ask for confirmation.

You don't have a button to edit the Kettle transformation/job, and that's because it's not possible to open Data Integration in the browser.

Starting to learn about CPK

Like we covered earlier, CPK is where almost all the magic exists. In reality, the plugins that you create with Pentaho App Builder are CPK plugins that might be created by Pentaho App Builder, the web interface that allows you to do so easily.

CPK lets you expose the Kettle jobs, transformations, and dashboards as a REST endpoint. You can call them using either of the following calls:

- ```
  http://<host>:<port>/<webapp>/plugin/<cpkPluginId>/api/
  {kettleFileName}
  ```

- ```
  http://<host>:<port>/<webapp>/plugin/<cpkPluginId>/api/
  {dashboardFileName}
  ```

Here:

- `host`: This is the hostname or IP of the server. It can be `localhost` when you have Pentaho installed on the same machine as the request.

- `port`: This is the port we can use to access the Pentaho server. It is `8080` by default.

- **webapp**: This is the web app's name, which by default is `pentaho`.

- **cpkPluginId**: This is the ID of the plugin that you specified when creating the plugin.

- **kettleFileName** or **dashboardFileName**: This is the name of the endpoint you are requesting. You can specify the name of the dashboard or the name of a Kettle transformation or job.

When we create a Kettle transformation or job using Pentaho App Builder, as explained earlier, you will get the following parameters automatically created for the job or transformation you have created:

Parameter	Default value	Description
`#cpk.cache.isEnabled`	`false`	This enables/disables the caching of results.
`#cpk.cache.timeToLiveSeconds`	`3,600`	This shows how many seconds a result will be cached for. Setting this value to 0 means the result will be cached *forever*.
`#cpk.executeAtStart`		This indicates whether the transformation is to be executed when the plugin is initialized or not.
`#cpk.plugin.dir`		This is the `plugin` folder.
`#cpk.plugin.id`		This is the ID of the plugin.
`#cpk.response.attachmentName`		This is the attachment name used when downloading a file from a result.
`#cpk.response.download`	`false`	This shows whether or not to mark the HTTP response body as an attachment.
`#cpk.response.kettleOutput`		This is the output format to be used by default. The possible values are: `Infered`, `Json`, `SingleCell`, `ResultFiles`, and `ResultOnly`.
`#cpk.response.mimeType`		This is the `mimeType` of the HTTP response. If this value is not set, the plugin will try to determine it from the file extension.
`#cpk.result.stepName`	`OUTPUT`	This is the default output step where the rows will be fetched for the result.
`#cpk.session.[sessionVarName]`		This is the value of the session variable named `[sessionVarName]`. It will be automatically injected when the variable is enabled.
`#cpk.session.roles`		These are the roles of the username executing this transformation.

Parameter	Default value	Description
`#cpk.session.username`		This is the username that is executing this transformation.
`#cpk.solution.system.dir`		This is the `pentaho-solutions` folder.
`#cpk.webapp.dir`		This is the `webapp` folder.

By default, all the parameters are disabled. To enable the parameter, you should remove the # from the beginning of its name. Otherwise, it will be seen as a comment.

Specifying the step of where to get results from

A Kettle endpoint (job or transformation) may have multiple steps or job entries where we can get the results from. You are able to choose which step to retrieve data from. This can be done by setting the name of the step/job entry to start with OUTPUT. Just prefix the name of your step with the referred string and see the results returned to the caller of the endpoint.

There is also another way. It is possible to specify which step entry we want to fetch the row results from — we just need to include the `stepName` parameter in the query string of the request. To make it easier to identify the step name where to pull the information from, we need to add to our URI `?stepName=OUTPUT`:

```
http://<host>:<port>/<webapp>/plugin/<cpkPluginId>/api/
{dashboardName}?stepName=OUTPUT
```

By default, CPK will try to find an OUTPUT step name. A bit later on, we will cover how you can change the step name directly in the jobs/transformations using the `cpk.result.stepName` property.

Specifying parameters' values

It's very useful that you can pass parameters to a transformation/job. To do so, you need to prefix the name of the parameter with `param`. If the parameter name is called `territory`, you need to use `paramterritory`, as shown here:

```
http://<host>:<port>/pentaho/plugin/<cpkPluginId>/api/{dashboardName}
?paramterritory=EMEA
```

Changing the output format type

CPK will try to guess the output type; however, you can specify the output type you desire. We may want to return data to the caller, or just return a file that can be downloaded. The available options are as follows:

- `Json`: This returns the result rows in a standard CDA-like result set format (`metadata / queryinfo / resultset`), just like a CDA data source.

- `ResultFiles`: This gets the files that were set in the result. For this to be enabled, we need to set the option **Add filename to the result set**.

- `SingleCell`: This returns the content of the first cell of the first row in the result. This allows us to return other format types, for instance XML.

- `ResultOnly`: This returns status information about the execution. This is usually the output of the executions of a job.

We can select the desired format by setting a query string parameter like in the following link. The query string name is `kettleOutput`:

```
http://<host>:<port>/pentaho/plugin/<cpkPluginId>/api/{dashboardName}
?paramterritory=EMEA
```

You want to avoid the use of the query string parameter, and you also have the transformation/job parameter `cpk.response.kettleOutput` that you can change. When the parameter `cpk.response.kettleOutput` isn't used, CPK will try to infer it. Take a look at the following diagram:

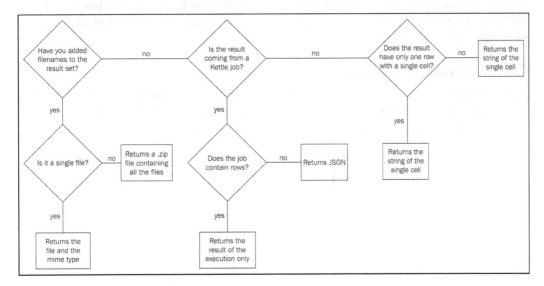

The previous diagram is the decision logic to determine which will be the result returned from the endpoint.

When the option `resultFiles` is used, CPK will compress all the files inside a `.zip` file, which is returned, but keep in mind that if the result only includes one file, CPK will not zip it and will return the files, so if you're using a browser, the browser will try to determine the mime type from the file extension. If the mime type is known, the browser will try to render the file and not download it. You can also force the file to be downloaded if it's a single file. This can be achieved by setting `cpk.response.download` to true.

If you also want to specify the mime type so that the browser can understand its content, you can do this by setting the parameter `cpk.response.mimeType` to the desired value (for example, an application/XML).

Specify the filename for the downloaded file

To specify the filename, you can use the parameter `cpk.response.attachmentName`, or set the query string parameter name `attachmentName`.

Returning a single cell

Let's suppose you want to return your own JSON or XML structure. How would you do so? To achieve that you need to return a single cell. You should follow the same behavior as for the result file. This will also behave as defined by the use of the parameters `cpk.response.download`, `cpk.response.mimeType` and `cpk.response.attachedName`.

Other considerations

Each CPK plugin has its own cache to store the results obtained from the execution of its endpoints. By default, caching is disabled and to enable it, you set the value of the transformation/job parameter `cpk.cache.isEnabled` to `true`.

The length of time that the results will remain cached can be set by setting the time in seconds using the parameter `cpk.cache.timeToLiveSeconds`.

Creating a dashboard

To create a new dashboard, just add the name of your dashboard and select the type *Dashboard*. You will also need to select its style between a clean dashboard or a Pentaho App Builder template dashboard. I advise you to use the clean dashboard and apply your own styles, or create your own style (similar to what was explained in *Chapter 7, Advanced Concepts using CDF and CDE*):

There is also a checkbox you can check if the dashboard should only be accessible only to Pentaho administrators. When you create a new endpoint, the dashboard will become available. The following image is an example of a row displaying a dashboard endpoint.

After the endpoint has been created, you will see the following image:

There are three buttons you can use for each frontend endpoint (dashboard):

1. **Open the dashboard**: This will trigger the execution of the dashboard.
2. **Edit the dashboard**: This will open the dashboard in edit mode.
3. **Remove / Delete the endpoint**: This removes the endpoint, and will ask for confirmation.

A dashboard is used like the Kettle endpoints are. The URL to call is basically the same, and the only change is the name of the endpoint, which should point to the name of the dashboard.

You can invoke dashboards using the following calls:

*   `http://<host>:<port>/<webapp>/plugin/<cpkPluginId>/api/{dashboardFileName}`
*   `http://<host>:<port>/<webapp>/plugin/<cpkPluginId>/api/{dashboardFileName}?mode=edit`

In the second call, you will see `?mode=edit`, meaning that we want to open the dashboard in edit mode, while the first one will open it in render mode.

There are some default endpoints already defined that you can use so you don't give the same name to the dashboards or transformations/jobs. The endpoints are as follows:

- `status`: Displays the status of the plugin and all its endpoints
- `refresh` or `reload`: Reloads all the configurations, endpoints, and dashboards, and also clears the endpoints cache
- `version`: Returns the plugin version (defined in the plugin's `version.xml` file or through the control panel)
- `getSitemapJson`: Returns a JSON object with the plugins sitemap (for dashboards only!)
- `getElementsList`: Returns a JSON object with the whole list of elements present in the plugin (dashboards and Kettle endpoints)

Folder structure

The folder structure of the plugins is as follows:

`dashboards | endpoints | static | resources | lib | plugin.xml`

Where, they are explained as follows:

- `dashboards`: Inside the folder are all the dashboards that have been created and that should be accessible to all users. Any dashboard that is placed inside the `admin` folder will only be available for administrators.
- `endpoints`: All backend endpoints, Kettle jobs, and transformations should be placed inside a `kettle` folder. When the name of a Kettle job or transformation is prefixed by _, the endpoint will not become available as an external endpoint. This makes it possible to have private endpoints that can only be used by another job and/or transformation.
- `static`: All CSS, JavaScript, and images can be placed here, and will be available to be used inside the dashboard.
- `lib`: This is where the Java libraries can be placed.
- `plugin.xml`: This is the file where all the configurations are set. Here you may uncomment the `menu-item` tag and make a menu item available to open the dashboard when the option is clicked:

```
<!-- Menu entry -->
<menu-items>
  <menu-item id="myPlugin_main" anchor="tools-submenu"
             label="MyPlugin" command="content/myPlugin/"
             type="MENU_ITEM" how="LAST_CHILD"/>
</menu-items>
```

Making use of Kettle endpoints on a dashboard

You may use some of the Kettle endpoints you have created for each of the plugins available on the server. When creating the dashboard, in edit mode of course, if you go to the data sources perspectives, you will find some data sources groups that are new to the list of data sources types. Inside each one of those groups, you will find a list of endpoints that you have created for your plugin, but also can be used in other plugins. Each plugin will have its own group, and the data sources inside are the data sources for each of them, as shown here:

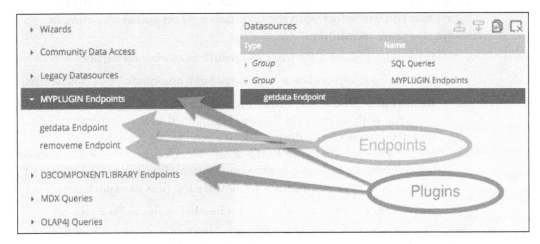

The previous image is one example of the groups that will become available, and you will also see your own data sources or the data sources you have created for your plugin. You can see in the following image two plugins: myPlugin and d3ComponentLibrary. There are two endpoints that belong to myPlugin: getData and removeMe:

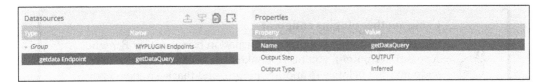

You can make use of this endpoint as another data source, except that you will have fewer options. The preceding image shows you that an endpoint provides three properties:

- **Name**: Used the same as with other data sources. This is the name of the data source that can be set on a component.

- **Output step**: This is where you can set the name of the step where you want to extract data from.

- **Output type**: This sets the output type of the data source. The available options that you can select from the dropdown when you start typing or clicking down are as follows:

    - **Inferred**: This lets CPK infer the result, as explained earlier.

    - **JSON**: The result will be a `Json` object like any other CDA data source.

    - **ResultFiles**: This will return a file, which may be the only one, or a `.zip` file with all the files that are being used in the dashboard. You will need to check the option `add filename to the result set` for the steps where the option is available. Doing so is not mandatory for all the steps but only for the ones where the files will be exported from. The filenames are used to identify the files to export.

    - **ResultOnly**: This is usually used when the endpoint is a job.

    - **SingleCell**: This is used when you want to get a custom result. You set the output that you wish for a single cell as a string. The result of the string of a single cell will be returned.

But how about parameters? Can't we use parameters and pass them to a transformation/job? Yes, you can, but you need to define them in the parameters of the component that is using the data source.

Using another plugins endpoint

When using another plugin transformation from another Pentaho App Builder plugin, you need to take care, because there will be an endpoint that belongs to another plugin, and that's a dependency. There is no problem doing so, you just need to make sure that you include the plugin as a dependency, so that users installing your plugin know that another plugin needs to be included.

When you use a data source (that is, a plugin endpoint) in a component, you may specify the parameters to pass to the transformation/job. Check the following image:

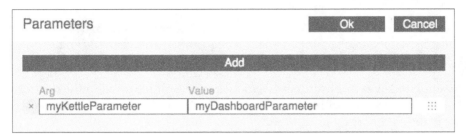

Let's suppose you have a parameter in your little transformation called myKettleParameter. You can send a value to the transformation by creating a mapping with the parameter of the dashboard. When using a table component, for instance, you may define the data source and the parameters to be sent to the data source.

The preceding image is one example of the image you will get when setting the parameters. On the left, you will need to specify the name of the parameters of the transformation, and on the right, the name of the parameter of the dashboard. This will create a mapping between both, and that's the way we can send a value to a Kettle parameter. You can add as many parameters as you need. Just don't forget that if you are adding too many parameters, you may be doing something wrong.

When creating a plugin, you don't always want a job/transformation to be used as a way to get data for the front end. You may want the dashboard of the plugin to perform some action. For that purpose, you can use a Kettle transformation or job. You can use your own code to do so, or you can use the button component.

The button component has a property called Action Datasource, where you can choose one of the data sources to execute when clicking the button. The action parameters property is where we can specify the parameters mapping between the Kettle job/transformation and the dashboard parameters. There are two callbacks you can use when setting Action Datasource:

- Success Callback: This will be executed when the job/transformation is executed with success.
- Failure Callback: This will be executed when the job/transformation fails to execute.

The functions that can be defined are as follows:

```
function(result) {
    ...
    // Make use of the result returned to the dashboard.
    ...
}
```

The function receives one argument, which is the result returned to the dashboard. Inside the function, you will need to write the code to parse the information and display it, or just interpret it.

How do I make the plugin available on the marketplace?

As soon as the plugin is developed and in a stable state, it is ready to be shared to the community. CPK is able to generate a .zip file with metadata information so it is able to be published to the marketplace. Of course, if you are building the plugin for a customer, you don't want to make it public, so you don't need to go through these steps.

To submit the plugin, you need to follow the instructions provided at the following link: https://github.com/pentaho/marketplace-metadata.

The following instructions assume that you have the git command line installed and available.

As you can see, there are three main steps:

1. Clone the repository:

    To do this, you first need to create a GitHub account, which can be created for free. Go to https://github.com/pentaho/marketplace-metadata and click on the **fork** button, which will create a fork of the repository in your account. You will then be able to clone the fork in your account. There are many ways to clone the repository, and one of these ways is to execute a line, as follows:

    ```
    git clone git@github.com:mfgaspar/marketplace-metadata.git
    ```

    This will create a folder with all the files needed. The file you will need to change is marketplace.xml. These steps are required to make it possible to perform the submit request.

2. Update the `marketplace.xml` file with your `market-entry`:

   You should edit the file and add an entry as explained in the instructions provided on the Pentaho marketplace metadata link we just mentioned. After you've filled out all the necessary information, you can proceed with the pull request, but first you will need to commit the changes to your repository. To do so, you can run the following in the command line:

   ```
   git add marketplace.xml
   git commit -m "Adding myPlugin to the marketplace"
   ```

3. Submit a pull request to have your plugin reviewed for inclusion on both the marketplace plugins and the Pentaho Marketplace website.

   To submit the pull request, you need to go back to your Pentaho Marketplace fork page, add click on **Pull Request**, and include a message.

Pentaho will need to categorize and approve the plugin before it becomes available on the marketplace.

Summary

As you can see, it's pretty simple to create a new plugin for Pentaho. I really hope you can have a brilliant idea that we can use, that becomes available on the marketplace.

In this chapter, you learned that you can build a plugin just by creating endpoints that are accessible from the browser, and this can be very useful when integrating Pentaho with third-party applications.

In the next chapter, we will cover what we have missed until now, for example, how to embed a CDF/CDE dashboard in a third-party application and how to perform debugging.

10
Embed, Deploy, and Debug

Usually, one of the request from customers is to embed dashboards in a third party application. Using RequireJS, doing so is simple and very flexible. You can build mini dashboards that you can easily embed into your application without interfering with the dashboard's default behavior. In this chapter, you will learn how to embed both CDF and CDE dashboards into third-party applications and will explore some considerations.

In all the earlier chapters, you learned how to build a dashboard using CDF and/or CDE. But when we are developing them, we may face some problems, and it would be great to know what should we be looking for. In this chapter, you will get information on how you can debug the dashboard using the developer tools in your browser.

One of the last phases of a project is delivery to the customer or internally to a department, or any other issue that you find. In this chapter, you will also learn some concepts that will help you deploy a project and you'll explore some considerations when delivering a project to a customer.

You may also know, if you've been paying close attention, that there are some CTools that have Pentaho support. If you are a Pentaho customer who has paid for support, you may raise a support case for CDA, CDF, CDE, and CGG, which are the supported tools. Otherwise, if you are a community user, you have other options that may not be as good and quick as support, but we will explore the options so you can find some help if you need it.

In this chapter, you will learn how to:

- Embed CDF and CDE dashboards
- Avoid cross-domain references problems
- Handle events from outside the dashboard
- Debug dashboards when developing them

Embedding dashboards

A frequent question or request that I get from customers is how to embed the dashboards in another application. To be honest, the process before RequireJS was introduced into CDF was quite hard and was not interesting. The possibilities, and I will not get into details of them, were to use an HTML iframe, but this came with a lot of problems later on, it was not really suitable for mobiles, and it was bad from the usability point of view. Another option would be to use html div integration, but that created conflicts in JavaScript libraries and in the CSS, so it might create a mess when styling your pages.

With the use of RequireJS, the process is much more simple and flexible, and does not cause big issues. Of course, you might find some minor issues, but they can be easily identified and fixed. The process of embedding a CDF and a CDE dashboard is different, even if the base concepts are quite similar.

Of course, the first step before embedding a dashboard, is to create that same dashboard. This is valid when embedding a CDE dashboard, because a CDF dashboard is created at the same time you are embedding it. The good news, which you should be expecting, is that you don't need to do anything different from what we've covered up to now to create a dashboard that can be embedded. A really good advantage is that you can embed the same dashboard multiple times in your application. And you may build a kind of mini dashboard that you can use multiple times.

Avoiding cross-domain requests

Before you start embedding your dashboards, you need to be aware of how to avoid cross-domain request issues.

When embedding dashboards in other applications and in earlier versions of CDF and CDE, you needed to have a reverse proxy working to avoid cross-domain request issues. Nowadays, the process is really simple. You can turn on an extra setting for CDF and CDE. To properly allow embedding, which usually requires cross-domain requests, you will need to add the following XML tag, and that's valid for both CDF and CDE.

Edit the settings.xml file of CDF and/or CDE, which you will find in your pentaho-solutions folder: system/pentaho-cdf-dd/settings.xml and system/pentaho-cdf/settings.xml. Then add the following property:

```
<allow-cross-domain-resources>true</allow-cross-domain-resources>
```

Depending on the configuration of your server, you may need to restart the server. If you don't know what I am talking about, just restart it and you will see it working without cross-domain request problems.

So now let's start embedding some dashboards.

Embedding a CDF dashboard

A CDF dashboard can be easily embedded in any HTML page hosted anywhere — you just need to include a script to embed CDF in your web page/application. The script will ask for CDF, and the request should be made to a Pentaho Server that has CDF installed. The script to include is as follows:

```
<script
  type="text/javascript"
  src="http://<server>/<webapppath>/plugin/pentaho-cdf/api/cdf-embed.
js">
</script>
```

Where:

- `<server>`: This should be replaced by the server name or IP and the port number when different from 80.
- `<webapppath>`: This should be replaced by the web app name. By default, it's Pentaho, but this can be changed.

If your Pentaho server is hosted on the same machine as your application and the web app is the default one, your request would be:

```
<script
  type="text/javascript"
  src="http://localhost:8080/pentaho/plugin/pentaho-cdf/api/cdf-embed.
js">
</script>
```

That's it ...

Okay, you must be asking, but how do I include the dashboard in my application/site, because I only saw how to call CDF's embedded capabilities?

Well, a CDF dashboard is nothing more than JavaScript code you have built, so you can include it on your web page/application now and it will work. From the *Chapter 3, Building the Dashboard Using CDF* you must remember that we had at least two files, but one of them was just to be used by Pentaho.

The main one is the .xcdf file, which is an xml file that identifies the dashboard when you double-click on it. It reality, it will be rendering a web page with the dashboard inside. This file will point to two more files, both HTML pages.

The first one is the dashboard itself, which is an HTML page where you can also include scripts (JavaScript and CSS, among others) and it is where the code of your CDF dashboard should be. The second one is just a wrapper for the first one. If you want more details, please refer back to *Chapter 3, Building the Dashboard Using CDF*. Please check whether the code of your dashboard (the code that .xcdf is pointing to) is like the following:

```
<div id="sampleObject"></div>
<script type="text/javascript">
  require(['cdf/Dashboard.Blueprint', 'cdf/components/
SelectComponent'],
    function(Dashboard, SelectComponent) {
      var myDashboard = new Dashboard();
      myDashboard.addParameter("region", "1");
      var selectComponent = new SelectComponent({
        name: "regionSelector",
        type: "select",
        parameters: [],
        valuesArray: [["1","Lisbon"],["2","Dusseldorf"]],
        parameter: "region",
        valueAsId: false,
        htmlObject: "sampleObject",
        executeAtStart: true,
        postChange: function() {
        alert("You chose: " + myDashboard.getParameterValue(this.
parameter));
        }
      });
    myDashboard.addComponent(selectComponent);
    myDashboard.init();
  });
</script>
```

If so, the code of your web page/application should be like this:

```
<html>
<head>
  <meta http-equiv="content-type" content="text/html; charset=utf-8"
/>
  <title>mySample</title>
```

```
    <script type="text/javascript"
      src="http://localhost:8080/pentaho/plugin/pentaho-cdf/api/cdf-
  embed.js">
    </script>
  </head>
  <body>
    <div id="sampleObject"></div>
    <script type="text/javascript">
      require(['cdf/Dashboard.Blueprint', 'cdf/components/
  SelectComponent'],
        function(Dashboard, SelectComponent) {
          var myDashboard = new Dashboard();
          myDashboard.addParameter("region", "1");
          var selectComponent = new SelectComponent({
            name: "regionSelector",
            type: "select",
            parameters: [],
            valuesArray: [["1","Lisbon"],["2","Dusseldorf"]],
            parameter: "region",
            valueAsId: false,
            htmlObject: "sampleObject",
            executeAtStart: true,
            postChange: function() {
              var choice = myDashboard.getParameterValue(this.
  parameter);
              alert("You chose: " + choice);
            }
          });
          myDashboard.addComponent(selectComponent);
          myDashboard.init();
      });
    </script>
  </body>
</html>
```

As you can see, one of the ways to embed the dashboard is really simple — just embed CDF by calling it as a script and include the code to create your CDF dashboard.

You have a mini dashboard that you want to reuse, so you can wrap it with RequireJS and reuse it as many times as you need — just don't forget that you also need the HTML elements on the page. I believe that, at this time, you should be able to find a way to do it. You have all the concepts, or you just need some more JavaScript and RequireJS knowledge, but that's not really the purpose of this book.

Embedding a CDE dashboard

Embedding a CDE dashboard can be quite simple. You really need to create your own dashboard using CDE in Pentaho. When you have your dashboard working, you just need to request it.

To make it possible to embed a CDE dashboard, we first need to embed CDE, just like we saw for CDF, but this time we request CDE to be embedded:

```
<script
 type="text/javascript"
 src="http://localhost:8080/pentaho/plugin/pentaho-cdf-dd/api/
renderer/cde-embed.js">
</script>
```

You can now embed a dashboard in one of two different ways. Using `RequireJS` in your web page/application, you will be able to include a dashboard as a module. The two ways to do this are:

1. Directly point to the `getDashboard` endpoint available in CDF:

    ```
    '/pentaho/plugin/pentaho-cdf-dd/api/renderer/
    getDashboard?path=/public/dash/sample.wcdf'
    ```

2. Use the `dash!` `RequireJS` loader plugin:

    ```
    'dash!/public/dash/sample.wcdf'
    ```

So, let's explore how to use it. The first step is to create a CDE dashboard. Only after you have a dashboard, do you need to include the dashboard in your web page/application.

Your dashboard and/or web page/application just needs to include the following code:

```
require([
  '/pentaho/plugin/pentaho-cdf-dd/api/renderer/getDashboard?path=/
public/dash /sample.wcdf'
], function(SampleDash) {
  var sampleDash = new SampleDash("content1");
  sampleDash.render();
});
```

Or it could include:

```
require([
  'dash!/public/dash/sample.wcdf'
], function(SampleDash) {
  var sampleDash = new SampleDash("content1");
  sampleDash.render();
});
```

If you look at both examples, you will notice a difference: the *link* to the module required. Both options will have a `RequireJS` module that contains a class for a specific dashboard. You can create new instances of that class, just to provide an element ID, or the element itself. The returned class extends the `Dashboard` class and adds some new methods:

- `render()`: This is used to render the dashboard, by first setting up the DOM, adding the components and parameters to the dashboard, and finally calling the `init()` function

- `setupDOM()`: This is used to set up a predefined layout inside its element

- `renderDashboard()`: This adds the components and the parameters to the dashboard, and then initializes it

You may use `render()` to render the dashboard; or, for better control, you may use `setupDOM()` followed by some logic of yours to manipulate the DOM, and finally call `element.renderDashboard()`.

When embedding a CDE dashboard, your page does not need to provide all the HTML elements needed for the dashboard, because you have created them. You just need to have one element where all the other elements will be placed.

Dashboard, component, and parameter events

One interesting feature that embedded CDE provides is the ability to manage events from the outside. For instance, we can create a link between dashboards. The way to do this is using dashboard events.

Let's suppose you have one instance for each of two dashboards. Both dashboards have one parameter in common, `productLine`. The first dashboard has one selector that allows you to change a product line, and the second dashboard has a chart that is listening to a parameter with the same name. The parameters from each of the dashboards will not automatically be linked, so we need to specify that connection:

```
require([
  'dash!/public/dash/selectorDash.wcdf'],
  'dash!/public/dash/lineChartDash.wcdf'],
  function(SelectorDash, LineChartDash) {
    var selectorDash = new SelectorDash("selector");
    selectorDash.render();
    var lineChartDash= new LineChartDash("lineChart");
    lineChartDash.render();
    selectorDash.on("productLine:fireChange", function (evt) {
      lineChartDash.fireChange("productLine", evt.value);
    });
});
```

Looking at the code, you will see that, in the first dashboard, the `productLine` parameter is being watched, and a change is triggered by the `fireChange` function. For instance, when the user makes a selection, the code inside the function will trigger a change for the `productLine` parameter of the second dashboard. This creates a link between both dashboards.

This feature is nothing more than an extension of `Backbone.Events`, so you can learn to use it to the fullest at `http://backbonejs.org/#Events`.

The events can be triggered by the dashboard or by the components. The following events are available:

- The events triggered by dashboards are as follows:
    - **Parameter changes**: When a parameter changes its value, the event `<parameterName>:fireChange` is triggered
    - **Dashboard pre-initialization**: When the dashboard finishes running the pre-initialization scripts, the event `cdf:preInit` is triggered
    - **Dashboard post-initialization**: When the dashboard finishes running the post-initializations scripts, the event `cdf:postInit` is triggered
    - **User not logged in error**: When CDF detects that a user is no longer logged in, the event `cdf:loginError` is triggered
    - **Server error**: If a call to the server returns an error, the event `cdf:serverError` is triggered

- The events triggered by components are as follows:

  ○ **Pre-execution of the component**: After the call to the `preExecution` function, the event `cdf:preExecution` is triggered.

  ○ **Post-execution of the component**: After the call to the `postExecution` function, the event `cdf:postExecution` is triggered.

  ○ **Error**: If an error happens during the execution of the component, the event `cdf:error` is triggered. This can be applied for each one of the components.

Managing events is important inside the dashboard, but the ability to manage events outside the dashboard becomes very important when we are embedding dashboards.

Debugging

When we are developing a dashboard, we may face problems and we need to know where to look for solutions. Many of the problems we face when developing a dashboard can be identified using the developer tools in your browser.

I usually use Chrome, so the examples here are based on the developer tools of this browser. The version that was used while writing this was 46.0.2490.86 (64-bit). Anyhow, if you are using Firefox, you also have developer tools, or you can install Firebug, a developer tool that does not come installed by default. To be honest, I find the developer tools of Internet Explorer to be very poor, even if they are getting better in the latest versions of the browser. Anyhow, we must use them when we are debugging problems that only exist in this browser.

Do not forget to test your dashboard on all of the browsers.

Browser compatibility

Like any other web page, a dashboard can work in one browser and fail to execute in another browser. Every browser has an engine, and they can be quite different. To check what each browser supports and does not support, and for which version, you can use the following site: http://caniuse.com. For instance, if you want to check which ones support SVG images, just search for SVG and you will see something like this:

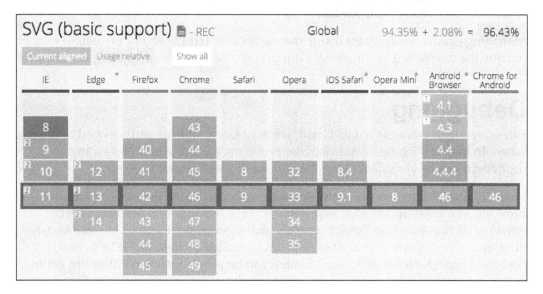

The preceding screenshot shows browsers and their versions; a red rectangle means that SVG is not supported and a green rectangle shows the versions that are supported.

Debugging with developer tools

Among other features, developer tools allow you to inspect, edit, and monitor CSS, HTML, JavaScript, and network requests in any web page. If you want to know more, the following links show how developer tools work:

- https://developer.chrome.com/devtools
- https://developer.apple.com/safari/tools/
- https://developer.mozilla.org/en-US/docs/Tools
- https://msdn.microsoft.com/en-us/library/dd565628.aspx

When a dashboard is rendered, the CSS and JavaScript files are minified; thus, when you are debugging the dashboard, you must add a parameter to your URL. The parameter to be added is `debug` and it needs to be set to `true`. You can add it as `?debug=true` if no other parameter exists or as `&debug=true` if another parameter already exists. Please look at the following two examples:

- `http://localhost:8080/pentaho/api/repos/%3Apublic%3Asample.`
  `wcdf/generatedContent?debug=true`

- `http://localhost:8080/pentaho/api/repos/%3Apublic%3Asample.`
  `wcdf/generatedContent?paramcountry=Portugal&debug=true`

Both examples will allows you to debug the dashboard the only difference is that one has a parameter and another one does not, so one uses the `&` to set the debug to true, and the other one uses a `?` to set the debug mode to `true`.

This will make CDF and CDE return non-minified versions of the code, and you will be able to check and understand the code. It will even be possible to add some breakpoints.

It is not the purpose of this book to teach you how to use developer tools, but I will give you some hints about the main and basic concepts to start with. This doesn't mean you should forget about your need to have a better understanding of developer tools for different browsers. On Chrome, open the developer tools using *Ctrl + Shift + I* (or *command + option + I* on the Mac) to open them. You will get something like the following screenshot:

In the preceding screenshot, you can see three numbers:

1: This is where you can get details about HTML elements, the network, and sources.

2: This is where you display the CSS of each element you can select in panel **1** when you are in the **Elements** tab.

- When you're in the **Elements** tab, you can to evaluate HTML and CSS, and you can also change HTML and CSS and preview the changes in real time. The changes are not saved to the dashboard, nor to file.

- When you're in the **Network** tab, you can get information about the requests made to the server. On the highest level, there are two types of errors you can expect here when using developer tools: the front end and the back end. When you get errors executing queries, it means that something went wrong when executing queries. You should first look at the request that is being executed; if it all looks fine, then you need to find the errors on the server side, and here the browser's developer tools can't help you. In these cases, you need to look at the errors on the server side and, if you're not getting the necessary information, you might need to increase the log level, but on the server side.

- When you're in the **Sources** tab, you can display each of the files loaded and needed for the execution of the dashboard. This is where is you can add breakpoints and pause the execution so that you can evaluate the code at a specific time. When the errors happening in the dashboard are not at the back end, then the **Source** tab is where you might need to look and to also interpret the logs being showed in the **Console** shown in **3**.

3: The console is where you can get the messages being sent from the dashboard. This is where you need to search for errors. If they're not shown, you can press on the *Esc* key. We covered some examples of logs in *Chapter 8, Visualizations Using CCC*.

Don't forget to learn a bit more about developer tools.

Short tips

Keep one eye on the console, as it provides you with a lot of information. You can see the order of execution of the components, which part of the dashboard is being executed, and even errors and which file we get the logged information from.

The previous screenshot also shows one error. If you click on the error, you will be redirected to the place where the error is coming from. If it's a JavaScript error, the code will be displayed in the source tab. If it's a network request, it will display details in the request. You can create a breakpoint there.

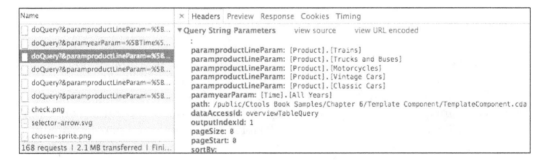

The preceding screenshot shows the details of one of the queries being executed. Before looking at the server-side logs, make sure all the parameters are correct, as the full request.

When using the **Source** tab, to create a breakpoint in the code you just need to click on the left side of the line where you want to stop. You will see a *blue sign* that identifies that there is a breakpoint, and the code execution will be stopped when that part of the code is being executed. You need to make sure that the code is executed so that the execution can be paused. You can then control the flow of the process by jumping into functions, to the next line, or to the next breakpoint. When hovering over the variable, its current value will be displayed.

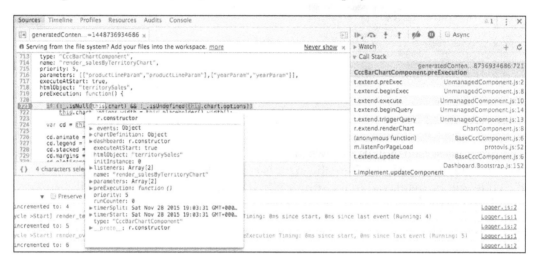

The preceding screenshot shows the code paused during the execution of the dashboard, and the mouse is hovering over the this variable, so we also see its value. In the top-right corner, you can see a toolbar, where you can jump to the next breakpoint, jump to the next line, jump into the next function, or jump out from current functions. You will also be able to disable breakpoints from pausing, among other options.

Delivering a solution

Before delivering a solution, you need to consider some aspects of the project. In reality, and as we saw earlier, they should be considered at the start of the project when everything is being planned. There are some phases of the project that are usually part of a successful project and can save you some time, but they can also help you create a better relationship with the customer and achieve a greater level of satisfaction. The documentation and knowledge transfer are two of those tasks, and another one is deploying a project and version control for our code.

Version control and deploying projects

You can't afford to lose your work, do you? Can you also spend most lots of lying changes for development to quality acceptance tests or production environment?

It's an important part of development that you keep all the code in a version control system. All content developed with or for Pentaho should be treated as a software artefact and tested and controlled as such. This is true even if we are talking about reports, such as the ones you can build with the standard Pentaho tools. For instance, a Pentaho Analyzer file is just an XML file that you can push into version control. The dashboards and CDA files that you produce with CTools are also files that you should push to the repository.

This also applies to the version of configuration files from your Pentaho system, and some custom extensions that are not deployed to the repository can be controlled via a external version control system. Finally, even though the DI repository does have version control, it lacks an advanced **version control system** (**VCS**) feature such as branching or tagging. For this reason, Pentaho recommends managing all artefacts with a VCS such as GIT or SVN.

The following diagram shows a conceptual architecture to deploy and test in different environments. Developers have the complete Pentaho stack on their development systems, or they might be developing on top of the development server. As artefacts are created and developer-tested, they get checked into VCS.

Once a set of functionalities are completed and checked, they are pushed from development to the **quality acceptance** (**QA**) server that is used for integration and testing. When QA is done, the artefacts are checked into a production environment using VCS. Here, you can use a specific branch and/or tags for an upcoming version or a patch. Finally, when a production release is ready, the branch or tag can be used to check out all of the artefacts.

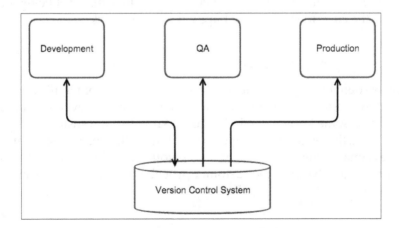

In order to isolate the developer work, it is useful to have a full copy of the development stack. Even some customers do not provide or allows to have a QA environment; the production and development environment should be exactly the same. Believe me, you won't deploy solutions from a development environment to QA or production if they do not match.

There is an issue with the way `.cdfde` files are saved to disk — the files are rewritten in such a way that the VCS will get confused and identify a lot of changes when in reality there was a small change. This can turn the process of merging files into a nightmare. When working as a team and working on the same file, there are merges that will be required, so be careful when committing changes and make sure you are doing the right thing.

Documentation

One important part of delivery to the customer is documentation. For you to be successful in your deliveries to the customer, you definitely need to include proper documentation. I agree that it's hard to create proper documentation, and that it's better to create interesting and useful stuff. Anyhow, it's not useful if people do not know how to make use of it or how to make it work.

You should train yourself to create documentation during some phases of the project. If you are not creating any documentation at the end of each completed phase of your work/tasks, you are doing something wrong. If you need to, you can break down your tasks into smaller tasks and schedule/spend some time building the documentation.

The truth is that it will save you time in the future, and it will also provide a better delivery for the customer, and enable you to reach the highest level of satisfaction for your customers. I'm sure you would prefer to select the most interesting projects and say, "I can't do it" or "I have no time" to a customer, rather than not being engaged again because the customer isn't truly happy with your work.

Knowledge transfer

Even if you are delivering proper documentation to the customer, it's possible and common that the customer will ignore it and archive it before even reading it. A good way to pass some knowledge is to make a knowledge transfer. And if you are asking why on earth you are building documentation, the answer is: because you are a good professional doing a great job and you wouldn't fail to deliver an important part of the project just because the customer probably won't give it any attention.

You won't need to spend a lot of time on the knowledge transfer, but you need to make sure that the customer has the necessary information to make proper use of your solutions and deliveries. This is a good opportunity to make it clear to the customer that the knowledge transfer does not replace the documentation and that reading the documentation is a prerequisite to the knowledge transfer. That said, we should never schedule a knowledge transfer before we can deliver the documentation.

I believe that it is also an advantage to request a list of questions regarding the documentation that the customer would like to be covered during the knowledge transfer. This removes their right to complain later about missing knowledge. Of course, that does not excuse you from creating proper documentation and preparing a proper knowledge transfer.

Some topics that you should cover during the knowledge transfer will be related to the project and the team you are delivering the project to. It's quite different when delivering a solution to an IT department than it is to a final customer, and your documentation and knowledge transfer should reflect this.

How to get help and help others

If you are an enterprise user, you have access to support (CDA, CDF, CDE, and CGG, which are the supported tools), but when you are not, how should you proceed? Well, you have multiple ways to solve your problem, and of course that will also be dependent on the problem you have found, the way you phrase the question, and how much information you are requesting. When you're not an enterprise user, you have some options. You will probably get a quick answer, but don't be disappointed if you don't—just try again.

For any and each of the ways to get help (even if it's enterprise support), you should always provide the most information you can. This includes the context of the problem that's happening. You should provide a good and clear description of the problem, a sample when ever possible (even if you need to create it with sample data), and/or screenshots when it makes sense to do so. You should also provide the configurations that are not there by default, because they might be important to replicate the problem.

You should always bear it in mind that people who are looking at your request or even trying to answer it might not guess what it's in your mind; alternatively, they may not be seeing the same as you. This might be the difference between getting a quick solution/response and not getting an answer.

When you want to get some help, you may want to ask the community, and you can use the forum to do so. You will find the forum at `http://forums.pentaho. com` and more specifically `http://forums.pentaho.com/forumdisplay.php?80-Community-Tools-CTools`.

The first step is to register as a user on the forum, so that you can create your own posts. First, you should search for your question/problem, which is also a good way to learn more. You might also want to search for JIRAs that are already closed and have a solution to your issue. If there is none, you can create a new post and wait for answers.

If you find some questions that you know the answer to, or have an idea how to solve them, you should reply with an answer, because you might be helping another user. This is the way you can help to build a strong community.

If you find that the problem is a bug, you should raise a JIRA. Go to `http://jira. pentaho.com/secure/Dashboard.jspa` and create a user. When you have a new issue, you need to select the project, so please ensure you select the right project. As said before, you should provide all the information that you are able to. You can see the selection of a project in the following screenshot:

The issues that you can create are not only bugs, but also improvements and new features. Improvements and new features are well received, and by suggesting these, you are contributing to a better product—a product that you are using.

For the JIRAs that you open, you will get notifications, so you will know their status. There is also a button that enables you to start watching some issues that you might be interesting on getting updates for.

You can also find some blogs that provide you with a lot of good content on how to use solutions and solve challenges. You should also be aware that having a good knowledge of the full Pentaho solution will be an advantage when trying to overcome some challenges. So don't discard any blog, help pages, or forums that might not be related to CTools, but that can provide information and knowledge about Pentaho, or even about front-end development, JavaScript, CSS, and so on.

A good way to get updates about new features or bug fixes is to look at the CTools change log at `http://www.webdetails.pt/ctools-changelog`. You will be redirected to the last change log, but you can select earlier versions. You can click on each of the lines displayed to get more information about it. You will even be able to get the code that was changed.

Summary

In this chapter, you learned how to embed CFD and CDE dashboards in third-party applications. You saw that we must first embed CDF or CDE and then embed the dashboards. When embedding a CDE dashboard, there are two ways to do it. When embedding, it might also be important to receive information from, and send it to, the dashboard or create links between dashboards, and for that we can make use of events.

We also talked about some aspects of the delivery of dashboards, which should also include documentation and knowledge transfers. Depending on who we are delivering the solution to, the technical level of the knowledge transfer and documentation might be quite different. Version control is an important part of the process when developing a dashboard; this is not part of the delivery, but it might be part of the deployment, so we discussed it in this chapter.

Finally, we covered where and how you can get help or a solution to your problems when developing dashboards using CTools. You can use the community to get help, report bugs, suggest improvements, and request new features.

Now that you have learned about CTools and how to create dashboards and Pentaho plugins, you should apply this knowledge to the dashboards that you already have, or just create new ones. Keep this book by your side while creating them, and you will see that it can be useful when you don't yet have a good knowledge of CTools.

You should go through the examples provided with the book, as this is important for you to get a better understanding of components, parameters, listeners, and so on. This book does not provides examples for all of the components, but now that you have an understanding of CDA, CDF, and CDE, you can take a look at the examples included when you install CDF and CDE. This way, you will develop knowledge of the available components, their properties, and how they can be used. You will also need to keep an eye on the backlog updates to the CTools, because they are getting better and better day by day, with new functionalities and improvements.

Index

A

add-ins
  creating 257-259
add-ins, filter component
  about 180
  group selection add-ins 181
  group sorting add-ins 181
  item selection add-ins 181
  item sorting add-ins 181
  post update add-ins 181
  root footer add-ins 181
  root header add-ins 181
  root selection add-ins 181
add-ins, table component
  cccBulletChart 215
  circle 213, 214
  clippedText 207
  dataBar 209, 210
  formattedText 215, 216
  groupHeaders 206
  hyperlink 220, 221
  localizedText 217, 219
  sparkline 207, 208
  trendArrow 210, 211
  using 204, 205
add-ins, template component 230-241
Asynchronous Module
    Definition (AMD) 62

B

Backbone
  URL 18

basis axis label
  formatting, scale based 302, 303
Blueprint
  URL 18, 274
bookmarkable parameters 279
Bootstrap
  URL 18, 275
bootstrap-select plugin
  URL 172

C

Cascade Style Sheets (CSS) 5
CCC (Community Charts Components)
  about **2**
  background 288
  charts, debugging 311-313
  charts, internationalization 299, 300
  component 290
  library, using in CDF dashboard 288-291
  references, URL 315
  URL 18, 288, 311
  using, in CDE 295, 296
cccBulletChart add-in 215
CDA
  about 21, 22
  cache 45
  data sources 23
  editing 43, 44
  previewing 43, 44
CDA cache
  and scheduler 45-47
  keys 47
  managing 45-47
  system-wide cache keys, configuring 48

short tips 347, 348
with developer tools 344-346
dimensions
about 308, 309
readers 309, 310
URL 308
visual roles 310, 311
Document Object Model (DOM) 60, 262
doQuery method 49, 50
Draw function property 196

E

editFile method 51
editor
operational toolbar 115
working with 113-115
Enterprise Edition (EE) 5
events, template component 242, 243
export button component
about 245
component name property 245
label property 245
output type property 245
export popup button component
about 245, 247
chart component to export option 246
chart export label option 246
chart export type option 246
content linking option 246
data component to export option 246
data export label option 246
data export type option 246
gravity parameter option 246
name for data export attachment
option 246
title option 246
extendable options, template
component 244
extension point
URL 302
Extract, Transform, and Load (ETL) 31

F

Fancybox
URL 18
filter component
about 177
add-ins, usage 180-185
configurations, advanced 185
data layout, expected 178
default messages, changing 185
options, advanced 185
properties, specific 179, 180
values, displaying 186
Font-awesome
URL 18
formattedText add-in 215, 216
formatters, template component 229, 230
forum
URL 352
frameworks 17
freeform components 253, 257

G

getCdaList endpoint 48
Git repository
URL 3
Graphical User Interface (GUI) 27, 111
groupHeaders add-in 206

H

help 351, 352
HTML 62
Hynds
URL 172
hyperlink add-in 220, 221
Hypertext Markup Language (HTML) 5

I

icon fonts
URL 212
identifier (ID) 23
internationalization 280-283

internationalization and localization, table
component
  Language property 195

J

JavaScript 5
JIRA
  URL 352
jQuery
  URL 18
jQuery i18n
  URL 18
jQueryUI
  URL 18
JSON
  URL 260
JSON object
  URL 195

K

Kettle
  URL 104
Kettle endpoint
  buttons 322
  creating 322
  parameters values, specifying 324
  results, getting 324
  using, on dashboard 329-332
Kettle transformations
  about 31
  KtrFile property 32
  variables property 32
Key Performance Indicators (KPIs)
  about 5
  components, using 66

L

layout elements
  references to 252, 253
layout perspective, perspectives toolbar
  about 122
  Bootstrap, used for creating responsive
    dashboard 136-139
  considerations 134-136

layout toolbar 122-134
responsive dashboards, building
    considerations 139-141
line charts
  URL 301
listeners
  inside components 75
listParameters endpoint 49
listQueries endpoint 49
localization 280-283
localizedText add-in 217-219
logger module 109

M

manageCache method 51
Marketplace
  URL 12, 13, 17
Modernizr
  URL 18
Moment
  URL 18
MomentJS
  URL 99, 101
Mondrian cubes 29-31
Mozilla Public License
  URL 3
multi-button component
  about 189
  Datasource 189
  ultiple selection 189
  value as ID 189
  values array 189
multi-tenancy
  URL 47
Mustache
  URL 18

O

Object-Oriented Programming (OOP)
    languages 263
open formula
  URL 37
operational toolbar, editor
  about 115
  new 115

W

X